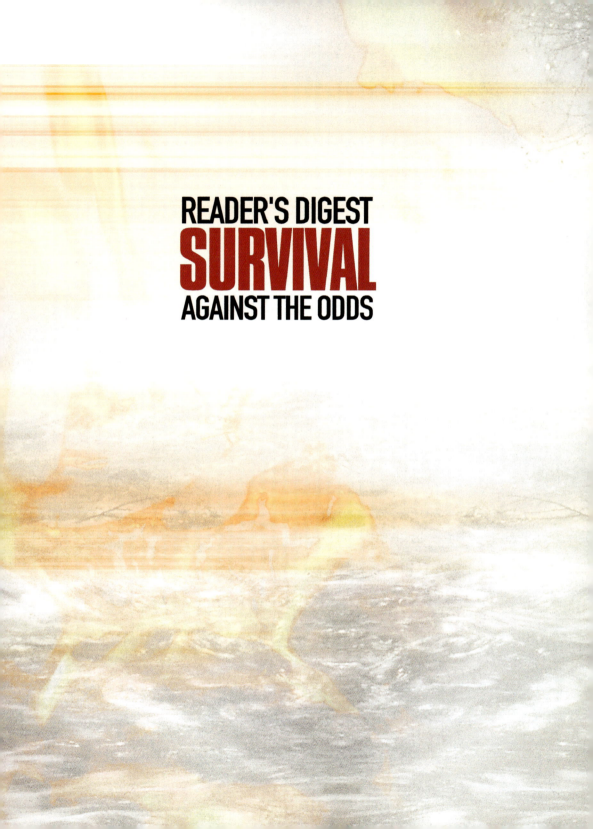

READER'S DIGEST
SURVIVAL
AGAINST THE ODDS

READER'S DIGEST
SURVIVAL
AGAINST THE ODDS

Contents

Foreword

There are moments and events that change all our lives, but few are as dramatic as those you will find in these pages. I will never forget Christmas Day 1996, when deep in the Southern Ocean between Australia and Antarctica, while on the Vendée Globe nonstop, single-handed round-the-world race, I heard that bleep on my laptop computer, my only link with the outside world. It was a distress call. French yachtsman and fellow competitor, Raphaël Dinelli, was in dire trouble. I was the only one close enough to save him.

You can read what happened to Raphaël and me in *Race for his Life* on page 150. This is just one of 40 stories of incredible survival against the odds taken from the pages of Reader's Digest magazine and its popular feature "Drama in Real Life". This book draws together a cast of characters from around the world who come face to face with death. It's hard to imagine anything more terrifying than Paul Connolly in Zimbabwe having to fight a leopard that comes crashing through his kitchen window, or the horror of Ivers Sims, who finds himself marooned in his crane cab 220 feet over a raging inferno in Atlanta, Georgia. Then there's 11-year-old James Leeds, trapped all alone in a cave in Cornwall, England, by a huge sea, while in Sierra Leone little Tenneh Cole walks 250 miles with a bullet in her head in the hope that she can find a doctor who will save her life. And in an icy Canadian wilderness, badly injured Reinhold Kaletsch displays extraordinary courage in *The Man who Refused to Die* (page 119).

These true tales of survival are also great stories of rescue. Many of the rescuers risk their own lives in avalanches, mountains, fires, floods and volcanoes. They leap in front of trains and dive into the darkest depths. They perform life-saving surgery armed with carpentry tools, coat hangers and blind faith.

I don't believe in heroes. Too often the word is used glibly by a society that accepts easy caricatures. But I do believe in bravery, and the moral courage that makes the people featured in these pages ignore the basic "me-first" survival instinct in order to save others. The stars of these stories are not Olympic athletes, nor have they been trained by Special Forces to conquer the elements and the life-threatening dangers they face. They are just good, honest, ordinary people to whom we can all relate. They may come from different countries and cultures and follow different religions, but what they all have in common, and what makes their stories so special, is the power of the human spirit.

I feel honoured to be numbered among the people in this book. Most are far braver than I. I know from my own drama in real life—during which I also had to perform an operation on myself at sea without anaesthetic, guided via e-mail by a surgeon in France—that facing these situations and making the right decision brings a great sense of inner peace and makes you realise what in life is really important. It's often the simple things, but most of all it is your family and those you love.

These stories are brought to you by some of the world's great action writers. It is not enough for Reader's Digest journalists merely to report the facts; they take you right to the heart of the drama. This is from John Dyson's *Rescue Under the Rainbow* (page 242), where miners are trapped by a giant rockfall: "In the boardroom . . . the gold mine's managers were discussing production targets when the windows rattled. The sudden jolt felt as if the world had run over a pothole." These are writers who make events leap from the page. They also take you into the minds and emotions of those in peril. It is impossible to read these stories without a lump forming in your throat.

You may pick up this book planning to read one story in a spare ten minutes. I suspect that once you start it you will be so gripped that you will carry on and read every single story, right through to the end.

Pete Goss
International yachtsman and Reader's Digest European of the Year, 1998

Please
don't leave me!

by Jim Hutchison

Surrounded by a wall of flames, the
12-year-old put all her hope and trust
in the pledge of a courageous firefighter.

"**L**et's go, Mum!" Shirley Young begged her mother. It was a Thursday in August—late-shopping night at Manukau City Shopping Centre in South Auckland. One of the highlights of the week for the 12-year-old Maori girl was to spend a few hours at New Zealand's biggest mall with her aunt and cousin. Her mother, Gaylene, a single parent struggling to improve her job prospects, appreciated having a few hours by herself to catch up on her studies.

Gaylene threw on a wool cardigan and drove the trio to the mall in her sister's white Cortina, stopping at the kerb on busy Wiri Station Road to drop them off. As Shirley headed across the car park to join the throng of shoppers she suddenly realized she didn't have her purse. "Wait, Mum!" she yelled, running back. "I forgot my money." Shirley opened the passenger door and leaned in to talk to her mother.

INFERNO: **searching the wreckage.**

Farther back along the busy road, Buddy Marsh shifted gears on his huge Scania tanker as he headed up the rise. The 40-tonne truck and trailer held more than 30,000 litres of petrol destined for a service station in central Auckland. A cautious driver, Marsh kept well to the left of the two-lane road but, as he neared the mall, a taxi, which had pulled out of the car park, blocked his lane. Marsh swung his rig away. A glance in his mirrors showed the trailer just clearing the front of the taxi. Then, as he looked ahead, Marsh gasped in horror. Not 20 metres away, directly in his path, was a stationary white car.

Marsh yanked on the steering wheel and hit the air brakes, locking up several of the 14 sets of wheels. The truck slammed into the rear of the car, spinning it round like a child's toy and rupturing its fuel tank. Petrol sprayed both vehicles and ignited instantly. Carried on by its momentum, the trailer jack-knifed, reared over the kerb and toppled on top of the wrecked car.

One second Gaylene Young was talking to her daughter; the next, she was whirling around in a vortex of crumpling metal. Gaylene sat stunned as flames poured into the car and a single, terrible thought rose in her mind. *Shirley! Where is she?* Gaylene groped frantically around in the darkness but the passenger seat was empty. *Thank God. She's made it out of here.* An excruciating pain shot up her legs: her sneakers and track pants were on fire. Gaylene struggled to open the buckled doors, but they wouldn't budge. "No!" she screamed, "I won't die like this."

"Brian!" Marsh called on his two-way radio to his shift mate Brian Dixon in another truck. "I've had an accident! I'm on fire! Call the emergency services!"

Marsh jumped down and ran round the front of the tanker to the burning car. Flames were licking the trailer's tanks. Worse, fuel was leaking from relief valves on the overturned trailer and spewing from a hole in its front compartment. The whole rig could blow.

Marsh reached the car just as bystander David Petera hauled Gaylene out, smothering her flaming clothes with his own body. Petera and other bystanders carried her to a safe distance.

Above the hiss of escaping compressed air and the roaring fire, Marsh heard a voice calling "Mum! Mum!" At first he could see nothing. Then, as he searched underneath the toppled trailer, he saw a young, dark-haired girl trapped in a tiny space between a rear wheel and the chassis. "Mum!" she cried. "Mum!" Marsh grabbed her beneath the arms. "You'll be all right. You're coming with me," he said. But he couldn't budge her: her lower body was pinned to the ground by the wheel assembly. "I want my mum!" she wailed.

Petera crawled in alongside and together they tried to find a way of freeing the girl. Through a gap in the chassis, Marsh could see a stream of fuel spilling from the tanker into the gutter. "We've got to get her out, *now*!" he told Petera.

"Try inching the truck forward," Peter suggested. Marsh ran back to the cab and jumped up into the burning seat; the interior was ablaze. He reached forward through the flames to the melting dashboard and twisted the ignition key. To his amazement, the engine roared to life. In low gear, he coaxed the rig gently forward. Shirley shrieked in pain. "It's no good," called Petera. "She's still trapped."

A wall of fire ran the length of the tanker, threatening to sweep round under the trailer where Shirley lay. Marsh grabbed a small fire extinguisher from the cab and ran back, spraying it around the girl in the hope of buying a few precious seconds. Then, from above the men, came a thunderous roar. An explosion tore a hole in one of the trailer's four fuel compartments. An immense fireball ballooned into the sky. Shoppers in the car park ran for their lives. Marsh and Petera, shielded by the tanker itself from the full force of the blast, crawled out. "There's a little girl trapped under the trailer," shouted Marsh.

"Let the firefighters handle it," a policeman replied. "Clear the area!" Truck, trailer and car were now lost in a cauldron of fire. "That poor little girl," Marsh said, holding his head in his hands. "She didn't have a chance."

With a blare of sirens, a pump and rescue tender from Manukau Station arrived. Immediately the vehicles stopped, senior firefighter Royd Kennedy had

TRAPPED IN A BLAZING HELL

The truck slammed into the rear of the car . . . rupturing its fuel tank. Petrol sprayed both vehicles and ignited instantly. The trailer jack-knifed, reared over the kerb and toppled onto the wrecked car . . . As firefighter Royd Kennedy searched underneath the toppled trailer, he saw a young girl trapped in a tiny space between a rear wheel and the chassis.

an armful of hose out of the locker and his partner, Mike Keys, was lugging foam containers down behind him. Driver Tod Penberthy was springing to connect the pump to the nearest hydrant. Waiting for the water, Kennedy saw his boots, fireproof overtrousers and the rubber on his breathing apparatus begin to singe. When they turned the hose on the fire, the heat was so intense that the water steamed away before it reached the flames.

Senior Station Officer John Hyland, in charge of the initial response, had never seen such potential for disaster in 19 years of fighting fires. The tanker was burning end to end, shooting flames 100 metres into the air. Petrol poured from holes and relief valves into a widening lake and a river of fire raced down the road into stormwater drains.

More fire crews arrived. "Concentrate on pushing the flames away from that tanker!" ordered Divisional Officer Ray Warby who had arrived to take control. As if to underline his words, the fuel in another compartment exploded in a monstrous fireball, forcing Kennedy and his crew mates back 20 metres. The vehicles in the car park around them had begun to melt, plastic bumpers and mirrors sagging and paint bubbling.

As the firefighters readied themselves for another assault on the fire, a long, high-pitched wail cut through the night. Kennedy's station officer, Graham Haycock, dismissed it as the sound of expanding metal. When the eerie sound came again it raised the hair on the back of Kennedy's neck. *I'll be damned*, he thought, *it's coming from the tanker*. Shielding his eyes, Kennedy peered into the glare, but saw only a flaming wall 50 metres high. Then, for a split second, the flames parted. From beneath the trailer he saw something waving. It was the hand of a child.

"Cover me!" Kennedy shouted to Haycock. He dropped his hose and ran into the inferno.

For ten minutes little Shirley Young had been slowly roasting in a sea of fire. *It's hopeless*, she told herself, *no one can hear me in here.* Giddy with pain and petrol fumes, she felt her mind begin to drift and suddenly saw a vivid image of her grandfather and her great-uncle, both of whom had died years before. *They're guardian angels now*, she thought. *They'll be watching over me.* The idea gave her new strength. Straining to see through the wall of fire, Shirley glimpsed moving figures. Mustering every ounce of strength, she screamed louder than she had ever done in her life.

As Kennedy neared the flames, the heat hit him like a physical blow, stinging his face through his visor. Shielding his head with his gloved hands and fireproof jacket, he crawled under the trailer. Shirley was trying to hold herself up by clutching a cable over her head, but her hips and thighs were under the wheel assembly and her legs were twisted up, like a grasshopper's, next to her chest.

"I'm scared. Please don't leave me," she wailed.

Kennedy tucked his air cylinder under her shoulders to support her upper body. "Don't worry," he told her. "I'll stay, I promise you."

Kennedy meant what he said; he had always made it a rule never to break promises to his own three kids. "My name's Royd," he said. "We're in this together now, so we have to help each other." He reached into the tiny space and cradled the small body in his arms. Having fended for himself since his teens he knew what it meant to be alone and afraid.

"Is my mum all right?" Shirley asked.

"She's a bit burned, but she got away. My mates will soon get us out, too," Kennedy replied.

The air was so thick with fumes that the two of them could barely breathe. Kennedy knew it would be only seconds before the vapour ignited. *Whoosh!* The firefighter braced himself as the air exploded around them. *This is it*, he thought. *Now we're goners.*

Shirley whimpered. Kennedy felt sick with helplessness as the flames washed over her. Then, for a moment, the fire drew back. "This is pretty rough eh, Shirley?" he said, unstrapping his helmet. "Put this on." *At least it may help save her face*, he thought. He pulled the strap tight under her chin and flipped down the visor. As he hunkered down he thought: *Where the hell is my cover?*

Haycock was running through the car park to the rest of their team, yelling at the top of his voice. "Royd's under the tanker. Get that hose up here!" Struggling with the water-filled hose, they took no more than a minute to get within striking distance, but it seemed an eternity.

A second wave of fire washed over Kennedy and Shirley. They fought back hard, beating out the flames. Then more explosions rocked the trailer, and Kennedy's heart sank.

We don't have a chance now, he thought. He looked down at the girl's tortured body. *I won't leave you. That I promise.* Then he wrapped his arms tightly round her and waited for the final surge of flame that would surely immolate them both.

Instead of fire, they were hit by an ice-cold waterfall. "My mates are here!" yelled Kennedy. Warby appeared through the curtain of water. "Don't worry, we'll get things moving," he told Kennedy, then he took quick stock. The two were shielded from the full force of the main fire above and beside them, but the burning wreckage of the car was in the way, hampering the firefighters' efforts to protect and rescue the pair.

RESCUER: **Royd Kennedy.**

Warby crawled out and ran to Peter Glass, an officer in charge of a rescue tender. "Get that girl out. I don't care how you do it as long as you do it *fast!*"

As firefighters sprayed the life-giving water that kept the fire away from Kennedy and Shirley, they were exposed to the full radiated heat of the main tanker blaze. It gnawed through their multilayered bunker coats as if they were tissue paper, and blistered their arms and hands. But they didn't dare back off. If the spray wavered, fire would instantly sweep back over. Even changing crews was too risky. Ironically, now Shirley and Kennedy began to shiver violently: 80 litres of freezing water cascaded over them each second. Soon they were in the first stages of hypothermia.

"I'll get someone to relieve you," Warby yelled to Kennedy.

"No," Kennedy retorted. "I must stay with her. I made a promise."

Peter Glass brought his rescue tender in as close as he dared while a crewman sprinted to the car and hooked a winch cable to the windscreen pillar. The winch was not powerful enough to drag the car out so they rigged it to the rescue tender's crane and, using it like a giant fishing rod, hauled the burning wreck away.

Assistant Commander Cliff Mears, from brigade headquarters, had now set up a mobile command post and called in a fourth, then fifth alarm. Any vehicle in the city that could be useful was on its way to the scene. However, the firefighters were facing yet another potential catastrophe. Fed by tonnes of fuel, a torrent of

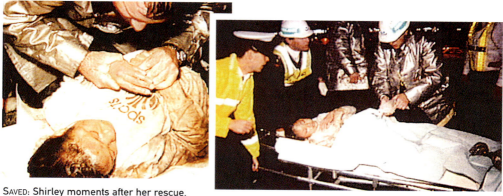

SAVED: **Shirley moments after her rescue.**

fire was pouring into stormwater drains in the car park and on Wiri Station Road. But what route did the drains take?

The answer came with a deafening explosion. A manhole cover blasted out of the ground at the main entrance of the mall, narrowly missing a woman and flinging her shopping trolley into the air. Rumbling underground explosions began lifting and blowing out manhole covers all over the complex. One and a half kilometres away, stormwater drains emptying into the Puhinui Stream sparked five separate fires in the scrub on the stream's banks.

The entire shopping centre was now permeated with petrol fumes. "Evacuate the centre," Mears ordered.

Back at the burning rig, Warby approached Grant Pennycook, a paramedic from a waiting ambulance crew. "There must be something we can do to ease the girl's pain—do you think you could make it under there?" he asked.

Biting back his fear, Pennycook donned a bunker coat and helmet and headed into the inferno. As he crawled into the tiny space where Shirley and Kennedy lay, he realised he wouldn't have room to get an IV drip going. He considered administering a pain killer, but decided against it: Shirley seemed to be coping and side effects such as the suppression of her breathing might hamper the rescue operation.

Trauma victims need to get to hospital within an hour of injury—dubbed the "golden hour" by emergency services—to have a decent chance of survival. Crawling out, Pennycook was conscious that timing was vital. Shirley had been under the tanker for more than 30 minutes. She could easily slip into shock and die.

Kennedy had been trying to take her mind off her predicament. "What do you watch on TV?" he asked, and they talked for a while about her favourite shows. "If you could go anywhere in the world where would you go?"

"Disneyland," she said emphatically, "I love Mickey Mouse."

Whenever she was startled by a sudden noise Kennedy would explain what the firefighters were doing. "How bad am I hurt, Royd?" she asked. Kennedy tried to reassure her: "You'd got a few broken bones and burns, but it's marvellous what the doctors can do." Occasionally she would let out stifled moans. "It's OK, yell all you want," he encouraged. "Bite me if it helps." The pain from the injuries to Shirley's lower body was becoming unbearable. She cried out, burying her hands in Kennedy's thick hair, pulling hard to ease her agony.

The steady flow of water wavered for an instant. *God no*, thought Kennedy, *the fire can't take us now*. Shirley barely managed to move her arms as the flames rolled in. Then the water came pouring back and Kennedy was horrified to see that several layers of skin on her arms had slid down and bunched up round her wrists. "I'm still with you, Shirley," he said. "Do you like horses?" he asked, desperate to get her talking again.

"I've never been on a horse."

"When we're out of here, I promise you a ride on my daughter's horse Gilly."

As Kennedy talked, he kept a finger on Shirley's wrist to check her pulse. Now it was growing noticeably fainter and more erratic. She'd been trapped for nearly 40 minutes.

With the wreck out of the way, Glass was trying to lift the trailer off the girl. He faced a knife-edge decision. A hydraulic jack would be quicker, but it risked tilting the trailer, tipping out more fuel and incinerating the pair. "We'll use the air bags. They'll give a straight lift," Glass told his crew. Only 25 millimetres thick and made of rubber reinforced with steel, the 600-millimetre-square bags could each lift a railway wagon 600 centimetres. They slid one under each set of rear wheels and began feeding in compressed air. As the trailer moved they slipped in wooden blocks to keep it on an even keel.

Kennedy felt Shirley's pulse flutter and she closed her eyes. "Shirley, talk to me!" he pleaded. She rallied for a couple of moments but her pulse was so faint now he could barely feel it. She lifted her head and looked into his eyes. "If I don't make it, tell Mum I love her," she whispered.

"We're losing her, Warby," Kennedy shouted. "Throw me an Air Viva!" Kennedy put the mask of the portable resuscitator over Shirley's face and forced air into her lungs. She stirred a little and opened her eyes. "You tell your mum yourself," he scolded. "I promised I wouldn't leave you. Now, don't you leave me!"

"I'll hang on," she murmured.

From his mobile control centre, Commander Mears had dispatched teams to chase down manhole fires. Firefighters gingerly lifted covers, careful not to cause a spark, and began pumping water down the drains to flush the fuel down to the harbour. Others carried fuel vapour-detectors around the mall, opening all doors and vents in an attempt to blow fumes out of the shopping centre.

The burning rig was in the final-approach path of Auckland International Airport and, with fireballs sending smoke and huge thermal currents into the sky, air-traffic control issued warnings to aircraft.

Peter Glass's rescue team had run into trouble. Part of the trailer was on soft ground that was sodden from all the water and the air bag under the wheel trapping her was sinking into mud instead of lifting. They blocked one more time and inflated the bag to its maximum, but the wheels had risen only ten centimetres. "We must have her out now," Warby told Glass.

Praying that it would give them that extra few centimetres of lift without tipping the trailer, Glass shoved a small hydraulic ram under the chassis. He flicked the valve open and held his breath. The trailer lifted some more. Now he had a 15-centimetre gap between ground and wheels; it would have to be enough.

"Go for it!" he yelled. Kennedy gently untangled Shirley's legs from under the wheel; they were crushed so badly they were like jelly in his hands. Warby helped him juggle her crumpled body from its prison. Then they carried her to the stretcher. Just before Shirley was lifted into the waiting ambulance, she smiled at him and he bent down to give her a kiss on the cheek.

"You've done it, Shirley!" he said. Then, overcome by fumes, shock and cold, he pitched forward.

For Shirley, the ordeal continued. As the ambulance headed for hospital, Pennycook bathed her burns in saline solution and gave her nitrous oxide to relieve her pain.

Back at the mall, firefighters were at last able to pour foam onto the tanker. Before, it would have endangered Kennedy and the girl; now they quenched the burning rig in just three minutes.

When John Hyland revisited the scene the following morning he saw something that would haunt him for the rest of his life. For 70 metres the top layer of tar had burned away, in places down to bare gravel—except for a

SHIRLEY YOUNG

Child of courage: Shirley's ordeal continued in Middlemore Hospital, South Auckland.

patch the size of a kitchen table so lightly scorched by fire that the painted line was still visible. This was where Shirley had been lying.

"It was as if the devil was determined to take that girl," Haycock said later, "and when she was snatched away, he just gave up."

"MIRACLE CHILD." Royd Kennedy kept his promise, taking Shirley for a ride on his daughter's horse, Gilly.

At Middlemore Hospital a team of surgeons worked through the night on Shirley. Orthopaedic specialists set her fractures and implanted a pin in her crushed right leg. Burns specialists saved what they could of the charred flesh on her legs. In another wing of the hospital, her mother lay with second- and third-degree burns to more than 20 per cent of her body.

Royd Kennedy finished his work shift, something many firefighters do when they have faced a life-and-death situation. Then he called his wife, Rosemary, and told her to put on bacon and eggs, and mounted his Harley-Davidson to ride home in the first pink light of dawn. Throwing caution to the winds, he opened the throttle wide. *If a cop pulls me over*, he smiled to himself, *I've got a good story to tell.*

For two weeks Shirley lay in intensive care. With tubes in her throat, she couldn't talk for the first few days. But as she drifted in and out of a sedated sleep, she scrawled a note: "I love you, Mummy." Five days after the accident they wheeled Gaylene into Shirley's ward. Mother and daughter held hands across their beds and wept with happiness.

Shirley slowly recovered, and began a series of painful skin grafts to her legs. Orthopaedic surgeons found the right calf muscle too badly damaged to repair and decided to amputate her leg below the knee.

Firefighters have an unwritten rule never to visit victims in hospital in case they get too involved and lose judgment on the job. But Kennedy visited Shirley often, eating her chocolates and writing on her chart, "This kid is far too noisy."

"She's a miracle child," says Kennedy. "No one knows how she survived in there."

But Shirley knows: "I had guardian angels watching over me," she explains.

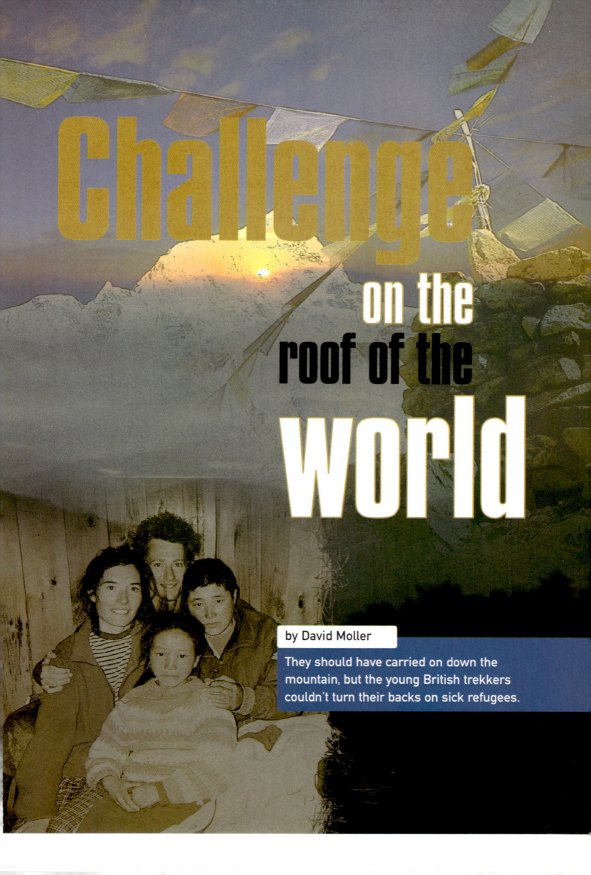

Challenge
on the
roof of the
world

by David Moller

They should have carried on down the mountain, but the young British trekkers couldn't turn their backs on sick refugees.

In the jaws of a crocodile

by Jim Hutchison

A man and a reptile were locked in a deadly
tug of war—for the life of a young woman.

The day had been hot and humid, and Sandy Rossi looked forward to her customary pre-dinner swim. With no running water at the remote African jungle camp, everyone bathed in the Epulu River.

Rossi, 27, had arrived three months before to be tutor and nanny for the two children of John and Terese Hart, naturalists from New York studying the vast Ituri Forest of central Zaire. Sandy, a former Peace Corps volunteer, told her parents back home in Missouri that the job was perfect for her.

Now, on this March 14, 1993 day, the five-foot, five-inch blonde took Bekah, ten, and JoJo, three, into the water. Ken Cockrane, a 28-year-old research assistant from California, joined them.

Sandy looked at her watch: 6:10pm. "Time to get out. It's going to be dark soon," she called. Ken herded the reluctant children ashore while Sandy waded out waist-deep, lathering up her thick, shoulder-length hair. Bending forward, she rinsed it with both hands.

A snout and two yellow reptilian eyes broke the surface of the river. The beast sensed prey moving in the water. Off in the twilight, it sighted splashing. Submerging without a ripple, the eight-foot-long reptile tucked its clawed and webbed feet against its 300-pound body. Its powerful tail drove it swiftly through the murky water.

Whoomph! Knocked off her feet, Sandy tumbled underwater. A crushing pain in her left forearm took her breath away. She sensed a malevolent, primal presence beside her. *I've been grabbed by a crocodile!*

Instinctively, she thought first of the children. *I've got to warn Ken.* Pushing her feet against the sandy river bottom, she thrust her head to the surface. Ken stood ten feet away, knee-deep in the water, his back to her.

Behind him, Sandy saw the children on the riverbank reaching for their towels. "Crocodile!" she gasped. Ken shot her a disapproving look. "Don't even joke about that," he admonished.

The crocodile jerked her under again, savaging her like a rag doll. Its great jaws were studded with 70 wicked teeth designed to penetrate flesh and hold a victim underwater until it drowned. She felt the bones in her forearm grind sickeningly. *I'm going to be dragged off and eaten by this thing and Ken doesn't believe me!* Reaching over the snout with her free arm, she clasped the fingers of her left hand protruding out the far side of its jaws, and locked her arms together. Again she pushed with her legs, staggering upright. Breaking the surface, she screamed, "Crocodile!"

Ken froze. Sandy stood in waist-deep water, straining to hold up the great, ugly green head, its frightful jaws clamped around her left arm. In a heartbeat she was gone.

Ken dived into the churning water, reaching her as she emerged spluttering, "It's got my arm!" Getting behind her, he grabbed her shoulders. Then he began pulling her backward toward the bank, reassuring her, "Hang on, Sandy."

Suddenly, the water stilled. Ken knew crocodiles rarely give up their prey. From such watery ambushes, the reptiles kill more than 400 people a year.

Ken's hand grazed something underwater. A chill ran up his spine as he realized it was the crocodile's snout. He fingered rows of frightful teeth clamping Sandy's wrist. *Oh my God, it's still got her.*

Desperately, he tried to pry the jaws apart, but it was as if they were welded shut. Without warning, the crocodile exploded into a frenzied roll, jerking Sandy away. Ken lunged for her waist and held on tight.

If I don't let go, it will rip her arm off. Reluctantly he released her and watched her corkscrew underwater, a blur of honey-blond hair and pale face entwined around the thrashing animal. He hovered over her spinning body, feeling helpless against the overwhelming strength of this monster. *How do you fight a crocodile with your bare hands?*

The sudden, wrenching torque snapped the bones in Sandy's upper arm like twigs. Anger at the brute ripping her body apart welled up through her fear and pain, and with it came a fierce determination to survive. *It can have my arm,* she resolved, *but not my life. I can't die like this!* Quick thinking and a cool head had got Sandy out of tough situations before. Once, in Mali with the Peace Corps, she was attacked by killer bees, and narrowly escaped injury by jumping into a ditch and pulling her jacket over her head. Now she struggled to remain calm. *What do I know about crocodiles?* A scene from the movie *Crocodile Dundee* flashed before her. Crocs drown their prey in a death roll, Mick Dundee had said. *It's not just trying to drag me off,* Sandy now realized. *It's trying to drown me.*

Abruptly, the spinning ceased. The reptile lay motionless, holding her underwater. Planting her feet on the bottom, she pushed to the surface.

"Hang on," Ken encouraged as her head surfaced and she filled her lungs. "We'll get you away from this thing."

The vicious spinning left her disoriented and sickened. She recalled hearing that punching predators on the nose made them let go. She rained blows on the beast's snout with her free arm.

Ken, probing beneath the water, located the crocodile's bony eye sockets. He gouged hard with his thumbs, but they just bent back against a triple layer of impenetrable, leathery eyelids. Cursing, he tore at the great reptile's throat with both hands. The beast never flinched.

By now, the crocodile had drawn them nearly 25 feet from the riverbank into the strong current. Already on tiptoe, Sandy could barely get her face above water.

HIDDEN MENACE

Lurking beneath the muddy waters of the Epulu River in the African jungle, the drab hide of a crocodile would have been hard to see as it swam stealthily towards Sandy Rossi. A crocodile has a variety of hunting techniques, ranging from simple, savage rushes to complex entrapment. If it can get a firm grip with its teeth, the crocodile will hold its victims in vicelike jaws, pulling them into deeper waters until they drown.

Ken was afraid of ripping Sandy's arm off if he pulled on her, so he seized the reptile's head and hauled for dear life, towing the crocodile toward the bank. Sandy helped as best she could, trying to ignore the crushing pain in her arm. Pure defiance burned in her blue eyes. "We're going to beat this thing!" she yelled.

Ken pounded the beast with short jabbing rights, but it was like punching the front of a tank. Sandy's face was pale, contorted in pain, but Ken saw her jaw set in grim determination. *She's counting on me. I can't let her down.*

Panting with exertion, inch by inch, together they gained a foot, then a yard, then another. When they reached waist-deep water, the bank was tantalizingly near. Ken looked over his shoulder. *Just six more feet.*

Whoosh! The crocodile snapped into another death roll, batting Ken aside.

Sandy gritted her teeth as she went under. *I'll tuck and roll with it, then when it stops, I won't be dead.* She feared drowning more than she feared the crocodile. With her good arm she tried to protect her head from the big rocks littering the river bottom. *One, two . . .* she counted the rolls . . . *three, four . . . ride it out then get air . . . five, six, seven . . . stopped!*

Ken hauled her up. He glanced over his shoulder at the riverbank, his heart sinking; they were chest deep again. It would be easy for the crocodile to sweep them out into midstream.

Frantically, he and Sandy heaved for shore. They worked in a yard or two. Then the crocodile spun wildly again.

This time Sandy managed to fill her lungs before being dragged under. She focused on counting rolls. *Two . . . five . . . eight . . . Sweet Jesus, help me, it isn't going to stop*, she prayed. At ten rolls the crocodile finally ceased and lay still.

Lungs bursting, she fumbled for the river bottom with her feet. Nothing. She flailed out in every direction in the murky water. Nauseated and disoriented, she couldn't tell up from down. A stream of air bubbles trickled past her face. *Follow them up.* She moved toward a pale glimmer.

A watery image of Ken's face appeared above her; she reached for it, but the crocodile held her in deep water now. She never knew it was possible to hold her breath so long. Scissor-kicking, she lunged for Ken with her right hand, catching his wrist. She clawed her way up his bicep, then his shoulder, heaving with all her remaining strength as he pulled her to him.

Her face broke the surface, mouth wide, sucking great, sobbing breaths. With his own six-foot, two-inch frame neck-deep, Ken knew Sandy could no longer touch bottom.

Not once had the great reptile surfaced. There was no need; it could stay submerged for up to an hour while its victim drowned. The brute's walnut-size brain knew nothing of giving in. Greater resistance prompted ever more violent and aggressive attack. When a crocodile, the closest living reptilian relative of the dinosaur, has prey in its jaws, no creature on earth can make it release its death grip.

The beast snapped into another series of rolls. In deeper water now there was no resisting the current as they spiraled downstream around a bend.

After the bend the water became shallower. Ken now stood thigh-deep, braced against a flood-gauge pole, wrestling the crocodile's head.

Growing even more frenzied, the creature twirled Sandy with such fury she smashed into the flood gauge, snapping it in half. The broken point speared through her left shoulder, driving deep into her rib cage and narrowly missing her

STILL WATERS: **The Epulu harbours killers in its murky depths.**

lungs. Stabbing pain shot through her. *If you black out you'll die*, she thought, fighting for consciousness.

Ken grabbed her waist, heaving backward for shore like a man possessed. With no thought now of saving her arm, he was locked in a macabre tug of war with the crocodile for Sandy's life. Heels dug into the mud, he strained against the monster as it lashed its great tail, its flailing razor-sharp claws slashing his legs, neither man nor beast giving an inch.

Sandy steeled herself and pulled as hard as she could, her legs kicking for the beach. Backs to the shore, legs hammering into the mud, they suddenly rocketed out of the water and sprawled onto land. Dazed, they lay with chests heaving. In the dim light, Ken looked down and saw a bloody, chewed stump of bone and muscle where Sandy's left forearm had been; what was left of her hand dangled by a few strands of sinew and skin. The ferocity of the attack had rammed her elbow and broken upper-arm bones into her shoulder, swelling her upper arm to three times its normal size.

The creature rose out of the water, swinging its huge head back and forth. It opened its jaws wide and gulped down Sandy's forearm. Then, with its cold reptilian eyes locked on Sandy, it slithered backward into the river.

They were only a foot from the water's edge, but before Ken could move Sandy he had to apply a tourniquet. Otherwise she'd bleed to death. Using a T-shirt, he tied a tourniquet tight around Sandy's arm, tucking what remained of her left hand against the pressure point.

Together, they ran up the embankment. At the crest, relief flooded over Sandy. *It can't get me now*.

Sandy's recovery was not assured, however. She had lost a lot of blood. At 6.50 that evening, Ken drove her to the village clinic, where a proper tourniquet was attached, and she was given antibiotics. It was 8pm before Sandy was placed on a mattress in a four-wheel-drive, and Ken set off across the rough jungle roads.

They arrived at the field hospital three hours later, where a Dutch doctor amputated the remains of Sandy's hand. The next day she was flown to Nairobi for more expert care, but the doctors there advised only rest, large doses of antibiotics and a transfusion to boost her strength before she returned to the United States for special surgery. Ken had the same blood type, so he donated some blood for Sandy.

"Ken risked his life to save mine," Sandy said. "He's like a big brother to me."

But Ken had the last words: "Sandy's alive because she refused to give up."

Sandy returned to the United States, where surgeons took muscle from her back and skin grafts from her leg to fashion tissue around the raw bone to support a prosthesis.

Volcano
chopper down

by Per Ola and Emily D'Aulaire

Scrambling from their doomed craft, the three stunned survivors were marooned by vents of hissing steam and a pit of boiling lava.

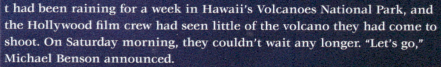

t had been raining for a week in Hawaii's Volcanoes National Park, and the Hollywood film crew had seen little of the volcano they had come to shoot. On Saturday morning, they couldn't wait any longer. "Let's go," Michael Benson announced.

Benson, 49, was in Hawaii to film background footage for the thriller *Silver*. He was accompanied by camera technician Chris Duddy, 31, and helicopter pilot Craig Hosking, 34. They planned to fly low over the volcano and zoom in on the crater floor with a special camera.

The site chosen was the smoking Pu'u O'o vent of Kilauea, the world's most active volcano. In ten years, its oozing lava had devoured villages and added hundreds of acres to the island as it hissed into the sea and solidified. Now, during a quieter period, the crater floor, larger than three football fields, was covered with a thin layer of hardened lava.

As they prepared to film that November 21, 1992, Benson decided to buy a little insurance. He knew some islanders believed in the powers of a volcano goddess called Madame Pele. They pictured her with fiery eyes, lava-black hair and a fondness for gin. So Benson—with a flair for the dramatic—decided to drop a bottle of gin into the crater. "We need only a few minutes of good weather," he explained. "Maybe with a little persuasion, Madame Pele will cooperate."

As Hosking circled the chopper above the steaming cone, Duddy tossed out the offering. He missed the opening, however, and the bottle exploded on the volcano's rim. "Close enough," Benson said. "She'll get the idea."

Hosking now hovered over the smoking caldera while Benson filmed the crater floor. "We got some good footage," Benson said. "But to be sure, let's do one more take."

This "shoot" was the kind of cinematic challenge that Benson, a veteran of such hits as *Terminator II* and *Patriot Games*, thrived on. Tall, lean, with brown hair and blue eyes, Benson knew he had a tough, winning team. With a craggy face and prematurely white hair, Duddy already had over 40 films to his credit. The gangling Hosking was known as one of the film industry's best helicopter pilots.

At 11.25am, they passed 300 feet above the crater's rim—right over the spot where Duddy had tossed the bottle. Suddenly, a warning light appeared on the instrument panel. "We've lost power," Hosking said. "We're going down."

They were descending to the left of a red-hot lava pond at 60mph. Clearly they were going down *inside* the volcano. There was no chance of clearing the rim and returning to the outside for an emergency landing.

Frantically, Hosking peered through breaks in the clouds, looking for a flat place to set the chopper down. Fortunately, he was steering away from the 2500-degree lava pool.

Heading for the edge: "Let's do one more take."

As he flared the nose slightly upward for a controlled landing, the main rotor hit a large boulder, causing the craft to drop the last few feet like a stone. The chopper's tail section broke off, and its batteries were smashed. The radio was dead.

Scrambling from the cabin, the three men fought for air in the sulfurous fumes. "We've got to get out of here before we suffocate," Benson said, gasping.

Steam hissed angrily from the ground. Nearby, the lava pond boiled ominously, and the heat beneath the thin rock warmed their feet. *If there's a hell,* Duddy thought, *it's definitely like this.*

With visibility less than 20 feet, they knew no one could spot them from the air. Indeed, no one would even be looking for them for another hour, when they were due back. "We'll have to hike out," Hosking said.

With Duddy in the lead, they picked their way toward a rock-strewn slope that angled sharply to the rim 300 feet above. In 15 minutes, they hiked about halfway up the crater wall.

Scrambling through layers of ash and crumbling rock, they sank to their knees, slipping backward with almost each step. As the slope increased to 45 degrees they had to crawl. "Keep three points of contact with the rock," Hosking said, recalling his climbing experience in the Rocky Mountains. "Two legs and one arm, or two arms and one leg."

Finally Duddy clambered onto a ledge. Above him, an overhanging rock face blocked his route. "I can't go any farther!" he yelled to the others, 50 feet below. "Don't come this way!"

Benson and Hosking crouched on another narrow ledge. "Hang on tight," Hosking told Benson. "I'll work my way back. Maybe I can get the chopper radio working."

"You'll suffocate down there," Benson argued.

"If we stay here, we'll either fall or choke to death," Hosking replied. "My going down is our only hope." And he disappeared into swirling steam below.

Reaching the crater floor, Hosking was engulfed by foul-smelling hydrogen sulfide and sulfur dioxide. He tore off his shirt and wrapped it around his nose and mouth to filter the fumes.

Hosking removed the battery from the movie camera. *If I could rig a connection,* he thought, *maybe that would power the radio too.* But he had to fight against blacking out. Again and again, he would crawl 50 feet up the slope where the air was less noxious, take a few deep breaths, then return to splicing the stripped wires to the camera battery.

Finally, after an hour, a spark signaled that the circuit was working. "This is Hilo Bay Three," Hosking announced. "Any aircraft in the vicinity of the vent? We're in the crater."

"You're *in* the crater?" responded the pilot of their backup helicopter.

"Roger. Aircraft not flyable, no injuries, but we can't climb out."

"We've notified Search and Rescue," the pilot replied. "A chopper's on the way."

Hosking shouted up to his friends: "I got through! They're sending help!" But Benson and Duddy could not hear him over the lava's grumbling, nor could they see him through the thick smoke.

At 1.30pm Don Shearer, a contract helicopter pilot on the neighboring island of Maui, received an urgent call from a dispatcher. "A helicopter's crashed in the Pu'u O'o crater. There are survivors."

Shearer had worked with park rangers on plane crashes, lost hikers, downed sightseeing helicopters—but never anything in an active volcano. He quickly fueled up and headed for the island.

As his Hughes-500 chopper approached the crater an hour after receiving the call, the radio picked up one of Hosking's appeals: "We need help . . . air."

This guy's on his last legs, Shearer realized. *If I don't get him out soon, it'll be too late.* "You'll have to direct me by sound."

Hosking answered that he understood. *But what about Mike and Chris?* he wondered. Reluctantly, he realized his best bet was to get out, then help rescuers pinpoint the whereabouts of Benson and Duddy.

Shearer moved cautiously in the blinding fog, unable to see either floor or walls of the crater. "To your right," Hosking said.

Edging sideways, Shearer spotted the wrecked chopper just 30 feet ahead. "I'm real close," he radioed Hosking. "Run toward the noise of the helicopter."

Hosking sprang forward, crawled onto the left skid of the hovering craft, and hauled himself into the rear seat. Barely able to breathe, Shearer maneuvered along the crater floor until he thought he was clear of any overhang. Pulling maximum power, he took the chopper straight up, high above the volcano. From the back seat, Hosking threw both arms around Shearer, tears of joy streaming down his cheeks.

When Hosking had first climbed down to the wreckage, Benson and Duddy could see him through breaks in the clouds. But then the fumes worsened, and an acidic, blinding fog surrounded each man. They took off their shirts and wrapped them around their faces to filter the poisonous air.

Later, Benson and Duddy heard a helicopter, but couldn't tell where it was. Benson yelled down to where Hosking had been. Maybe he knew what was going on. No reply.

"Is he dead?" Duddy called.

"I don't think anyone could survive down there this long," Benson replied.

A feeling of doom overcame Duddy. Divorced, with two young children, he thought, *I don't want to die this way. I want to see my kids grow up.* One by one, he pictured every person in his family. Out loud, he told them he loved them.

CAUSTIC CAULDRON

They were descending to the left of a red-hot lava pond at 60mph. Suddenly, the main rotor hit a boulder: the craft dropped like a stone.

With Duddy in the lead, the three men picked their way toward a rock-strewn slope that angled sharply to the rim 300 feet above . . . nearby the lava pool boiled.

Park rangers Jeffrey Judd and Neil Akana worked their way to the rim above Benson and Duddy. Extremely unstable, the area could slough off at any moment. Visibility was no more than an arm's length. Fumes at the rim were so pungent they corroded the stainless-steel clips on their climbing ropes. The rangers had to wear gas masks.

Akana snapped himself to a rope and crept to the crumbling edge of the volcano. Judd and several firefighters held the rope's other end. "We're going to throw ropes over the side!" Akana called. "If you see one, grab it, and we'll haul you out!"

Duddy's heart leaped. "We're down here!" he shouted.

Again and again, Akana threw a bright orange rope over the side, fishing blindly for the men. Duddy's voice echoed off the crater wall, making it difficult to pinpoint his location. Benson couldn't hear Akana's voice over the lava pit's roar.

The rangers were soon joined by Hosking, who insisted on helping. As darkness fell, however, they returned to their base camp, hoping to come up with another strategy.

Huddling on the cliff, Benson and Duddy shivered as a rainstorm drenched them and temperatures fell to the 50s. Duddy, consumed by fear, called to Benson, "Maybe it's smarter and quicker just to jump into the crater!"

"Don't do it!" Benson shouted back. "Be patient."

Benson's confidence gave Duddy second thoughts. *If Mike can take it, so can I.*

On Sunday morning, Shearer learned that corrosive fumes had damaged his chopper's turbine the day before, grounding him. And poor visibility stymied the rangers' efforts to help the trapped men.

Duddy couldn't stand the prospect of another night on the ledge. He looked at his watch: 3pm. "I can't take it anymore," he called down to Benson. "I'm climbing."

Benson heard his determination. "OK," he said. "Good luck."

Duddy stood up, reeling from vertigo. He wriggled his fingers into a crack in the cliff. His feet found a toehold. The rock was wet and slick. His arms and legs shook with fear—but he hung on. He could see the top of the rim now. Forty feet to go.

Six feet from the top, he was stopped cold by a wall of compacted gravel and stone. Rocks crumbled in his hands as he groped for a hold. *It's over*, he thought. *I can't go up or down.* He looked above him. The top was so close. *I have to try.*

Carefully, he sank both hands into the gravel up to his elbows. In one final, mighty pull, he heaved himself up and landed on his stomach on top of the rim. He lay a moment, gasping in disbelief, then yelled to Benson, "I made it! I'll make sure they know exactly where you are." Benson heard nothing above the whistling wind and lava.

Following a rope that rangers had left as a marker, Duddy stumbled down the outside of the cone to the overjoyed rescuers. "Mike is 150 feet below the rim, just to the right of where the ropes are," he told them. "You've got to get him out!"

As a stopgap measure, rangers decided to drop packages of food, water, clothing and portable radios over the rim. They hoped that Benson might be able to reach one of them. It would help him through the night.

In the fading twilight, Benson saw something hurtling through the mist. It looked big, heavy and striped. *Oh my God!* he thought. Duddy had been wearing a striped shirt. *It's Chris!* Then he heard a sickening thud on the crater floor. "Chris!" he screamed. *Why didn't I try to stop him?* Suddenly Benson felt responsible for the whole disaster. *Why did I insist on that final shot?*

Waiting for sunup on the third day, Benson strained to breathe. His throat was so sore he could no longer call for help. He caught rain water in the half-inch depression on his light meter's face and sipped every drop. He thought of his wife of 25 years and their two children. They were telling him to be strong. *We love you,* they seemed to say. *You're going to be rescued. Stay put.*

The gases he breathed caused strange thoughts to race through his head. As the swirling mist parted briefly, Benson saw a human profile on a distant rock. *Madame Pele! You're not going to win. I'm getting out of here!* Then he prayed for a miracle. *Please, God,* he pleaded, *make the day clear so they can see me from the air.*

Members of the film crew had managed to track down Tom Hauptman, a daring rescue pilot. Early Monday, Hauptman flew to the crater rim with ranger Judd in the copilot's seat.

Hearing a loud noise overhead, Benson peered upward. Suddenly the air cleared, and 80 feet above him he made out the tail rotor of a helicopter. Frantically, he waved—and the pilot waved back. Benson couldn't believe his eyes.

The craft vanished again, but a voice boomed over the chopper's public-address system. "We're lowering a rescue net!" Benson thanked God for the miracle.

Hauptman programmed his satellite navigation system to home in on the exact spot where he had seen Benson. Now the pilot eased down to rim level and hovered delicately, lowering the net into the swirling clouds below. Hauptman waited ten seconds, then climbed to where he could check his "catch." The net was empty. Benson had seen it, but it was just out of reach.

Hauptman waited for another opening in the clouds. He lowered the basket and hovered above the side of the cliff.

This time the rope dangled within Benson's reach. When he pulled it toward him, however, the net snagged on a rock. Hands trembling, Benson struggled to free it. But before he could climb into the net, it began to rise. *There goes my last chance,* he thought glumly.

However, the net came back, this time dangling ten feet in front of Benson. Without a moment's hesitation, he dived into it. When Hauptman broke into clear air, he let out a whoop. "We've got a live one!" he screamed to Judd.

Benson, Duddy and Hosking all suffered dehydration, minor abrasions and pulmonary problems. Duddy and Hosking made a full recovery before Benson, who continued treatment for some time. Rangers believe that his 48-hour survival ordeal inside the active volcano was a world record.

The experience had a profound effect on each of the three men. As Benson summed up at the time: "They say a cat has nine lives. If I were a cat, I would've used at least five of mine in that volcano. I'm not about to squander what's left."

"YOU'RE IN THE CRATER?": (left to right) Hosking, Duddy and Benson.

Typhoon!

by Peter Michelmore

It blew out of the sea, smothering ship and mates. On deck, four divers were trapped in a cage of death.

S he had been running northeast toward safer waters for hours—a 20,000-ton, four-level-high dead weight strung on a towline behind a tugboat. But the typhoon was too swift. Shrieking winds had overtaken Derrick Barge 29, and by daybreak on August 15, 1991, she was floundering through the South China Sea at less than two knots of speed.

Many of the 195 men aboard were still below in their cabins when control-tower operator Craig DeJean, 33, an American originally from Texas, saw waves loosen two ten-ton steel anchor buoys on deck. They hammered at the planking around the hatch leading to the barge's water-desalination plant. Suddenly there was a screech of metal and DeJean was shouting, "We've lost the hatch!"

Sea water poured down on the desalination units as first engineer Graham Wheeler raced into the adjoining room, which contained the barge's main pumps. Wheeler and several crewmates ripped up floor plates and tried to weld them to the desalination-room door, but the force of the water was too great. Now, turning to the pumps, already in swirling water, Wheeler opened wide the outlet valves. A big jet pump shot water overboard like a fire hose.

But the flood was creeping up over Wheeler's knees. Once it reached the jet pump's air-intake valves, the machinery would shut down. Swamping seas would sink the barge. In a delaying action, Wheeler left the jet pump running and sealed off the two rooms by shutting a watertight door leading from the pump room.

"I don't think we can save her," an exhausted Wheeler told the chief engineer.

The alarm spread quickly by word of mouth. "Put on your life jackets! Get on deck! We're in trouble!" Up and down the already listing barge, steel corridors rang with the sounds of running workers who were pulling on orange life jackets.

On deck, DeJean pushed into the hard wind, heading for the saturation diving chamber. A sickening pit formed in his stomach as he thought of the four men trapped inside the 10-by-28-foot chamber. The divers, who had been working on the ocean floor, had another two days to go before their bodies would be conditioned to air pressure at sea level. If they were taken out of the chamber now, helium gas dissolved in their tissues would bubble up inside their bodies. The "bends" could kill them or leave them paralyzed for life.

For emergencies such as this, many offshore construction vessels carry self-propelled hyperbaric lifeboats that attach to the diving chambers. Divers stay inside, cramped but safe, until they depressurize.

But such lifeboats are not required by law, and DeJean knew that Derrick Barge 29 had none. *How do we save the divers?*

Craig DeJean was one of the hardy, self-sufficient breed of men who work offshore oil fields the world over. Most toil 90 days straight, take 30 days off, then eagerly come back for more. DeJean himself had enjoyed the routine, and the money, since graduating from high school.

His present job was to help lay pipe on the ocean floor leading to an oil-drilling platform about 100 miles southeast of Hong Kong. The field was Chinese. It was being developed by a multinational group, which had hired the giant New Orleans-based McDermott International marine construction company to build the platforms and pipelines.

Derrick Barge 29 was commanded by Billy Young, 47, also from Texas. The work force was mostly young Malaysian and Filipino riggers and welders. Many of the 40 or so Westerners aboard were engineers, technicians or divers.

On Tuesday, August 13, nearly four months into the project, which was running behind schedule, a tropical storm blew in from the direction of the Philippines. Young called up the divers from 360 feet down and ordered the barge to be readied for departure.

Derrick Barge 29 had no seagoing power of her own, so Captain Robert Zwart, 40, a stocky, bearded Dutchman, brought his tugboat *Typhoon* alongside. Crewmen attached the towline coming from the barge, and they headed northeast, away from the storm's path—9500 horsepower of tugboat muscle pulling the 420-foot barge.

There was disappointment aboard, but no fear. Several times before on this mission the barge had run from typhoons. Young had done it so often that his men called him Typhoon Billy. For DeJean, it just meant a delay in getting back to his wife, Tania, and his three young daughters in Aracaju, Brazil, where he had chosen to live.

Graham Wheeler, 46, a British-born New Zealander who worked the night shift with DeJean, was overdue for leave. "It's my three-year-old grandson," growled Wheeler, a six-foot-two-inch oak of a man. "He can only handle me being away two months."

These two men slept through most of Wednesday, awakened to rough seas and made their separate post-midnight patrols under the arc lights of the barge. By Thursday's misty dawn, the tropical storm had become Typhoon Fred, with winds of 80 miles per hour. The barge was 78 miles north of the typhoon's direct path, but this storm was casting its fury wide.

A swarm of off-duty divers and technicians was gathering at the saturation diving chamber when DeJean got there at seven o'clock. "We're trying to get the guys into the diving bell," one of the divers told him.

It was a makeshift plan of evacuation. The bell could be lifted overboard, then recovered later and towed to Hong Kong, where the divers could continue their decompression. But the tension showed in the faces of the half-dozen divers outside the chamber. The bell always remained depressurized on the deck for possible emergency use, and the divers in the chamber could not be moved until the pressure and gases were restored.

"I'm going to need 15 hours, Graham," the diving boss said to Wheeler, who had reached the scene.

Wheeler's heart sank. "If I can give you 15 hours, I can give you 100," he replied. "It doesn't look good."

Wheeler thought of John Lyons, one of the divers inside the chamber who was also from New Zealand. Like his fellow divers, Lyons loved the sea but talked often of home and his dream of settling down with his wife and children.

Billy Young and several divers talked to the men in the chamber by intercom in an effort to keep their spirits up. The four divers could be seen moving about behind the small view ports. As the situation deteriorated, the diving boss opened the chamber's valves and began emergency decompression. Everyone knew what this last-ditch, risky effort meant, and nothing more was said.

Wheeler saw a foreman hurrying from Young's office. "Billy's asking the Singapore office how much list we have before we capsize."

"It will start to go at 17½ degrees," Wheeler said quickly.

The foreman reeled, his face dead white. "We're at 18 now."

"Then we're going over!" cried Wheeler, turning on his heels. Plunging below, he and several engineers darted through the corridors of the barge, closing off watertight doors. "We have to give her buoyancy," he called as he ran.

Wheeler clung to the hope that she would not flip over completely and sink. His mind was insistent, driving him on. *I've got to save her to save the divers.*

Bounding back upstairs, Wheeler and an electrician cut life rafts free from the barge. They saw the towline separate from the tugboat and, immediately, the barge swung broadside into the surging seas. As it went into a slow roll, shouts and screams rose above the gale. "She's going over! Jump! Jump!"

Then the port side and bow of the barge became a storm-tossed litter of falling men and life rafts. Some rafts deployed on the deck or in the water. Others hit the water and turned over or only partially inflated. Those that popped open all the way threw up orange canopies, ready to take a full complement of 26 men if they could reach them.

Racing up the slanted deck, Wheeler looked back for the electrician. Horrified, he watched the starboard gantry crane jump its tracks and slam into the man, crushing him against the pipeline-assembly tunnel.

Then the bow deck under his boots suddenly gave a mighty heave, and Wheeler was thrown 150 feet. He somersaulted through flying containers and steel plates. It was chaos, yet he heard nothing. To his mind, it was the silence of death. *This is it!*

SWAMPED ALIVE

Epic rescues by tugboat and helicopters saved 173 men from Derrick Barge 29 . . . 22 men perished. The saturation diving chamber, welded to the deck, never detached from the barge . . . the four divers inside were trapped in a terrible limbo as the capsized barge floated on the surface.

Wheeler saw a hole appear through the blizzard of debris. Flapping his arms, he bellied into the sea, head over heels.

Breathless and gagging on diesel-fouled water, Wheeler came to the surface. His legs were immovable, locked in spasm. His lower back twinged at every move. Bobbing near his face was a piece of timber, eight inches square and about six feet long. He curled his arm over it and hugged fiercely. *I'll never let go.*

A dead body, still tied in an orange life jacket, washed toward him. He pushed it away but, nightmarishly, the body kept returning. Then came another and another, until there were five. *Is everybody dead?*

Rising and falling on his piece of wood, Wheeler saw an upside-down raft floating by. As he struggled to reach it, two Filipinos popped their heads over the side and hauled him aboard.

Craig DeJean struggled in the water on the other side of the slowly capsizing barge, clinging tightly to a line running alongside an inverted raft. He had plummeted from the starboard rail just as the steel lip of the hull broke clear of the water. It caught him across the back of the thighs and pitched him into the ocean. De Jean managed to glance at his watch. It was 8.34am.

His mind flashed back to the horror of seeing the diving chamber with the men still inside. In anguish, he raised his eyes to the wind-driven surf. "God help us," he groaned.

The prayer was on his lips when a hand came over the side of the raft and closed on his own. Then he felt a body splash at his side and an arm encircle his shoulders. "I've got you, mate," said a voice in a quiet British accent.

At the lift of a wave, Tim Griffiths eased the American into the arms of New Zealander Mark Rusden, who set him down in the folds of the damaged raft. Rusden winced at the effort. He, too, had hit the steel lip of the hull. "Caught it right across the buttocks," Rusden said.

Griffiths, a diver and life-support technician, tried to fashion a splint for DeJean's mashed right thigh from a sodden work vest. He could not make it secure. Sea water sloshed into DeJean's open wounds, sending bolts of agony through him.

But the wound in his heart was deeper. He was alive, still with a chance. The divers were sealed in a tomb, facing inevitable death.

Raising his hand, DeJean looked into the faces of Tim, Mark and two Malaysians. "We ought to say a prayer for our lost mates," he said hoarsely. As the raft swept away on the sea, the five men huddled in its folds, heartsick and silent.

"LIFE RAFT AT 12 O'CLOCK." How many were dead?

Soon a raft with a raised canopy floated toward them. "We're going to get you under cover," Griffiths told DeJean. "When that raft gets closer, I'm going to swim for it." Calmly, he looped a rope around his life jacket and knotted it in front.

The others looked at the raging ocean, then back to the Englishman in amazement. But when the distance closed to 150 feet, Griffiths handed the free end of his lifeline to Rusden and dived into the foaming, mountainous sea.

With a cry of dismay, Rusden felt the rope come loose from Griffiths's body. Then the dark head in the water turned and headed back. "Me and my bloody knots," he joked.

After retying the line, he was over the side again, disappearing into the waves, until he reached the raft. A Filipino and two Malaysians helped Griffiths haul in the damaged raft and put DeJean in a sheltered corner. *Bravest thing I ever saw*, DeJean thought, looking at a man who swam through typhoons.

On the bridge of the tugboat, Captain Robert Zwart had hit the distress button on his satellite telephone as soon as he saw the men jumping into the ocean. By 9.08am, he was on direct voice line to the Maritime Rescue Coordination Centre in Canberra, Australia. "I'm alongside Derrick Barge 29. She has capsized and is sinking. I have over 100 people in the water and require immediate assistance."

Canberra immediately telephoned the details to the search-and-rescue office in Hong Kong. Search coordinator Trevor Berry took the message and gave a single command. "Launch everything!"

Eighteen minutes later, helicopters of the Royal Hong Kong Auxiliary Air Force took flight into fierce head winds from Kai Tak airport. British Royal Air Force crews scrambled at their base in Hong Kong's New Territories; on mainland China two choppers from a private company joined the search.

Flying in and out of rain squalls, the pilots had periods of near-zero visibility. But the view was clear for a fixed-wing aircraft that arrived first on the scene. Its pilots saw waves breaking over the disappearing keel of the barge and orange rafts and life jackets and debris littering the sea for miles around.

A Chinese container ship, *Ming Plenty*, alerted by radio and already close by, agreed to stay on site as a reference point for incoming choppers. The Soviet freighter *Ulan-Ude* signaled readiness to take survivors aboard.

"Life raft at 12 o'clock." RAF Master Air Crewman Adrian Jones, 41, checked his harness and winch line as the pilot of the helicopter hovered, nose to the wind, 65 feet over a canopied raft. Launching himself into the gale, Jones aimed directly at it. After three attempts, his boots touched rubber, and he saw eight men. "You first," he said, fitting harnesses under the arms of the two nearest and buckling them firmly.

At a signal tug on the line, Jones, Griffiths and Rusden were up and away in a triple harness. In less than a minute Jones was headed down again.

As he homed in on the raft this time, a 40-foot wave caught him in a full body blow, flinging him sideways. Jones swung back, steadied in the wind, and

"I WAS SPARED BY A MIRACLE." **Graham Wheeler (far left) reasoned. It also saved Craig DeJean (left) while John Lyons (right) and Billy Young perished in the storm.**

continued down. He was drenched, breathing hard, with still six men to save. *I'll never make it this way,* he thought. *It's too difficult to reach the raft.*

Making a crucial decision, he unhooked himself from the line and sent DeJean and another man aloft by themselves, and then two more. He rode up with the last two, and the helicopter turned for Hong Kong.

The 12 crewmen of the tugboat *Typhoon* were still picking their way through the flotsam, plucking men from the sea one by one. Approaching an overturned raft, Captain Zwart cut his motors and let the sea wash his tug close. Crewmen pulled Graham Wheeler aboard and moved him to the shelter of a corridor. His arms were shaking, and his body heaved with vomiting.

Wheeler knew he was going to make it. But he could not fathom why. *The barge is gone. The divers are gone.* Over and over, his mind played the tortured thought *I shouldn't be here!* There, on the tugboat, Wheeler gave in to tears.

Epic rescues by tugboat and helicopters saved 173 men from Derrick Barge 29. Of the 22 who perished, Billy Young and three radio operators died at their posts.

The saturation diving chamber, welded to the deck, never detached from the barge. The four divers were trapped in a terrible limbo for hours as the capsized barge floated on the surface. It was a quiet and somber time of writing last letters of love to wives and children.

Suspended at a depth of 40 feet, they had only one chance—an act of desperation. It is thought that they opened the roller door of the chamber, allowing water to come in slowly around the edges. Once water filled the chamber, three divers managed to struggle through the hatch. As they neared the surface, the pressure on their bodies fell rapidly, and the "bends" proved fatal.

"What happened on Derrick Barge 29 will go around the world like a whiplash," says Graham Wheeler. "Never again should an oil barge leave dock without life-boats for divers."

McDermott International launched an investigation to determine the facts surrounding the incident.

Craig De Jean was hospitalized in Hong Kong with severe internal hemorrhages and puncture wounds to his thighs, then flown to America to recuperate at his parents' home in Bridge City, Texas. He cannot escape flashbacks of horror, but his mind also plays images of heroism. Forever, he will remember that, when all seemed lost, a man appeared at his side in the stormy seas. He still feels the embrace and hears the quiet voice: "I've got you, mate."

Though Wheeler soon had the solace of home and family, his nights have been haunted by the ghosts of the men who died aboard the barge he tried so hard to save. "I was spared by a miracle," he says. "There must be a reason. I must find what it is."

Has anyone got a drill?

by Tess Redgrave

A young footballer lay dying in a remote Australian town, and British doctor Steve Hindley had no tools to save his life.

HALLOWED GROUND: **where the Ravensthorpe Tigers took on the Lake King Raiders football team.**

The sweet perfume of eucalyptus trees wafted through the open window of the doctor's house in Ravensthorpe, a small outback town in Western Australia. Steve Hindley gazed out at rain-soaked bushland and sighed with satisfaction. Saturday, June 27, 1998, was the 41-year-old English doctor's first day in Ravensthorpe, 310 miles southeast of Perth, and his presence here was the realization of a long-held dream.

For years, attracted by the Australian lifestyle, he had been thinking about migrating from Cornwall.

After eventually securing visas and a two-year posting in Tasmania, he went ahead of his wife and three children, having agreed at the last minute to work for a month as a locum in Ravensthorpe first. The slim, dark-haired and bearded newcomer spent his first day unpacking and meeting the local hospital staff, all of whom were welcoming. The town of 400 people felt exotic and strange with its wide streets, sprawling bungalow homes and gum trees, but Hindley savoured the new experience.

Just under a mile away, despite the cold, drizzly midwinter weather, 150 enthusiastic spectators had turned out at the local sports ground to watch the Lake King Raiders Aussie Rules football team take on the Ravensthorpe Tigers. Among the onlookers was 47-year-old Karen Sinclair, a nurse at the town's 11-bed hospital, taking a break for the first time in two years from her usual Saturday shift to cheer on two of her three sons, both players for the Raiders.

"Ouch! I bet that hurt," Karen said to her husband as one of the Raiders players, Hayden McGlinn, took a hard hit to the head and had to be helped off the field, walking groggily. Minutes later she noticed the injured footballer had collapsed and now lay sprawled on the ground.

"Hayden's not looking too good," the blonde, bespectacled nurse told her husband with concern in her voice. "I'm going to check on him." She had known the curly-haired 23-year-old since he was five. Hayden had played with her boys as a child and she still regularly saw him at the shop he managed at Lake King, thirty-seven miles from Ravensthorpe. He always went out of his way to greet Karen and chat with her, and insisted on carrying her goods to her car.

By the time Karen reached Hayden, the team trainer was helping to manoeuvre him onto a stretcher. "Are you all right?" she asked, grabbing the young man's hand.

"No! Please give me something for the pain in my head, it's so bad," Hayden said, slurring the words. "Don't let me die, Karen," he pleaded.

"Call an ambulance," Karen told the stretcher-bearer. "We've got to get him to hospital."

At 5.15pm, as the ambulance left the sports ground, Hayden seemed fully conscious and was calmly looking up at Karen. *I hope he'll be OK, she thought.*

In the hospital's small casualty department, nurses attached Hayden—still wearing his mud-spattered yellow, red and blue striped jumper—to a cardiac monitor and measured his blood pressure and pulse rate. His vital signs were normal. Still, as part of the usual routine, the nurse in charge went to call the new doctor.

When the nurse finally got Hindley on the phone, she explained the young footballer's condition. "We've done the routine tests," she told him.

"I'll be over soon," replied Hindley.

But minutes later, Hayden began to toss his head about and cry out: "My head! My head!"

Something is seriously wrong with this kid, Karen thought. His pulse showed that his oxygen level had dropped and the cardiac monitor showed his heartbeat had begun to slow.

By the time Hindley arrived in casualty, Hayden's condition had deteriorated. His pulse was down to 70, and his blood pressure was elevated at 130 over 90. Hindley made a quick clinical assessment. Hayden was losing consciousness and the doctor realized that, with his pulse falling and his limbs becoming increasingly rigid, the young man was bleeding into his skull. It was the worst possible scenario. "I think he has a serious head injury," said Hindley.

When someone suffers a severe blow to the head, the jelly-like brain is thrust against the opposite wall of the skull, then bounces back again. This can damage veins on the dura mater, the tough outer layer of the meninges, the lining of the brain. Blood from the broken veins begins to collect inside the skull, forming a haematoma and increasing pressure on the brain.

The haematoma eventually puts so much pressure on the brain that it presses down onto the brain stem, the vital control centre for the heart and lungs. The effects include a falling pulse rate, rising blood pressure and paralysis. If the pressure continues to increase, the pulse slows still more and irreversible brain damage follows. Finally the victim's heart and breathing stop altogether.

Hayden was now unconscious, his body rigid and twitching. *A closed head injury!* thought Hindley. *This young man needs a neurosurgeon, and quickly, but the nearest is 300 miles away.*

An IV inserted into Hayden's arm trickled a strong diuretic into his bloodstream. This would help remove water from brain tissue, hopefully relieving the pressure of the haematoma. Hindley then administered a powerful steroid, also to reduce pressure, hoping to stabilize Hayden.

Realizing his patient needed to be moved, Hindley phoned the closest Royal Flying Doctor Service base at Kalgoorlie, 215 miles away. The Flying Doctor Service specializes in transporting seriously ill people from remote communities. A plane had just come in but would have to refuel. The service, Hindley was informed, would call back with an estimated time of arrival at the small airstrip six miles outside Ravensthorpe.

Next, Hindley rang the Sir Charles Gairdner Hospital in Perth. He explained the situation to Dr Steve Lewis, the neurosurgical registrar, who agreed to put a surgical team together and await Hayden's arrival. In the well-equipped hospital, doctors could use high-tech imaging equipment to find out exactly where the bleeding was, then cut away a section of Hayden's skull to relieve the pressure before draining the clot and tying off veins. "Keep me posted about his condition and let me know of any deterioration," said Lewis.

Before Hindley could reply, a nurse called out, "Quickly doctor! He's having a fit."

Hayden jerked and twitched. His head lolled back, then he stopped breathing. Working with desperate speed, Hindley extended Hayden's neck to check his airway, while Karen prepared a breathing tube for insertion into his windpipe. The tube was attached to an oxygen cylinder and a face mask and bag. This could be used as a manual ventilator to breathe for Hayden. But, luckily, the shock of passing the tube into his airway caused him to start breathing again. *He's deteriorating fast*, Hindley realised.

Finally, Hindley injected his patient with a sedative that would stop the fits.

By now, light rain was tapping on the hospital's metal roof. If the weather worsened, Karen feared, the flying-doctor aircraft might not be able to land on the small airstrip.

Hayden's pulse rate was down to 50, his blood pressure 150 over 95. Hindley could see that the young man's left pupil had "blown." It was widely dilated and did not respond when a light was shone into it.

The doctor knew this was a critical turning point: it meant the brain was being pushed down onto the optic nerve of the left eye. At this rate, it was a matter of time, an hour at most, before death became inevitable. Even before that, the brain could suffer permanent damage. With the Flying Doctor Service estimating arrival time at 8.15pm, Hindley guessed it would take another half an hour to move

"HAS ANYONE GOT A DRILL?" **Karen Sinclair asked the waiting crowd.**

Hayden to the plane, then at best another two hours before he got to the hospital in Perth. *There isn't enough time!* he thought. *If I stand here and do nothing he's going to die.*

Hindley was no stranger to medical challenges. In England, as well as running a general practice he had worked as a police surgeon, sometimes being called out up to five times a night. From his training, he knew the only thing he could do to save Hayden was to make a burr hole in his skull to relieve the pressure on his brain—an ancient technique first used by Stone Age medicine men who drilled into people's heads to release evil spirits. The procedure is usually done by neurosurgeons with specialized tools. "We'll need a drill big enough to make a decent-sized hole, and quickly," Hindley said, turning to the nurses.

Knowing there were no drills in the hospital, Karen ran into the lobby where an anxious crowd of 25 people was waiting for news. "Please, has anyone got a drill? Perhaps in their car?" she said loudly. "We need a drillbit about this size." She held up her little finger. "I don't care what type of drill it is, we just need it now.".

Twenty-one-year-old Nathan Gardiner, one of Hayden's best mates, had been in the waiting room since 5.30. For two years, the two had shared a flat and worked together at the same shop. At school, Nathan had used a variety of tools in his woodworking class.

There are bound to be some drills at the school, he thought, and ran off.

Hayden's blood pressure was now dangerously high at 190/100 and his pulse rate was 30. He could suffer cardiac arrest or stop breathing any minute.

At 7.30pm, Hindley phoned Lewis in Perth, told him he intended making a burr hole and asked for advice on the best place to drill. Without a CT scan, he could not know the clot's precise location. Lewis suggested that Hindley drill just above the patient's ear, where no major blood vessels would be in the way. "Even if it goes wrong, you're doing the right thing," the neurosurgeon assured him. "Time is crucial."

While waiting for a drill, a nurse began to shave the left side of Hayden's head. "The clot must be on the side the pupil has blown," Hindley told the nurse. "We'll go in there. If we miss, we'll try again further back." Using a tape measure, Hindley bent over Hayden and marked out a spot with a pen.

Realizing he'd need a key to the school woodworking shop, Nathan roared along gravel backroads to the woodwork teacher's house. It was in darkness. Nathan sped to another teacher's house. It, too, was dark. Finally, he found a teacher with a master key. At 7.35pm, he pulled up outside the hospital and dashed inside, clutching two hand drills. The larger of the two, about 16 inches long, had a crank handle similar to the spanner motorists use for removing wheel nuts when changing tyres. The bit, almost half an inch in diameter, was rusty.

"This will do," said Hindley. "It's about the right size. Karen, would you scrub it clean, please, and swab it with antiseptic? We haven't got time to sterilize it."

It was a long time since Hindley had held such an implement. He carefully positioned the rusty point of the bit above Hayden's left ear. He placed the round cap at the base of the drill against his stomach and began to turn the handle. It squeaked as the drill bit into Hayden's head.

In the back of his mind, Hindley knew that plenty of things could go wrong. Even if Hayden survived, he might have already suffered brain damage. The

OUTBACK ORDEAL

Indian Ocean

WESTERN AUSTRALIA

Perth

Ravensthorpe

Southern Ocean

The small wool and sheep town of Ravensthorpe, 310 miles southeast of Perth, houses approximately 400 people. When British doctor Steve Hindley, working as a locum in the town's small hospital, saw Hayden McGlinn's head injury, he knew the Flying Doctor Service could not transport the youngster to a neurosurgeon in Perth in time to save his life. INSET: in the words of the local tourist bureau, the "welcoming wilderness" surrounding Ravensthorpe was once the site of a nineteenth-century gold rush.

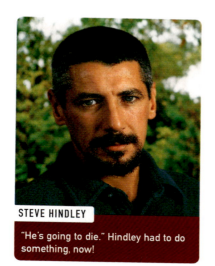

STEVE HINDLEY

"He's going to die." Hindley had to do something, now!

unsterilized bit could expose him to infections of the brain, like meningitis or encephalitis. Or the position he'd chosen could miss the haematoma. Then he would have to drill more holes, wasting precious minutes.

As she watched intently, dread gripped the pit of Karen's stomach. She had seen this procedure once before. The patient had died.

Hindley continued to crank the drill as four, then five minutes passed in silence. Suddenly Hayden flinched. At the same time, Hindley felt resistance slacken as the bit eased through the bone and into the skull cavity.

Hindley slowly unscrewed the drill bit. For a second, nothing happened. Then a dark clot of blood shot out from the small hole in Hayden's head.

Blood continued to ease from the skull as Karen glanced at the pulse reading. It rose a few points, and Karen felt a surge of elation. But suddenly it dipped again. Another large clot began to well out onto the bedsheet. Again the pulse picked up—to 40, then 50, then 60 beats a minute. Karen's hope began to rise again. "Blood pressure's coming down," she said. It was now 130 over 85, close to normal. She pressed the unconscious man's left arm and thigh. Some of the stiffness had gone.

Hindley put the drill aside and the tension drained from his arms and shoulders. He had bored directly into the haematoma at his first attempt. There was only one further thing to do. Hindley administered a large dose of antibiotics to protect Hayden from infection. The young man could still die before he reached Perth, but he had been given another chance.

Hayden arrived at the Perth hospital just on midnight. A CT scan showed his haematoma had been caused by two ruptured veins inside the dura mater. A neurosurgical team operated immediately, draining more blood and tying off the veins. Six days later Hayden was sitting up in bed, smiling.

As the news of Hayden's recovery spread, the town of Ravensthorpe treated Hindley as a hero. In the street, strangers shook his hand. In the pub, locals competed to buy him drinks.

Hayden McGlinn spent five weeks at a Perth rehabilitation centre before returning home to recuperate. He has completely recovered and keeps the life-saving drill in his bedroom.

Several weeks after returning home, Hayden visited Ravensthorpe Hospital to

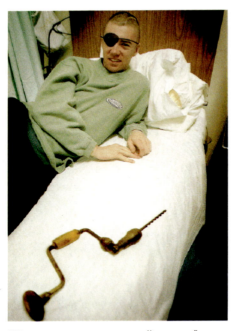

"WITHOUT THAT OLD DRILL AND YOU, I'D BE DEAD."
Hayden McGlinn after his op.

thank Karen and the other nurses. He also rang Hindley in Tasmania where the doctor had taken up his posting. "Thanks for saving my life, mate," he said. "Without that old drill and you, I'd be dead."

Dr Michael Besser, president of the Neurosurgical Society of Australasia and head of the department of neurosurgery at Royal Prince Alfred Hospital in Sydney, agrees. "Dr Hindley undoubtedly saved Hayden McGlinn's life. He made an accurate diagnosis and had the guts to act on it."

Modestly, Hindley says he was just doing his job. "It was a team effort, where everybody pulled their weight. We all did our best for Hayden, and I'm proud to have played my part in that."

Child lost
in the desert!

by Donna Elizabeth Boetig

Five hundred searchers couldn't find little Derrek Clay. His only hope was Kallie, an untried tracker dog.

Shelley Clay glanced out her kitchen window to check on Damien, four, and Derrek, two. "Hide and seek," they chanted, crouching under shrubs in the yard of their trailer home in Maricopa, Arizona, a desert community southwest of Phoenix. Satisfied the boys were all right, Shelley turned her attention back to the roast she was preparing that warm Saturday, April 27, 1991.

It wasn't until later, when her husband, Curtis Clay, an auto mechanic, arrived home and Shelley went outside to greet him that she noticed Derrek was no longer in the yard.

"Where's Derrek?" she asked her older son.

"That way," Damien replied, pointing toward the desert.

"Derrek, Derrek!" the Clays called again and again as rising fear gripped them. They well knew the desert's dangers: scorpions, rattlesnakes, mountain lions and coyotes. Finally, their frantic calls unanswered, Shelley ran inside and called the police.

By the time Pinal County Deputy Gene Berry arrived, the desert was filled with neighbors looking for the youngster. In their zeal, they'd obliterated the boy's tracks.

Help was summoned, and one of the biggest searches in the county's history was set in motion. Rescue teams were organized to cover sections of a three-mile circle around the Clay home. That night, a helicopter swept the area, and early Sunday morning volunteers on horseback scoured the shoulder-high web of vegetation for any sign of Derrek. Then a helicopter crew spotted a disposable diaper decorated with little elephants. From Shelley's description, police knew it must be Derrek's. Spirits soared.

By Sunday night, National Guardsmen and the Border Patrol were on the scene, forming part of a human chain across the desert. Heading up the operation was James Langston, coordinator for the Maricopa County Sheriff's Office Search and Rescue team.

The searchers, over 500 in total, found nothing. Even bloodhounds from the Arizona State Department of Corrections failed to turn up a clue.

DANGEROUS DESERT

The desert of Maricopa, Arizona, southwest of Phoenix, is home to scorpions, rattlesnakes, mountain lions and coyotes, as well as the resilient local population. In the searing heat, thorny shrubs and cactuses grow to extraordinary heights. INSET: the parched desert gives way to distant mountains.

By early Monday morning, more than 36 hours had passed since Derrek was reported missing. Stepping outside the command post, Jim Langston watched the sun rise over the mountains. *How are we ever going to comb every inch of this terrain?* he wondered. Then an idea struck him.

Inside a tiny, windowless office at Utah's Department of Human Services in Salt Lake City, computer analyst Nancy Hachmeister, 35, was working at her keyboard when her beeper sounded. Reaching for the pager clipped to her waistband, she saw the number belonged to Don Hornecker, Arizona's emergency-services coordinator.

For the past ten years, Nancy had volunteered in searches for persons lost in the wilderness—assisted by Utah's Rocky Mountain Rescue Dogs. *Whatever it is, I just can't go this time,* she thought. *They will have to find someone else.*

As the youngest of five daughters, Nancy had enjoyed endless hours with her dad when she was growing up. But on June 11, 1979, he was flying a DC-3 that crashed into a remote river. The bodies of the copilot and five passengers surfaced the first week, but her father's corpse could not be located. Nancy agonized over his fate for 33 days, until rafters finally discovered his remains. Vowing to try to spare others such pain, she began to think about becoming a search-and-rescue volunteer.

Now, as she heard that a two-year-old boy had been lost in the desert for two days, a chill swept over her. *How long can a child live without water?* she thought. *I've got to go.*

Lingering Doubts

Until recently, Nancy had been assisted by Aja, her talented German shepherd. But Aja was injured, and her daughter, Kallie, had replaced her. Nancy had begun to doubt, however, that the daughter possessed her mother's fearless nature—a trait crucial for a search dog. Although Kallie had assisted in several live wilderness finds, there had been a few occasions when she had seemingly lost her nerve.

In one instance, when Nancy's pickup truck was broadsided by a drunk driver, Kallie disappeared for several hours. Nancy found her in the brush, shaken and suffering from a massive chest wound. The dog's ordeal had left her unpredictable and fearful.

That Monday afternoon, Nancy and Kallie flew to Phoenix, then took a bus to the Clays' home. At the command post, she studied a map with colored overlays denoting areas that were already being searched.

"Our deadline is 6pm tomorrow," Jim Langston said. "After that, chances of finding the boy alive are bleak."

Nancy quickly decided that it would be pointless to allow Kallie out into the 85-degree temperatures. Dog and searchers would probably be quickly exhausted in such weather.

Desert scents: "Let's go, girl!"

"We'll wait till sunset," Nancy told Jackie Vernon, 31, an Eloy homemaker whose first search-and-rescue assignment was to be Nancy's partner. "Derrek's track should rejuvenate in the cooler air."

When Nancy asked the Clays for something with their son's scent, Curtis handed her a pair of tiny white ankle socks retrieved from under the boy's bed.

"Find, Kallie!"

Nancy held out the socks for Kallie to sniff. "This is Derrek. Wanna work?" Kallie could barely contain her excitement. Nancy clipped a chemical light stick on the dog's collar to make her visible, then called, "Find, Kallie, find!"

Kallie bounded across the desert, looping around mesquite and cactus, her nose high. Here in the cool sands bleached by moonlight, Derrek's scent lingered.

"She's working well," Nancy told Jackie. When they reached the area where the diaper had been found, a search helicopter suddenly swooped by so low Nancy swore she could touch it. Kallie froze, eyes glazed with fear.

"Let's get back to work, girl," Nancy coaxed. The shepherd cowered, her confidence shaken.

"Let's go, girl," Nancy repeated forcefully. Slowly and cautiously, Kallie began tracking again.

With every passing hour, hopes of finding Derrek alive diminished. Nancy pictured the toddler wandering in the dark, stumbling, calling out to his mother. She removed Derrek's sock from her backpack and put it close to Kallie's nose. "Check it out, Kallie. Is this Derrek?" The dog's eyes met hers as if to say, "I'm doing my best." She stroked the animal's coat. If Kallie sensed her handler doubted her, the dog's confidence would fade completely.

As the temperature dipped into the mid-50s, the

three returned to camp, exhausted. At 1am Jackie was sent home to get some rest. If necessary, she would return the next morning.

Nancy and Kallie woke at 5am that Tuesday and resumed the search. Vultures were circling in the distance, and Nancy feared they might be too late. Suddenly, Kallie began to yip in pain. Cactus spines had pierced the padding on her paws.

"Roll over," Nancy ordered. She removed a pair of surgical pliers for just such an emergency from her backpack and pulled out a dozen spines. Kallie's paw puffed immediately. "I'm not budging," she seemed to say.

"Come on, girl, let's work," Nancy coached. Kallie rose slowly, determined to please her mistress.

By late morning, Kallie had become paralyzed by the heat, and Nancy was feeling drained. The two returned to the command post to rest.

Faint Cry

When the sun set, Nancy and Kallie resumed work, joined by Jackie. The deadline for finding Derrek had come and gone. Like the other volunteers, the women knew Derrek probably wouldn't be alive after 75 hours in the desert, but they all refused to give up hope.

About 9.45pm Kallie caught a scent in the still air and raced up a hillside. Again, she yelped in pain. A jumping cholla cactus had released an army of needles into the dog's legs and stomach. Nancy removed the spines she could see, but minutes later Kallie was struck again.

Exhausted, her paws sore and swollen, Kallie strained to keep going. *How much longer can she push herself?* Nancy wondered.

Then an astonishing thing happened. As if propelled by an unseen force, Kallie raised her nose into the air and began to track furiously. She led the women to the base of a mountain more than three miles from camp, where they heard a faint cry—and another.

"Find Derrek!" Nancy shouted. But the dog, already racing ahead, had stopped at a paloverde tree and was on point.

"Got something to show me, Kallie?" Nancy shined a light into the tree branches. Nothing. She shifted the beam to the left. Was that just a branch? Or a leg? *Yes!* There, in a tangle of creosote bush, peeked a golden halo of hair. The small body was so dirty it blended into the earth.

Derrek lay with his eyes closed, wearing only a T-shirt and one sandal. His forehead was gouged and bleeding, his body scratched from head to toe. Nancy gently touched his arm. He didn't move.

Her heart sank. *Were they too late?* She leaned over and stroked Derrek's forehead, and the child looked up with the most beautiful blue eyes she'd ever seen. Peering over Nancy's shoulder, Jackie fought tears.

"Don't Die on Me!"

Nancy pulled Derrek into her arms and hugged him close. Knowing he was severely dehydrated, she rationed him a few drops from her water bottle. Too much too soon, she feared, could damage his brain.

A few feet away stood Kallie, her tail wagging a mile a minute. "Did I do good?" she seemed to ask. Nancy patted the shepherd and gave her a sip of water too.

By now Derrek was on the verge of delirium. Nancy radioed the base, but got no response. "Don't die on me!" she cried as she looked into the boy's sunken eyes.

The two women took turns carrying Derrek as they hurried toward base. Finally, at 10.32pm, Nancy made radio contact. "I have a find. He's alive," she reported, her voice shaking. Minutes later, a helicopter settled in the sand.

The rescue hadn't come a moment too soon. "It's remarkable he survived," said Dr David Tellez at Phoenix Children's Hospital. "He couldn't have lasted much longer."

Kallie herself was barely able to walk. A veterinarian back in Salt Lake City removed more cactus spines, soaked her feet and treated her with antibiotics.

About a year after the rescue, Nancy and Kallie drove up to the Clays' home. Derrek's eyes lit up as he ran to the shepherd and threw his arms around her. Soon, the two were rolling around in the back of Nancy's truck.

Nancy will always cherish the memory of Derrek's rescue—and of Kallie's heroic effort. "I doubted whether she had the temperament to be a good search dog," she said. "Now I know she does. We couldn't have found Derrek without her."

"DID I DO GOOD?" Kallie with Nancy, and Derrek.

Alone
in a rolling sea

by Jim Hutchison

She survived a capsized ferry, but now she
faced even greater peril during her rescue.

After an eight-hour lineup for tickets and a mad dash by taxi to the Cebu City wharf, the two young Canadians half expected to miss the ferry. Cindy McCluskey, a blond 23-year-old from Barrie, Ontario, and Nicole Chaland, 27, a slim, dark-haired university graduate from Vancouver Island, had met in the Philippines four months before. Participants in the Canadian Co-operative Association's Youth Experience International, the two were stationed in Cebu City and had become close friends. Now, to celebrate Christmas 1999, they were headed for a ten-day vacation on the resort island of Boracay, one of the most idyllic of the 7,000-plus Philippine Islands.

"We made it!" McCluskey whooped as they spotted the white hull of the M/V *Asia South Korea*. At 6.30pm, a half hour past sailing time, the 2,840-tonne ship was still loading lumber.

Among rows of cots in the main deck's forward section, the girls stowed their gear. On both sides of the deck, rectangular cutouts in the hull served as windows. The ceiling above was the floor of the upper deck.

At 9.30pm, the ship finally set sail, heading northward. The passenger manifest listed 459, far less than the maximum capacity. In fact, the overloaded ferry carried far more.

Turning in at 11pm, McCluskey and Chaland were soon lulled to sleep by the throbbing engines and warm sea breezes. They slept soundly until, hours later, a sudden shuddering crash jolted them awake. The ship's deck began listing to starboard. McCluskey's watch read 5.24am.

To make up for lost time, the girls would later find out, the captain had taken a shortcut from the main shipping channel between Bantayan and Panay islands. Poor navigation, rough seas and strong currents had driven the vessel onto a hidden reef.

OVERLOADED, **heading north: the M/V "Asia South Korea".**

The engines cut out and then the lights went off. "What's going on?" McCluskey shouted, fumbling for her flashlight. A woman beside her replied in a trembling voice, "Put on a life jacket and pray."

With too few life jackets to go around, the women had to settle for children's vests that came up under their chins. They strapped them on and joined hundreds of other passengers gathering on the port side.

At least we're good swimmers, McCluskey thought. The two often went snorkelling, and McCluskey had earned a bronze lifesaving cross.

Five minutes later the ferry was listing so heavily the starboard windows went under. In the grey, predawn light, an orange life raft drifted by. There were no screams; just hundreds of people praying, in rising tones of panic, "Hail Mary, full of grace . . ."

FERRY FIASCO

The captain of the M/V "Asia South Korea" had taken a short cut from the main shipping channel . . . poor navigation, rough seas and strong currents had driven the vessel onto a hidden reef.

The deck tilted to 45 degrees. "You've got to jump!" McCluskey pleaded with the people around her. But the shocked passengers stood rooted in fear, families huddled together, mothers clutching children.

The two Canadians helped people over the side. "Go, go, go!" they yelled. The bow rose higher as water flooded into the stern from a huge gash on the starboard side of the hull.

"Time to leave, Cin!" Chaland yelled. The women scrabbled along the steeply pitched deck towards the middle of the ship, where there were fewer people. But they lost their footing and slid across the deck, banging into a mass of metal cots.

McCluskey grabbed a rope hanging from a canvas cover and climbed back up the deck to the port side. "Come on, Nicole!" she shouted, repeatedly encouraging her friend.

Clambering onto a window ledge, she found a terrified man clutching the edge, unable to leap to the water below. "Take my hand," McCluskey ordered. Hands clasped, they slithered down the rusty hull and plummeted into the water.

Surfacing, she looked up for Chaland, but she was nowhere to be seen. McCluskey soon heard a loud whoosh of escaping air and felt the suction of the sinking ship pulling her under. Swimming clear, she turned to see the ferry slip stern-first towards the depths.

As Chaland scrambled to follow McCluskey, a man above fell, knocking her over. She rocketed down the slanting deck. As she clawed her way back, a scream turned her head. A young woman lay frozen with fear, helpless against the steep angle of the ship. Behind her, a huge wave rushed towards them from the submerged starboard side. Another surge of water approached from the port side.

The waves hit Chaland like a hammer blow, slamming her underwater then tossing her around like a rag doll in a washing machine. Kicking furiously, she surfaced and swam for the nearest window.

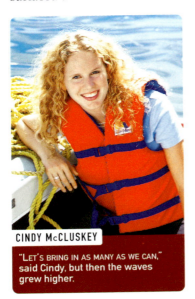

CINDY McCLUSKEY

"LET'S BRING IN AS MANY AS WE CAN," said Cindy, but then the waves grew higher.

McCluskey swam through three-metre swells towards a life raft. She felt numb. Twenty minutes ago she'd been sound asleep. Now she was floundering in the ocean, her closest friend missing.

"Help me!" an elderly woman implored. McCluskey towed her to the life raft, but it was full. As she left the woman clinging to the rope around the inflatable raft and swam out to bring in more people, she spotted a familiar face bobbing in the waves.

"Nicole, over here!" she shouted. Chaland paddled over.

"I didn't think you made it," McCluskey said. Back together, the pair grinned from ear to ear.

With the waves batting them against the life raft, they found it easier to move away and tread water. More people drifted past. "Let's bring in as many as we can," said McCluskey.

Stationing themselves at opposite ends of the raft, they encouraged survivors to join them whenever they saw someone go by. But the debris and ship's cargo of lumber, with screws and protruding nails, threatened the growing number of survivors, so the pair had to work hard at pushing it away.

The waves grew higher; with the roller-coaster motion, first McCluskey, then Chaland began to throw up. Their life jackets continually rode up, chafing them under the arms. Swarms of jellyfish stung them.

After an hour, 70 survivors were jammed inside the life raft, while 20 more clung to it and another half dozen men treaded water with the two women. When current and wind threatened to separate weaker swimmers, they all joined hands in a chain, clinging to pieces of debris that held them afloat.

At 7.30am, a boat appeared. The alarm raised, a flotilla of cargo and fishing boats were heading to the scene. The boat sailed past a kilometre away to pick up survivors in another raft. "We're next for sure," said Chaland.

After an hour the boat sailed away. "They must have seen us," McCluskey murmured, bitterly disappointed.

They checked with those in the raft; there were six flares aboard. Next time they would make sure they were seen.

An hour later another boat was spotted. "Light two flares only," ordered McCluskey. But the men in the raft didn't know how. Chaland shouted directions. The first flare skipped uselessly across the water. "Aim straight up!" McCluskey shouted. The next arced skyward, but the boat sailed on. Now all they could see was endless, windswept ocean, flint-grey under cloudy skies.

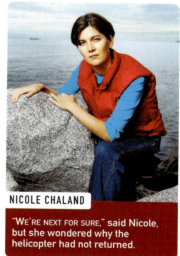

NICOLE CHALAND

"WE'RE NEXT FOR SURE," said Nicole, but she wondered why the helicopter had not returned.

After four hours in the water, McCluskey and Chaland whooped with joy when a chopper marked "Rescue" swooped in and hovered 20 metres away. The crew dropped a life raft, but it skipped away on the wind. Two men in wet suits then jumped out and swam to the group as two ladders were lowered.

McCluskey was closest, so a crewman motioned her to climb the ladder. Near exhaustion, she dragged herself up the first three rungs and waited for the crew to pull her in. Two male survivors climbed onto the other ladder.

Suddenly the engines roared and the helicopter lifted skyward. Chaland watched amazed as it sped away with McCluskey clinging beneath it like a stuntwoman.

"Hoist me up!" McCluskey screamed, but noise drowned out her voice. She looked back and saw the raft disappearing.

As she held on against buffeting winds, the men on the other ladder repeatedly crashed into her, ultimately knocking her from her perch. Falling towards the sea 30 metres below, she instinctively crouched into a ball. *I'm going to die!* was her last thought as she hit the water.

Seconds later, she came to with her broken life jacket around her head. Cushioning her fall, it had saved her life. She looked up and watched the helicopter vanish in the distance.

Searing pain from massive bruising and a broken rib engulfed her left side. Now she was injured and alone, the powerful current carrying her farther south. *No one will look for me this far out*, she thought.

Chaland couldn't understand why the helicopter had not returned. They'd even left the two crewmen in the water. Over the next two hours, she grew so weak she could no longer swim, and clung to the raft. Next to her, the elderly woman McCluskey had saved moaned softly. "If you get in the water now, you'll get wet. If she stays in the water, she'll die!" Chaland shouted angrily at those in the life raft. Shamed, two young men jumped into the water and helped the woman aboard.

Finally, after eight hours, Chaland and the others were picked up by a fishing boat. She lay on the deck, teeth chattering. "Thank you," she mumbled over and over to the crew.

McCluskey tipped her head back, trying to lap a few drops of water from a passing rain shower, but it only intensified her thirst. As the hours wore on, she sang to keep her sanity. The current was so strong she could feel herself being swept along. Now and again she heard the clatter of helicopters and waved at one in the distance without response. Ships sailed by on the horizon but never came near.

Something dark swam beneath her. She reached down and scooped it up. It was a turtle. Grateful, she held it for a moment, gathering strength from the presence of another living creature. Then she let it go.

She began to hallucinate, seeing ships that vanished on the next wave. As the afternoon wore on, fatigue claimed the last of her energy. She thought of her boyfriend. Always when they went skiing and she got cold, he'd say, "Keep moving, get warm." She heard his voice now and forced herself to kick her legs.

As one endless hour ran into another, she began to lose hope. *It would be so nice to just let go*, she thought. She said her good-byes to family and friends, then snapped to her

ANXIOUS VIGIL: **friends and relatives wait for loved ones.**

senses. *Come on! You can at least make it till dark.*

Exhausted, she steeled herself to face the approaching night. Suddenly she saw a boat a kilometre away. Blinking, she looked again. *It's real,* she thought. Shrugging off her orange life jacket, she waved it frantically overhead. The boat sailed on, growing smaller by the second. Gritting her teeth against the pain, McCluskey whip-kicked high on the wave tops. *This is your last chance. Keep waving!*

Coast Guard Lieutenant-Commander

STRETCHER CASE: an injured passenger is carried to safety.

Joel Dela Cruz scanned the rising seas breaking over the bow of his gunboat. It was 5.45pm. In 15 minutes it would be dark. He was familiar with the treacherous currents in this interisland channel, and when they'd arrived on station at 4.30pm and not spotted a single survivor, he suspected some might have been swept out of the search zone. But now 20 nautical miles south of the grid, he was sure no one could have drifted this far.

As he turned northward to join the other ships, his first officer shouted: "Floating object starboard side!"

McCluskey saw the ship come about and waved even harder.

"Survivor in the water!" the lookout called.

The vessel drew closer and a crewman tossed McCluskey a life buoy.

"What are you doing way out here?" Cruz asked, amazed, when McCluskey, chest heaving with pain and exhaustion, was carried into the wheelhouse.

"I fell from the helicopter," she gasped.

"You're the one!" he exclaimed. "It's a miracle you're alive."

With shaking hands she wrote her name and then Chaland's. "Please find out if my friend is safe," she croaked.

Of the more than 700 rescued that day, McCluskey was the last to be plucked from the ocean. Various reports indicated that more than 50 people lost their lives, but the real number will never be known.

On Christmas Eve Chaland flew to Cebu City and waited anxiously at the house of her boss, Ann Mills. At 3.30pm, McCluskey arrived, limping through the gate. The two hugged for a long time.

It wasn't the beach at Boracay Island, but for the two survivors it was certainly a Merry Christmas.

Ordeal on

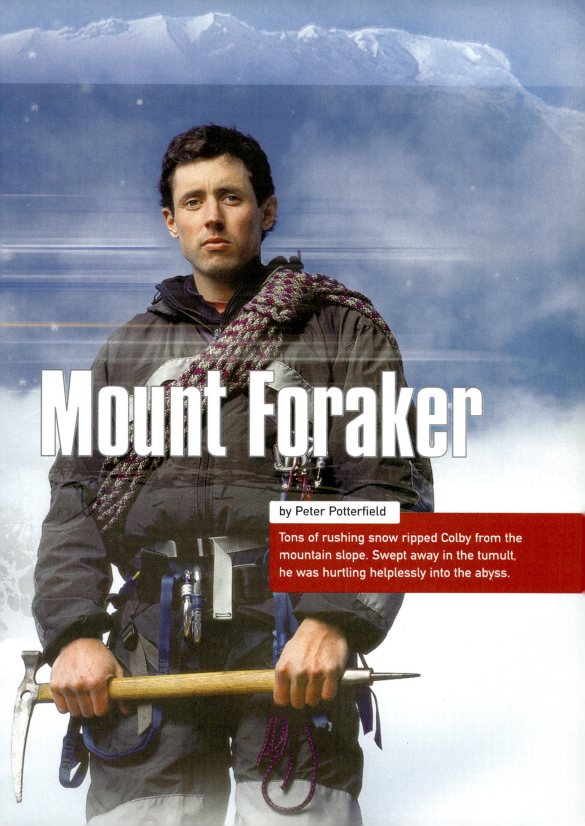

Mount Foraker

by Peter Potterfield

Tons of rushing snow ripped Colby from the mountain slope. Swept away in the tumult, he was hurtling helplessly into the abyss.

The small, single-engine Cessna circled the snow-covered summits of the Alaska Range. After one circuit the skiplane descended and floated onto a relatively flat section of the sprawling Kahiltna Glacier 7200 feet above sea level.

Throughout the spring of 1992 a steady stream of Cessnas had been arriving. They were crammed with climbers from around the world. All had come to scale the awesome, 20,320-foot-high Mount McKinley—known to mountaineers by its Indian name of *Denali*, "the tall one"—or one of its towering neighbors.

As the bright red plane coasted to a bumpy stop, the passenger door popped open. Out climbed Tom Walter. Tall, lanky and balding, although still in his 30s, he waved to Colby Coombs and Ritt Kellogg. Standing on a snowy rise near their tent, they waved back.

All three men planned to make the first ascent of an unnamed ridge on Mount Hunter. It was Tom's idea—he had tried the route once before and failed. But as they trudged toward the campsite with his gear, Tom announced, "I'm afraid I've got some bad news. I took a good look at the ridge from the plane. It's in terrible shape. Quake damage maybe. Anyway it looks really unstable. I think we should take a pass."

Colby and Ritt had also had a chance to look over the proposed route, and they agreed. Experienced climbers all, none wanted to take any foolish chances in these mountains. Already it had been one of the most deadly climbing seasons in memory in the Alaska Range. Persistent bad weather and multiple accidents had resulted in an all-time high of 11 fatalities on Mount McKinley alone. It was a grim reminder of the severe demands Alaskan mountains make on climbers, and the ultimate price they can exact.

Fortunately, the surrounding peaks offered over a hundred alternatives. That evening the three climbers sat around their tents enjoying the area's beauty and discussing their options. They were part of a small village of tents on a vast ice table, surrounded by majestic peaks. Lording over them was the imposing Denali, rising more than two miles above the surrounding wilderness of rock and ice. The "tall one" was a beautiful sight in the lingering June dusk.

Ever since Colby was a little kid, he'd remembered his mother's advice to always, always have a plan. Now, almost instinctively, he opened his copy of *High Alaska*, a climbing guide for the area. As he glanced through it, his eye fell on one entry. "What about Mount Foraker?" he said. "Somebody put up a new route on the big buttress coming off the Southeast Ridge in the early '80s."

"Yeah," said Tom, "I heard about that. It's a long one, probably five or six days in decent weather. That might be the one to do."

"What route is that?" Ritt asked.

Colby raised his arm and pointed. "There."

Rising directly across the glacier from their camp was Foraker, at 17,400 feet, the sixth-highest peak in North America. Colby pulled out a pair of binoculars, and the three climbing partners took turns examining the mountain in the fading light.

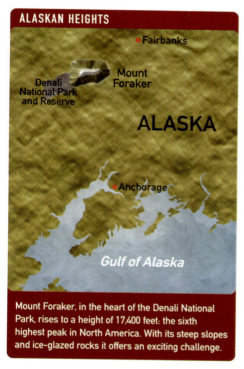

ALASKAN HEIGHTS

Fairbanks

Mount Foraker

Denali National Park and Reserve

ALASKA

Anchorage

Gulf of Alaska

Mount Foraker, in the heart of the Denali National Park, rises to a height of 17,400 feet: the sixth highest peak in North America. With its steep slopes and ice-glazed rocks it offers an exciting challenge.

The route up was known as the Pink Panther because the party that made the original ascent had carried a stuffed panther for good luck.

It looked to be about the right challenge.

The route along the mountain's huge flank required over a mile of nearly vertical climbing. Almost the entire massive East Face was exposed to potential avalanches from hanging glaciers, except for that route. It was rugged, arduous and quintessentially Alaskan in character—steep ice slopes and ice-glazed rocks—and for those reasons was rarely attempted.

Their decision made, the climbers spent the next day sorting gear and hardware, packing food and preparing for the week-long climb ahead of them. By six o'clock that evening—June days in Alaska are virtually endless, so daylight activity is possible around the clock—they were ready. The three clamped on their skis, roped themselves together to minimize the danger of falling into unseen crevasses, and set out across the five-mile-wide stretch of glacier. Colby was pulling a child's red plastic sled loaded with a week's worth of food and stove fuel.

As the men were leaving, Annie Duquette happened to be standing in front of her shelter. A combination air-traffic controller and base-camp manager, she spent the entire climbing season—from April to July—on the glacier. She had seen her share of old hands and first-timers come and go. In the softening light of dusk, Duquette watched the group move quickly across the glacier.

She couldn't help but recall the other times she had observed people setting out toward Foraker. Sometimes, if the group was not particularly well-prepared, she got a bad feeling. Foraker is a dangerous mountain.

These guys struck her as strong and confident and very capable. Yet for some reason she felt compelled to watch them for a long, long time.

TROUBLE IN VIEW: Colby took this photograph as menacing snow clouds formed.

In the Clouds

The small party reached the base of Foraker at eleven o'clock that first night. Colby gazed at their route, which rose upward another 6000 feet. "Awesome," he said to his two companions.

As the trio began to divide gear and supplies among themselves, clouds gathered around Foraker's peak. Soon snow was falling in discouraging abundance. The group decided to wait it out.

The snow finally let up the next day, June 15. Around noon they eagerly got under way with Tom in the lead. The men were tied together with two ropes. Using ice axes and the front points of their crampons—racks of metal spikes attached to their boots—they moved quickly up the lower reaches of the mountain.

"We're cruising!" Ritt exulted.

"Let's keep it up," came Tom's voice from above.

After more than 12 hours of continuous climbing, they reached the foot of a narrow ridge and decided to stop. With amazed delight they realized they had covered almost a third of the route in one day.

On the second day, June 16, the pace was equally quick. Excited and energized by their progress, the trio continued climbing right into the dusky light of the Alaskan summer night. By early morning on the 17th, they were some 11,000 feet high.

They would have liked to press on, but clouds began to cling to the mountain, obscuring the route ahead. The next thousand feet, they knew, would be the hardest, most treacherous part of the climb.

Reluctantly they prepared another bivouac: a snow cave they dug into the slope. Each of the three took turns digging out a space big enough for all of them. It took almost an hour, but when finished, it offered a snug haven.

Huddled inside, the men waited out the storm. As always, their meal that night was instant soup sprinkled with a little Parmesan cheese. And although they were 11,000 feet up, squeezed into a tiny cave, they were content. It is what they lived for: to be up in the clouds with fellow adventurers.

"This is great," Tom said, sipping a mug of Earl Grey tea. "I just wish we'd see a little blue sky and midnight sun."

Ritt looked around at the cramped, frigid quarters and its dirty, unshaven occupants and shook his head. Before opting for this excursion, he'd been planning a South American vacation. "What a place for a holiday," he said in mock complaint. "And to think I could be sailing instead of being stuck in this icebox with you two."

Colby smiled. A few weeks before, he had run across Tom at the National Outdoor Leadership School headquarters in Lander, Wyoming, where they were both instructors. Colby had done some climbing with Tom and knew him to be an exceptionally skilled, laid-back companion. Tom's mountaineering résumé was impressive. He had pioneered several routes in the Alaska Range and had

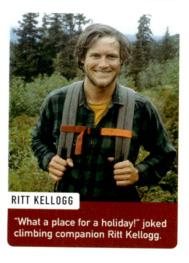

TOM WALTER

"This is great," said outdoor leadership instructor Tom Walter.

RITT KELLOGG

"What a place for a holiday!" joked climbing companion Ritt Kellogg.

climbed mountains in Pakistan, India, Nepal and South America. When Colby asked Tom to join him and Ritt on their Alaskan adventure, Tom jumped at the invitation.

Colby was pleased to see how well Ritt and Tom got along. In the few days they had been together, they enjoyed each other's company and had clearly come to respect each other's abilities. Although Ritt was somewhat quiet and introverted and Tom was more outgoing, both were easygoing men without the big egos common to many climbers.

Colby had always enjoyed Ritt's company. Their climb up Foraker was the most recent in a series of adventures the two had been sharing since they were students at Colorado College in 1986. Because of their love of the rugged outdoors, the two men had found they were kindred spirits, and soon became fast friends.

Now Colby added snow to the pot to make hot water. Every so often one of the threesome would stick his head out to check conditions, only to retreat under a blustering snowfall.

Finally, around noon the following day, June 18, the wind died down, and traces of blue sky appeared through the ragged, windblown clouds. This was their chance.

The men got ready carefully. Facing them was a thousand feet of a high and treacherous rock buttress. In places it was coated with thin, unstable layers of ice. Elsewhere the mountain jutted outward, creating precarious overhangs.

Tom and Colby swapped leads as they went. Ritt was happy to let the others set the pace—Tom, the old hand, Colby, the gung-ho natural-born climber. They moved slowly but steadily. The three men had to use their full mountaineering repertoire, at times going barehanded for more dexterity.

DISH OF THE DAY: **Tom Walter cooks dinner in the snow cave.**

About 300 feet short of the top of the buttress, the weather turned mean. A strong wind kicked up, rolling in clouds and fog. They could see only a few feet above them. With no place to stop, the group had to feel its way along the rock face. By midnight they reached the top of the buttress. The men had been going nonstop for about 12 hours.

Relieved to have this part of the climb behind them, the three faced a new problem. They found themselves at the bottom of a 1200-foot ice slope that rose up at a 50-degree angle. Visibility was almost zero, and the wind was gusting at about 40 miles an hour. In that kind of weather, death from exposure was a real risk. They had to get sheltered quickly.

The group discussed their options. One was to stay where they were and dig in. But hacking a ledge out of the steep ice was not much of an option. It would take hours, and the ice slope was far too steep. That left another possibility: to climb to a more protected site.

They turned their hooded jackets against the building wind. "What do you think?" Colby shouted to his companions. Tom glanced into the whiteout above them. "I'd forget trying to make camp here."

"Agree," Ritt added.

Colby nodded toward the ice slope and said, "I figure we'll be at the top in an hour or so. It should be less windy on the other side."

Though steep, the slope before them was far less demanding than the terrain they had just climbed. And once they were over the top, they could set up a bivouac. With plenty of food and fuel, they could wait out the worst of the storm.

As the blizzard raged around them, the three began carefully working their way up the icy slope. Tom led, tied to Colby with a 165-foot length of red 9mm climbing rope. Colby in turn was tied to Ritt with a 165-foot length of slimmer, 7mm white line.

Their experience and technique mattered. They knew a single slip by one man could prove fatal for all three, since a falling climber could drag the other two down with him.

As he moved up, Colby stared straight ahead at the red rope linking him to Tom. It lay a few feet from his face. If the rope stopped momentarily—meaning that Tom had paused to rest, place his ax or perhaps scratch his nose—then Colby stopped as well. When the rope started moving again, so did he. That way no slack developed in the line to snag on anything.

DEADLY PASSAGE: the climbers' route was more than a mile of ice-covered treachery, straight up Mount Foraker's flank.

There was no conversation among the climbers as they worked their way up. They were on autopilot. Although there was still plenty of daylight, the soupy whiteout made it almost impossible for them to see one another. Each man was essentially alone, isolated in a small world of fog-enshrouded ice and snow.

With about a third of the slope remaining to be climbed, Colby noticed the rope stop. As before, he paused. His calves were beginning to burn from the steady exertion.

Something was wrong. For a brief moment Colby thought he saw the rope above him move in a peculiar way, as if it were going slack.

His brain screamed an alarm. Before he could shout a warning, the cloud-shrouded ice slope changed to a world of utter confusion as a wall of ice and snow smashed into him. Tons of debris pummeled him with such force that he hurtled down the mountain on his back like a flipped-over turtle.

Avalanche! Its power was irresistible. The noise was unlike anything Colby had ever heard. It was the sound of death.

Into the Abyss

The next time Colby opened his eyes, he recognized the clear, bright light that was distinctive of an Alaskan morning. It was June 19.

Beginning to collect his thoughts, he knew he was Colby Coombs; he knew he was on a climb, but he was uncertain about other details. Pain permeated his entire body. He was freezing, the cold penetrating through to his bones. His hands were numb. He looked down and saw he had lost his mittens and had only thin glove liners protecting his hands. In a flash it started coming back. The avalanche. The fall.

As he looked around, he realized he was on the steep slope, hanging from the end of a rope. Groggy, he peered up and saw the red 9mm line was caught on a protruding rock above him. Now he looked sideways, and there, not ten feet away, was Tom Walter, hanging from the other end of the same rope. The line must have gotten caught on the rock as both climbers fell. Colby could only see the back of Tom's parka, but the way his partner hung from that rope aroused in Colby an unbearable sense of dread. Tom was absolutely still.

Suddenly Colby remembered Ritt and glanced down. The 7mm rope still trailed below him, but loosely. The end of the line was out of sight somewhere farther down. There was no sign of his friend.

Colby couldn't believe he was still alive, but when he tried to move, he felt a sharp, breathtaking pain in his left shoulder. His left ankle ached, and his neck was so immobilized with pain that he couldn't turn his head. To look around, he had to rotate his upper body, which generated more pain from his injured shoulder. And he was so thirsty, his mouth and throat were raw.

His mind raced. Could he get to Tom? Could he get to Ritt? Could he ever get down? Life-and-death questions for which he had no answers.

Although Colby did not know it at the time, he and his friends had fallen nearly 800 feet and had crashed to a halt just above the rock buttress they had climbed a short time earlier.

Colby grabbed an ice tool and edged clumsily over to Tom. His movements were slow and painful. When he arrived next to his friend, Colby could see Tom's body was cold and stiff. He felt for a pulse but detected nothing. When he turned him, Tom's face was covered completely by what appeared to be snow.

Colby tried to brush it away, but it remained in place. Looking closer, he was shocked to realize a hard mask of opaque white ice was frozen onto his friend's face.

The effect was eerie, as if Tom's identity had been taken along with his life. Below the body, a bloody streak stained the frozen slope as far as he could see.

The realization that Tom had been killed was horrifying. Colby remembered that his friend's wife was arriving in a few days to meet him. Earlier in the climb Tom had commented on his good luck. He and Lisa, his bride of ten months, had planned a sea-kayaking trip from Anchorage in late June, so a few days' climbing would be a perfect prelude. He planned to be back down just in time to meet Lisa's flight from Montana, where the couple attended college.

Now, hanging beside Tom's lifeless form, Colby started to feel overwhelmed by the enormity of the tragedy. Then he stopped himself. He was in bad shape and knew he had to focus on what was necessary to survive. Grieving would have to wait. He had to decide what to do next.

Colby knew he had to get moving. First, he'd need to replace gear he had lost in the fall. Slowly and painfully, he removed Tom's right mitten with its shell and liner. Colby put the shell backward on his left hand and put the liner on his right hand. Next he removed Tom's pack and the ice screws hanging from a sling around his neck.

Colby also knew he was going to have to somehow extricate himself from the rope before he could attempt to climb lower to look for Ritt. It wouldn't be easy. The knots would be impossibly tight after the force of the fall.

He decided to cut the red rope just above his own harness. That would leave him with almost the full length of usable climbing line—assuming he could dislodge it from above and cut it off his friend. Colby half-stood on the slope, clipped to his ice tool. He was partially hanging from the rope and partially supported by his good leg. He took a knife out of the front pocket of his bibs, opened the blade and began sawing.

What happened next shocked him. As soon as Colby severed the line, Tom's body, with the rope attached, dropped away, rocketing down the mountain and disappearing over the edge. Stunned, Colby stared down the mountain where Tom's body had gone.

It brought him back to reality: if he weren't careful, if he didn't think clearly, he might follow Tom into the abyss.

Tragic Discovery

Gathering his wits, Colby knew he had to try to find Ritt. But thirst, pain and fatigue had clouded his thinking. He first had to recoup his strength while he figured out his next moves. He desperately needed to get warm.

Some ten feet away was a tiny ledge that seemed just big enough to support him. So, carrying Tom's pack as well as his own, he took a few tentative steps toward it. With one shoulder useless and an ankle that could bear almost no weight, the slightest movement radiated pain.

Digging his ice ax into the slope at shoulder height and holding on while shuffling his feet, Colby slowly made his way to the narrow platform. Once there, he drove his ice ax firmly into the slope and tied himself to it with a rope. He was exhausted. *If moving a few feet is so hard,* he thought, *how will I ever get down this mountain?*

Next he pulled a foam pad from Tom's pack and lay on top. He tried to crawl inside a sleeping bag but managed only to get his legs in. Loose snow blew all around him in the freezing wind. It had been approximately 12 hours since the avalanche.

Colby's head pounded. The pain in his neck signaled to him that he had a serious injury. His left shoulder, he was certain, was fractured. The extreme discomfort in his left ankle continued even at rest, and he suspected more broken bones.

Looking down, he could see the white 7mm line descending below him. Somewhere down there was his best friend. "Ritt!" he shouted.

Silence. He shouted again, but there was only the sound of the wind.

Half in his sleeping bag, Colby tried to rest on his uncomfortable, tilted perch. But the down-sloping rock made a poor shelf, and he kept sliding off until he was hanging from his tether. Although his miserable bivouac afforded no sleep, it did offer the chance to rest and gradually restore body warmth. And so the hours went by.

By the morning of June 20 the wind had died down. Colby had warmed sufficiently so that he was no longer shivering uncontrollably.

He was now ready to discover the fate of his friend. His plan was to find Ritt, then climb back up—with him or alone. Then they, or he, would traverse to the crest of the ridge and begin the long descent to base camp.

Moving stiffly, Colby crawled out of his makeshift shelter. In an irrational act of neatness, he rolled up Tom's bag and stowed it beside his pack. It was as if he expected his friend to come back to get his gear, and Colby wanted it to be in good order.

As he prepared to get moving, Colby realized he still had on his climbing helmet. When he removed it, he saw that the hard plastic shell had been shattered. Touching his head, he discovered his hair was matted with dried blood. The lightweight helmet may have saved his life, but the fact that his head had bled despite the protection showed him how powerful the avalanche's impact had been.

Methodically, Colby dug Tom's ax into the slope next to his own. Then he secured his end of the white line to these anchors and clipped on to the rope. Satisfied with his setup, he put his weight on the rope and began descending slowly, using his good right leg to control his body angle.

The white rope was perilously thin. As Colby rappelled, he was alarmed to see that big chunks had been torn out of it. The farther he went, the more damage he saw. If the rope suddenly snapped, he would plummet off the mountain. But he knew he had to keep going. He had to find Ritt.

Colby descended more than 100 feet below his ax anchors and had just come over a ledge when he saw Ritt. His friend was lying upside-down and motionless at the bottom of a steep snow slope. The last 20 or 30 feet of rope was wrapped tightly around Ritt's torso. Colby's heart sank. It looked bad.

When he reached his friend, he saw that his body was rigid. He touched Ritt's neck, pressing hard. There was no pulse. The person with whom Colby had shared so much of his young life, so much fun and adventure, was dead. Gone in an instant.

Alone

Colby Coombs had clung to the forlorn hope that his friend was alive. But now Ritt Kellogg's death was a cold, irrefutable fact. Colby was on his own.

He decided he had to survive, not only for himself but for his mother. She meant everything to him. After his father left his family when Colby was a child, she had to raise him and his two sisters alone.

Colby's mother was emotionally devastated by the breakup of her family. As a single parent, she made a special effort to teach her children to take responsibility for their actions, helping them to become as self-reliant and independent as possible. Try to be prepared for the problems that life throws at you, she taught.

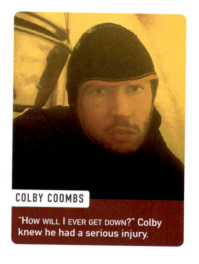

COLBY COOMBS

"How will I ever get down?" Colby knew he had a serious injury.

His mother had always been there for him. Now she became the focal point for his survival. She had never let him down. Just vanishing without a word to her was unacceptable. Colby made a silent vow that he would get off this mountain.

He realized he would need a stove, a tent and, above all, water. More than 24 hours without a drink in the cold, dry air had dehydrated him dangerously.

Perched precariously on the steep slope, and leaning on his good leg, Colby tried to open the drawstring at the top of Ritt's pack, but the rope wrapped around the body held the pack too tightly. Remembering how Tom had tumbled down the mountain, Colby attempted to slip his hand into Ritt's pack without dislodging the body from where it lay.

Slowly he tugged Ritt just a few inches toward him to gain better access to the pack. But even at that slight movement, his friend's body immediately started to slide over the ice-covered rock and hurtle down the mountain. Before he could react, the line tied between them went taut.

"No!" Colby screamed in horror. Then the force of Ritt's falling body yanked him off his feet and slammed him against the slope.

Shaken and dangling, Colby could not believe he had made another mistake in judgment. For a moment he lay there listening to the sound of his own breathing as he clung to some rocks. He looked down. Ritt's body lay about 30 feet below at the end of the line.

Carefully Colby eased himself down to Ritt. Being next to his friend's body again, Colby felt horror and sadness sweep over him. Taking a deep breath, he forced himself to reach into Ritt's pack.

He retrieved a half-full water bottle from the pack, unscrewed the lid and gulped down the contents. Next he retrieved the tent, a stove, fuel and some food, and stowed it all in his own pack. When he had what he needed, he removed an ice tool from Ritt's pack, drove it into the icy slope and tied his friend's body to it with a length of rope for search parties to find.

Now he had to plan. Thirty-six hours had passed since the avalanche hit. The long day and night he had spent on his rock had given him a chance to get a good look at the lay of the land. He decided to set off sideways toward the ridge's crest on a course that would take him off the mountain.

Colby's first steps were excruciating and made him wonder if his damaged ankle could take the stress of climbing. He imagined himself having to crawl down Mount Foraker. But after a little experimentation, he found his ankle could bear weight if he held his foot at a right angle and moved with a sideways step. It was slow going, but at least he was going somewhere.

After all the traumatic events, Colby found some comfort in climbing again. The difference this time was he was not climbing for the thrill of it but for his life.

He fell into a regular, if halting, rhythm of hiking that seemed to work. Then, half-way to the crest, he stumbled and twisted his foot. His ankle roared with pain. As he steadied himself with his ax, his shoulder throbbed. The misstep and the pain snapped Colby back to alertness. There could be no lapse in attention on the mountain.

At the end of nearly a day of painful climbing, Colby found a flat spot beneath a small ice wall, a perfect campsite. He pulled out a small two-man tent and crawled inside. Quickly setting up the stove, he soon was gulping down warm potfuls of water melted from snow, and mugs of hot, thick soup. His body radiated deep, debilitating pain. He had got this far, but he still had a long way to go.

Colby had the habit of praying on his climbs when he felt close to nature. Now tragically alone, he said a simple prayer: "God help me. Please let my body hold out. Give me the strength to get out of this alive."

Deadly Detail

Completely exhausted, Colby gingerly lowered himself to the sleeping pad for rest. As he did so, his neck exploded in agony. The pains in his neck, shoulder and ankle were relentless. He lay for hours, unable to sleep.

In the middle of the night, he tried to sit up to take a drink of water. The pain in his neck was so bad that he realized he would have to learn to sit up all over again. Experimenting with different techniques, he found that if he grabbed his hair with one hand—taking weight off his neck—he could rock himself up into a sitting position by the fifth or sixth try.

On June 21, seven days after the expedition began, Colby finally reached the shoulder of the Southeast Ridge in late afternoon. His energy spent, he rested on a small ice platform. He had hoped to put more terrain behind him, but this was as far as he could go. He was beat, but he took heart from the fact that from here on, it was all downhill—4000 feet down an ice-covered ridge to the glacier and camp.

To battle dehydration, he consumed mug after mug of hot water and soup. After dinner he lay down warily, not knowing whether he'd have the strength to get back up. Despite his exhaustion, sleep still would not come.

The silence that enveloped him was in stark contrast to the laughter that filled the tent of the three climbers such a short time ago. There was the ribbing they gave Ritt when his just-washed laundry flash-froze in the arctic air. Then came his and Ritt's belly-laughing protests as their sunburned lips cracked in response to another one of Tom's signature tales of foolishness in the wilds. He could still hear Ritt erupting in bursts of laughter as he came upon another piece of outrageousness in a Ken Kesey novel.

Three laughing friends, full of life. And now this.

The weather had cleared enough for him to see his base camp from where he lay. He could actually make out Cessnas landing on the glacier airstrip a little over six miles away. Down there climbers were going about their daily routines. There was no life-or-death struggle, no tragedy.

He started thinking how easy it would be for rangers in a low-flying helicopter to pluck him off the mountain in this clear weather. *Maybe I could lie here and wait*, he mused. But the idea was pure fantasy. He was virtually invisible, just a speck on Foraker's massive flank. No one knew where he was or of his desperate efforts to stay alive. Everything led back to the same conclusion: if he was to survive, he would have to get off the mountain himself.

By the next morning he realized he was weaker. The pain, the little food and the sleepless nights were all taking a toll. After a mug of his last remaining oatmeal, he started down.

The route he faced was a nightmare. Somehow he would have to make his way down a series of small cliffs, drop-offs and jumbled sections of glaciers. Some of it would require negotiating by rope and rappelling. Colby would have to do it all with a bad ankle and shoulder, using only the frayed line that had bound him to Ritt.

Warily he made his way along a 1000-foot-high cliff. Three Japanese climbers had been killed near that spot when a small avalanche of ice from overhanging glaciers fell on them with no warning.

Moving carefully, Colby came upon dozens of avalanche chutes where years of ice debris sliding from above had carved icy bowling alleys into the slope. On either side of each chute was a low ridge of debris. Agonizingly, Colby climbed up and over each ridge, down into the avalanche chute, across the treacherous ice, and finally up and over the other ridge. It was slow going.

Just when he thought he was making good progress, Colby stepped into one of the last chutes, and his right boot slipped. In an instant he fell and was heading down the slick ice, skidding toward the cliff edge. He was sliding straight for a 1000-foot drop to the glacier below.

No! Colby thought. *Not after all I've survived.*

Instinctively he slammed his ax into the ice and rolled on top of it, hoping his weight would drive the blade in deeper. Screaming to himself, *Stop! Stop! Stop! Stop!* he tried to position the ax so it was exerting the maximum drag.

Nothing happened. He felt the rough-textured ice skip underneath him at a frightening speed, accelerating all the time. The abyss was only seconds away.

Suddenly the ax grabbed hold. Colby's skid stopped with a jarring jolt. The force of his self-arrest racked his body. It felt as if his fractured shoulder blade had ripped apart. The pain was so spectacular, he feared he might pass out.

Minutes passed while he tried to recover his composure. Slowly he rose to his feet, trembling with adrenalin and relief. He climbed out of the deadly chute and resumed his journey.

When at last he reached the end of the traverse, he found his next obstacle: a sheer 70-foot drop. Colby would have to rappel again. He twisted an ice screw into place, rigged the line—it barely reached the ground—and descended slowly.

Once down below, he tried to retrieve his frayed rope by pulling on one end. It jammed.

Uh-oh, Colby thought. He pulled again as hard as he could, but the rope wouldn't budge. He yanked on the other end. That did nothing. Somehow the rope had become snared around the ice screw and would not come loose.

He knew the only way to free it was to climb back up and untangle the line. He also knew he did not have the strength. He stood there futilely staring at the jammed rope, his lifeline, realizing he would have to abandon it. From that point on he would have to climb down without the security and support of a rope. Depending on what he would be facing, that might be impossible or deadly.

Colby stared at the rope one last time. *Is this the detail that kills me?* he wondered.

Final Options

The exhausted climber knew that trying to push any farther that day would be a serious mistake. He set up camp in a flat spot and tried to rest, with little success. As he lay there, he wondered how long he had been without real sleep—four days? Five?

It hardly mattered to him anymore. His rope was gone. His food was gone. And the rest of the way down would be no easier. How long could he keep going like this?

He roused at the first bright light of morning. With no breakfast to prepare, getting ready was simple. And with no food or rope to carry, his pack was that much lighter now. So much for the good news.

Gingerly Colby began walking down a shallow slope that he guessed would lead to the glacier. Halfway across, he heard a muffled *whump!* He froze. In alarm he watched as the whole slope sank and dropped underneath his feet. Cracks radiated, terrifyingly, everywhere around him.

He had seen big slab avalanches—whole fields of shifting snow—and knew this slope might go at any moment. If he were standing on it, he would be buried alive under tons of snow and ice.

Colby stood absolutely still. Walking across the slope could set off an avalanche, so he dared not continue. This meant he would have to climb all the way back up to where he began and find a different way down.

Colby had spent the whole morning getting to where he was, and now all that was for nothing. Yet he knew he'd been lucky, and he wasn't going to squander his reprieve. Reaching deep inside, he summoned new reserves of willpower. He had made it this far and was determined not to make a mistake that would kill him. Turning uphill, he slowly retraced his steps to start over again.

By the time he had struggled to the top of the slope, it was near evening, and he could feel his strength almost completely spent.

This time his new course showed no ominous signs of fracture. He had made the right decision. As he worked his way downhill, he soon found himself on relatively flat ice.

He was on the Kahiltna Glacier. Colby had done it; he was off the mountain. But he could muster no jubilation. Days of the hardest physical work he had ever done and the most anguished psychological stress he had ever endured had left him hollow.

In just an hour he reached the place where he, Tom and Ritt had stashed their skis. He could hear the Cessnas descending to land at the distant airstrip. It was the evening of June 23, five days after the avalanche.

Now for the last, and still dangerous, obstacle: crossing the glacier to base camp. He knew that hidden under the glacier's snowy cover were a hundred huge crevasses, any one of which could swallow him up without a trace. Thinking it would be the most awful irony to die within sight of safety, he stepped into his skis.

It was late when he began across the ice. The diffuse evening light of the midnight sun shone on him—a solitary figure moving slowly, wearily against the backdrop of the vast grandeur of the Alaska Range, hauling a red plastic sled loaded with some of his friends' gear.

He stabbed at the ground with his ski poles every step of the way to uncover fragile snow bridges before they might drop beneath him. Several times the sled turned over and began sliding into a crevasse, threatening to pull him with it. With each step his anxiety rose. He knew he was reaching the end of his endurance. He was gasping for air. But he skied on, dragging his injured foot behind him like a character in a bad horror movie.

Finally the base camp lay just ahead. Trudging closer, he saw a couple of climbers setting up their tent. Colby felt uneasy, like a man with a terrible secret.

He skied past. They said nothing to him, and he said nothing to them.

Soon he came to Tom's red tent, which they'd left standing when they left for Foraker. It was 5am on June 24. Exhausted, he collapsed inside.

Later there was a knock on the door of the airstrip manager's shack. Annie Duquette opened it, smiling. Then she took one look at the lone figure and her expression changed. She recognized him as one of the three she'd seen set off for Foraker ten days earlier. The man she remembered as a fit, self-confident climber stood before her, looking ravaged, his left arm clutched up like a raven's claw.

"What happened?" she asked.

Colby made no reply.

Then in a lower voice she asked, "Where are the other two?"

All the emotion he had consciously bottled up throughout his long ordeal was suddenly released. Colby felt a wave of tears coming; his throat tightened. Finally he managed the awful words: "They're not coming back."

Tribute

Colby was flown off the glacier on the first available Cessna. At Valley Hospital in Palmer, Alaska, X-rays revealed he had fractures in his leg and shoulder. He was immobilized and immediately taken to the regional hospital in Anchorage, where CAT scans pinpointed dangerous fractures in his vertebrae.

As he was to learn, he had climbed down the mountain with a fractured shoulder blade, a broken ankle and a broken neck. The doctors immediately stabilized his neck and limbs and scheduled surgery for his ankle.

At the hospital a steady stream of people came to offer encouragement. Colby's spirits soared when his mother and sister Sayre arrived. The joy and relief in his mom's eyes were especially palpable. For a long moment they embraced wordlessly.

Then came the day when Tom Walter's parents and wife visited. Looking up at them, understanding their grief and knowing that he was somehow an agent in their horrible loss, was the hardest moment in Colby's life.

"I'm so sorry, so sorry," he kept repeating.

They would have none of it. Donna Walter, Tom's mother, said gently, "Colby, we thank God you're alive, that one of you made it. Now tell us what happened to our beautiful Tommy."

And so he did, even though the retelling was like reliving the catastrophe. If he could only change the order of events, the sadness could be lifted from these good, loving people. If only . . .

When he was done and his visitors departed, he fell into a deep sleep of emotional exhaustion.

A short time later Colby learned there was to be a memorial service for Tom in Anchorage, where he and his wife, Lisa, lived when not attending school in Montana.

"I'm going," Colby announced. The prospect brought immediate protests from his doctors, but Colby would not be swayed. "I'm going. I owe him that," he said with finality.

When he wheeled into the nearby church where the service was held, Colby was nervous, suffering from survivor's guilt, wondering if the others would look at him and ask themselves, "Why him and not Tom?"

As he entered the sanctuary, everyone turned. One glance at the beaten figure in the wheelchair was vivid evidence of the violence that the mountain had inflicted. Support bars held Colby's left foot in place. His left arm was in a sling, and his head and neck were rigidly secured in a scaffold-like brace.

The service was simple, with friends and family rising one at a time to tell stories about Tom and how they missed him. The loving testimonials went on for an hour and a half. Finally it was Colby's turn.

He wheeled to a place in front and, damp with sweat, began to address the sad gathering. He told them that climbers understand danger might await at the next crevasse, ice field or ridge. But they willingly accept that danger, not to blithely put themselves in peril, but rather to know the satisfaction that comes from doing a hard thing well and on their own.

They accept it because it is the price to be paid for viewing some of the most

AT REST IN THE MOUNTAINS: a memorial to Ritt, Tom and other climbers stands in Talkeetna.

breathtaking sights on earth. They accept it because with the danger comes the clarity of God's hand in nature.

Never is a person more alive than when moving upward to the summit, he said, and that's where his friend was when it ended. "Tom's death is a terrible tragedy," Colby declared, "but you have to know that Tom was doing something he loved, something that gave him life."

FRIENDS AND NEIGHBOURS: **Annie Duquette and Colby Coombs today.**

When Colby finished, Tom's father rose and began to clap. Soon he was joined by everyone in the room. The sound of it, the emotion of it, washed over Colby like an absolution.

Once released from the hospital, Colby flew to his mother's home in Massachusetts to recuperate. A week later Ritt's younger brother, Kirk, arrived to talk about Foraker.

From long conversations with Ritt over the years, Colby knew that Kirk had looked up to his adventurous big brother. During his visit Colby found the strength to detail the events of the climb again. When he came to the avalanche, Kirk listened attentively—wordlessly.

Afterward Kirk wheeled Colby into the dining room, which had been temporarily converted to serve as his bedroom. Kirk's eyes fell on a large photo near Colby's bed, a dramatic shot of the East Face of Foraker. He paused for a moment and then, tears welling up, asked, "Where did he die, Colby?"

Colby pointed to the ice wall high up the face. So small, so insignificant. So utterly devastating to so many.

Then Kirk stood up and squeezed the other man's shoulder. Looking him in the eye, he said, "I'm glad you made it, Colby."

A ranger flying over Mount Foraker spotted an ice ax stuck in the snow at the place where Ritt Kellogg and Tom Walter were swept from the mountain. The two climbers' bodies were never located.

Colby Coombs today works as a guide on Mount McKinley and teaches climbing at the Alaska Mountaineering School, which he opened in Talkeetna, along with Alaska Denali Guiding. His solo descent of Foraker is regarded as one of the great feats of modern mountaineering survival.

The fight

to save

Tenneh

by David Moller

She had walked 250 miles through a war zone with a bullet in her head. Could a British surgeon save the little girl's life?

HEALING HANDS

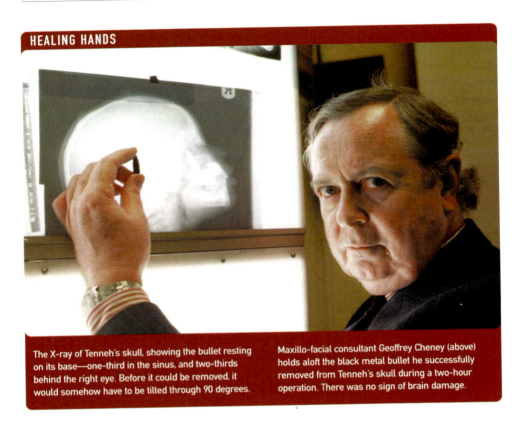

The X-ray of Tenneh's skull, showing the bullet resting on its base—one-third in the sinus, and two-thirds behind the right eye. Before it could be removed, it would somehow have to be tilted through 90 degrees.

Maxillo-facial consultant Geoffrey Cheney (above) holds aloft the black metal bullet he successfully removed from Tenneh's skull during a two-hour operation. There was no sign of brain damage.

the greyish-black tissue, which simply broke away as his forceps played over it.

Eventually, when he had removed some 80 per cent of the infected tissue, he called a halt. Intravenous antibiotics would take care of any lingering infection. Deftly, he replaced the wedge of bone in Tenneh's face. On top of it, he fixed a curved titanium plate with five tiny screws to hold the bone in place and help re-form the damaged margin of the eye. At 10.45am, the surgery was complete.

Luckily, there was no sign of brain damage and in time the stitches under Tenneh's eye would fade to a faint scar.

Just two days after the operation, Tenneh was again busily helping the nurses, as observant and imitative as ever. Blowing bubbles with a plastic ring, she dropped some of the soapy liquid on the floor. "Look what you've done, Tenneh," a nurse laughed. Immediately, she went off to get a paper towel, just as the nurses did, to wipe the floor.

At the end of May the time came for her to return home to the Makeni orphanage. The Cooks wondered how Tenneh would adapt after all the attention, the media interest and the deluge of presents that had arrived from all over

Britain. But she cheerfully accepted yet another massive upheaval in her life. Back with her friends in the familiar surroundings of the orphanage, she blossomed.

Since her return, Tenneh has received two special visitors, Malomoh and Mariama Cole, who have moved from the Brickworks refugee camp into a temporary home with relatives. The Coles love Tenneh as their own child and are delighted with her progress. While occasionally frustrated at her lack of hearing, she has responded well at the local school for deaf children, where she is learning to use a hearing aid and lip-read in English.

In October 1996, came another reunion, when Mark and Caroline Cook went to open a new purpose-built orphanage in Makeni. When they arrived, the

A SAFE HAVEN (left): the Makeni orphanage in Sierra Leone, which Mark and Caroline Cook had set up through their charity, Hope and Homes for Children. It was here they located Tenneh, then flew with her to England.

HAPPY TO BE BACK (below): Tenneh hugs Nurse Helen Shorten after recovering from her operation.

children were lining the track to the entrance of the home. They had just returned from school and were dressed in their blue-and-white uniforms. As the Cooks greeted them, Caroline spotted a slim six-year-old, a white handkerchief over her braids to protect her head from the midday sun. The little girl looked up and, slowly, a look of shy recognition transformed her face into a smile of pure joy as they embraced her.

For Mark Cook it was a precious moment. Tenneh's courage and determination had become a symbol of all the children he'd encountered, all victims of war. Tenneh Cole had lost her home, her parents, the sight of one eye, most of her hearing. Yet she had clung to hope.

As he watched, Tenneh scampered off across the dusty, sun-baked compound to keep watch over Ibrahim, a two-year-old she has taken under her wing. Like herself, he is an orphan. She washes him, dresses him, feeds him, trundles him about happily in a plastic cart—perhaps recreating the role she once played for a younger brother, or instinctively trying to compensate for horrors of which neither of them might ever speak.

Joyous outcome: one year on, the Cooks were reunited with Tenneh at their new, purpose-built orphanage at Makeni.

Face
beneath the water

by Lee Maynard

With no feeling in her legs and only fear in
her mind, she sank back into the darkness.

The late spring sun was dropping into the high, golden desert west of Las Cruces, New Mexico, as Colby Stadjuhar steered his four-wheel all-terrain vehicle (ATV) along the dirt path beside a huge irrigation ditch.

In parts of New Mexico they call such ditches *acequias*, after the ancient canals dug by the Spanish and Indians centuries ago. In winter they are empty and dry. In spring they swell with cold high-mountain runoff. This ditch was swollen now, but Colby, enjoying his ride, barely noticed the mud-laden, silent flow.

Any way you looked at her, Jeanine Cook was an exceptional woman. She was nearing completion of her doctoral studies in electrical engineering at New Mexico State University. Laughter spilled out of the 35-year-old as she told people that her degree would allow her "to operate her household appliances better." But she was serious about her studies, about teaching and, as a graduate assistant, about mentoring other students. And she did it all confined to a wheelchair.

The accident that took away the use of her legs happened 16 years ago. One moment she was watching the hypnotic movement of her headlights on the narrow country road as she drove home late and tired from a lab. The next moment she was tumbling down a steep incline. Her Toyota finally smashed into heavy brush—in that instant her life changed.

Following Colby along the canal that mild evening of May 17, 1999, were Melissa Girard and Jenni Brown, both 13, riding together on another ATV. The three friends were going nowhere slowly, puttering along the canal, happy to be out on one of those evenings that made you glad to be alive and living in New Mexico.

After her accident, Jeanine struggled through weeks of hard, sometimes frightening physical therapy. She especially dreaded the sessions in the swimming pool. She had never liked the water, and failed basic swimming tests three times as a child.

ELEMENTAL FEAR: **Jeanine was terrified of water.**

On a fishing trip with her father when she was ten, Jeanine was standing on the bank of a pristine Colorado river. Water rushed clear and cold from the mountains. Looking down, she saw the smooth, undulating shape of a fish. Fascinated, she gripped her rod, leaned forward—and fell.

The numbingly cold water closed over her, filling her nose and mouth. The current began to take her. But at the last moment, her father grabbed her and plucked her out. She was shivering violently from cold and fear.

Those feelings were still with her years later during physical therapy. Aides attached floats to her useless legs and lowered her into the water. But inadvertently the floats would tip her forward and water surged into her mouth. She bit back the fear, refusing to let it defeat her recovery.

Colby Stadjuhar was just an eighth-grader at Picacho Middle School in Las Cruces, but he was a big kid, and still growing. At 14, he was already five-foot-11, 200 pounds. In little more than a month he would be graduating from middle school. It was a confusing time for Colby. He had grown used to being "on top" in middle school. He was a football player, and that counted for something. But in high school he'd have to prove himself all over again with new kids, new rules. It worried him.

Jeanine married Jonathan Cook in 1995 and delighted in their home life. She was a ball of energy at school, home and outdoors. An avid rider, she had bought a horse and cared for it herself whenever Jonathan was away. When she wasn't riding River Fox, she was out on a specially built bicycle that she propelled with her arms. She loved all physical activity, except water sports. Laughing, she told Jonathan she even hated spray in her face when she showered.

Colby was a good kid, but there were times when he pushed the limits, got cross with his parents, pulled one too many pranks—or forgot the rules and made a mistake.

One morning he absentmindedly picked up a small pocketknife, took it to school and got caught. It was a serious infraction, and he was suspended for one week. He could have been expelled. The incident shook him up. It made him question whether he was too impetuous and could make the right decisions. Self-doubt made him hesitant.

May 17, 1999, was the first day of a week's vacation for Jeanine. Jonathan, who also taught at the university, was away at a conference. All she planned to do was relax, catch up on her reading, ride River Fox and take Charlie—a big, lovable greyhound-and-Irish-wolfhound mix—for his daily run beside the canal.

There was no one else in sight when Jeanine rolled out in her motorized wheelchair that evening. Charlie padded ahead of her along the narrow path. They went in silence for a while before Jeanine saw the other dog on the opposite side of the ditch.

It was a boxer—large, muscular and waiting. Its eyes fastened on Charlie. Jeanine had seen the dog before, but it had always been behind a fence. And at first she didn't sense any danger. They were separated by the ditch—wide enough here to accommodate three rowboats side by side. But then the boxer leapt into the water and came for them.

It burst onto the muddy bank and tore into Charlie. The huge dogs fought in a blur of motion, teeth flashing. Then Charlie's leash tangled around the handle of the wheelchair. As he lunged and thrashed, the chair began to slide in the soft earth.

Jeanine's mind was clear and analytical. *Got to stay calm.* She thought of turning off the chair's power, reasoning that its dead weight of nearly 140 pounds would anchor her. But she had no chance to react. The dogs clawed themselves off the path and down the slippery side of the canal.

"Charlie," she yelled. And she screamed at the other dog to go away. But Charlie's lunging force began to turn the wheelchair toward the ditch. Its wheels dug into the soft earth, but still it was pulled inexorably toward the edge.

Now the dogs were fighting in the ditch, and the heavy chair skidded quickly. As the foot plate hit the water, Jeanine was thrown from the chair. The black water hit her like a slap in the face.

She sank immediately.

Colby rode beside the canal, looking at nothing in particular, just having a good time riding. The girls followed closely behind. He had no particular plan or destination. No particular time to turn around and head home.

The water was nearly five feet deep and unexpectedly cold. Powerless to stand or kick her legs to swim, Jeanine sank into a dark world so laden with silt that she could not see and in which no one could see her from a distance.

Squeezing her eyes shut, she flailed her arms, and felt her face break the surface. She gasped in as much air as she could before sinking back into waving, rotting weeds. Still she fought the downward pull by grabbing for weeds along the bank with one hand, while trying to wave with the other.

Fear. She fought it. *Fear.* It was there twining around her like the waving, rotten weeds ensnaring her powerless legs. She had to keep her mind clear and use all her upper-body strength to raise her face out of the water one more time.

"Somebody please help me!" she gasped. There was no one in sight. Her face barely broke the surface, for just a moment, and then she sank back into the nightmare darkness.

ANCIENT LAND: in parts of Mexico the huge irrigation ditches that cut swathes through the land are modelled on the ancient canals dug by the Spanish and Indians centuries ago. In spring they are filled with cold, mud-laden water.

As the three teenagers continued along the path, Colby glanced occasionally at the broad band of water, some 12 feet wide. Then he saw something white flash on the dark surface.

He looked again. *What was that?* he wondered. It moved like a tiny white flag, a waving hand. It could have been a flare of sunlight on the water.

But maybe it wasn't.

Jeanine stretched upward for air, but the water was so cold it was stealing her strength. It was only a matter of moments before she would not be able to rise again.

Then, breaching the surface, she glimpsed in the distance someone riding along the ditch on an ATV.

Questions flashed in her mind: *Can I stay above the surface? Will he see me? Can I yell loudly enough?* Gulping air again, she struggled to force sound through her aching throat, and slowly moved her arms to stay up. But she slid under again.

Quickly scanning the chocolate-colored water, Colby saw a metal handle in the water. Then something broke the dark surface. A face. White, immobile, blank. A woman's face. She looked directly at him and seemed to be saying something.

What in the world? he wondered. *What's she doing?* Swimming—in the ditch? He didn't understand, but before he could even think it through, he found himself reacting. He jammed the ATV to a halt, leapt off the machine and ran to the edge of the ditch. His feet dug into the mud as he slid down into the black water.

Where is she? Her face had disappeared. Then he saw it: a frail white hand in the water.

Colby thrashed through the ditch, the cold of the water through his clothes making him gasp. He swung his arms back and forth under the water, searching for the woman. She was under there somewhere.

And then he touched something. *Clothing?* He grasped her under her weakly waving arms. He lifted her, even as her weight drove his feet down into the sucking mud.

JEANINE COOK

"WILL HE SEE ME?" Colby and Charlie the dog with Jeanine after her rescue.

Hands. Jeanine felt hands. In one swift motion her whole body seemed to break the surface. He had her, and she could breathe!

Colby pulled his feet from the silt and drove hard toward the bank. The woman hung limply in his arms. He reached the bank, but the soft earth gave way and he slid down again. Wrapping the woman tighter in his arms, he charged the bank again and again.

Looking up he saw Melissa and Jenni, reaching for the woman. Together the three friends struggled to the top of the bank, carrying the limp, dangling woman who gasped in great mouthfuls of warm, fresh air.

Today, both Jeanine and Colby have had a chance to reflect on the rescue. At Jeanine Cook's house, Charlie the dog wanders into the room and drops his head into her lap. She absentmindedly strokes his grizzled head, laughing. Her laughter is sparkling, infectious, but now her voice drops low and soft.

"Every time I get into a bad spot, God keeps me alive. He must have some use for me," she says, laughing again. "I love students, love to teach. Maybe that's what he has in mind. I don't know. But I do know this—somebody sent me Colby."

At his house, Colby leans back in a wooden kitchen chair. His face is lit by the pale afternoon light. He seems comfortable with himself and how his life is going. He still loves pranks, but there is an inner seriousness too.

"The biggest thing I learned is that you can't practice deciding. You can't practice the will to take a risk. So when something like this happens, it's good to know it's in you."

As he talks, unconsciously his arms come up, as though he's again lifting Jeanine Cook out of the dark water.

Mayday!

I don't know how to fly

by Robert Kiener

His pilot had collapsed. The young
man stared uncomprehendingly
at the controls of the tiny plane.

n the radar room at Cardiff Airport, an urgent cry suddenly blared from the overhead speaker: "Mayday! Mayday!" Air traffic controller John Hibberd, 41, flipped the radio switch on the control panel in front of him. "Mayday go ahead." "I think my pilot has had a heart attack," came a man's shaky voice. "And I haven't a clue what to do!"

It was 6.39pm on Monday, March 30, 1992. Just a few hours earlier, Alan Anderson, a 26-year-old mechanic from Llandow, South Wales, had accepted an invitation from his girlfriend Alison's father, Les Rhoades, to "come on up for a bumble"—a short "aimless" flight.

Alan, who has a fear of heights, had been so terrified when Les took him up in a four-seat plane the year before that he had sworn he would never fly again. But it was difficult to say no to Les.

In the two years since they had met, Alan and the 63-year-old former mechanical engineer had become like father and son, both delighting in "taking the mickey" out of one another. So Alan knew he'd never hear the end of it if he refused a ride in the 22-year-old, single-engine Rallye Minerva, known as "Gaydog" after its call sign "G-AYDG", that Les owned with five friends.

Sitting beside Les, dual controls in front of him, Alan felt his fears begin to melt away as they flew west from Cardiff along the coast towards Swansea. There was hardly a cloud in the windless sky, and the evening sun bathed the Welsh countryside in a warm glow. *This is brilliant*, thought Alan. *It's like flying with my guardian angel.*

After 30 minutes or so, they turned back towards Cardiff and Les reset the plane's radio to Cardiff Airport's approach frequency. Then he pointed to a lone cloud ahead, some 200 feet above them. "Let's chase it," he said.

GROUNDED: **Cardiff Airport was now closed.**

"Do we have to, Les?" joked Alan. "It's bad enough being up here."

Suddenly Les's head fell forward and he let go of the control stick. *Good joke, Les*, thought Alan. Then the plane began to lose altitude and go round in smaller and smaller circles. "Come on, Les, stop messing around," said Alan. "I'm getting scared." Les still didn't move.

Gaydog slipped into a dive, dropping to 1,700 feet . . . 1,500 feet . . . 1,000 feet. Terrified, Alan put his hand inside Les's jacket and felt for a heartbeat. There was none.

Through the windscreen Alan could see they were heading straight for the three chimneys of the vast Port Talbot steelworks. Now less than 600 feet from the ground, he pulled on the dual control stick in front of him as he had seen Les do. Gaydog began a steep climb. They missed crashing into the steelworks by seconds.

"Oh God, please help me," Alan prayed. A jumble of thoughts filled his mind: *How am I going to tell Alison about her father? . . . I wonder if she knows how much I love her? . . . What am I going to do now?*

GAYDOG: **a single-engined Rallye Minerva, such as this.**

He shouted into the radio headset he'd been wearing since take-off: "Help! Help! Mayday!" When no one answered, it dawned on him that his headset was merely for communication between pilot and passenger; it could not transmit. Shakily he removed Les's headset and put it on.

What now? Better pull Les's feet off those two pedals. (Though Alan didn't know it, they were the rudder controls.) Reaching across, he bumped into a black knob protruding from the centre of the control panel. Without realizing it he had hit the throttle. Gaydog was now flying at more than 120 mph—near top speed— along the coast.

Again Alan shouted "Mayday!" into his headset, this time pressing the button on the top of the pilot's control stick as Les did when he radioed the tower. Now his headphones crackled into life. *Thank God*, thought Alan as he heard John Hibberd's voice.

The instant Hibberd received Alan's Mayday call, he checked the control console's directional finder. It told him Alan was to the west of the airport, but he still had to establish Gaydog's exact position; it could be any one of the five aircraft on his radar screen.

"Can you look at the dials ahead of you and see what heading you are on?" he asked Alan.

The compass was unmistakable, hanging at eye level. "Number 12 next to the east," Alan read.

"That's fine," Hibberd told him. "You're heading directly back to the airport. And how is the pilot now?"

"He's cold," said Alan shakily.

Hibberd asked Alan if he knew what his altitude was. He was taken aback at Alan's reply: "Whereabouts on the dial is that one?"

"See if you can see something that says A–L–T."

"Yeah, I can see that. The little hand is just about on the two, the other one is just below the seven."

Hibberd was reassured that Alan was flying at around 2,600 feet, high enough to avoid television masts, high chimneys or other obstructions. (In fact, Alan had misread the altimeter; he was only at 1,600 feet.)

Briefing all incoming planes to keep clear, Hibberd urgently paged his fellow air traffic controller Colin Eaton to come and help him.

To Alan, it seemed ages since Hibberd had last spoken. *Why doesn't he tell me how he's going to help me?* he thought. As long as he clung to the control stick the plane flew steadily and level, because Les had fully "trimmed" the elevators and rudder. *But I'll never manage to land*, he thought in panic. He decided he would circle over the Bristol Channel until the plane ran out of fuel. Then, just before it hit the water, he would unstrap himself and Les, and jump.

Still heading east along the coast, he spotted Cardiff Airport; from 1,600 feet it looked like a small table-top. He pressed the radio button and blurted, "Cardiff Airport, I'm just coming over the runway now."

Meanwhile, John Hibberd had just been contacted by the pilot of a light aircraft—"Charlie Echo" in radio shorthand—flying some five miles north of the airport, offering his assistance. Miraculously, the pilot was an experienced flying instructor, 26-year-old Robert Legg, who with his student Martin Leighton had been listening to the drama unfold since Alan's first audible Mayday call. Hibberd now acknowledged Alan's message and immediately told Legg to head south towards the airport, where he should be able to spot Alan heading towards the Bristol Channel.

Adrenalin surging, Legg turned his single-engine Piper Warrior II to the southwest and began scanning the skies for Gaydog. At last he and Martin spotted Alan's tiny plane some 1,000 feet below them. Robert put Charlie Echo into a shallow full-power dive to catch up with him.

Running back from his tea break, Colin Eaton, a stocky RAF veteran of 38, slipped into the left-hand seat at the radar-room console. Hibberd, busy instructing incoming planes to switch to the airport's spare frequency and leave the normal one free for Alan and Robert, passed the emergency over to him.

Eaton radioed Alan, speaking slowly and carefully. "This is the air traffic controller . . . There is an aircraft about four miles to the west of you. He is rapidly approaching you to draw alongside, and then he will be speaking to you on this frequency."

"OK," replied Alan. "I've never done this before, mind."

Robert Legg radioed Alan to tell him he was coming up behind, and asked how much fuel he had. "Half a tank on both sides," said Alan, reading the plane's twin gauges. "How much longer are we gonna be?"

HARROWING DESCENT

Approaching Cardiff Airport, Alan Anderson, a 26-year-old mechanic, listened on his headphones to instructions from a pilot in a nearby plane. It was his first flying lesson and he was alone at the controls.

In the calm, reassuring tone he used with all his students, Legg replied, "I'll get you down as quickly as possible." He didn't know *how* he was going to get Alan down, but he did know it made no sense for him to keep heading over the Bristol Channel; contrary to Alan's belief, he would have little chance of survival if he crashed into the water.

"Hold the control column in front of you," Legg told Alan. "Rotate it gently to the right and put the aircraft into a bank turn to the right."

He was closing in on Gaydog, now heading north towards the coast. "If you look to your right, just behind your wing, you may see my aircraft," he radioed Alan. "We're going to circle over the airfield in a nice wide circuit and then we're going to bring you down on to the runway."

Listening to Robert Legg's precise instructions, John Hibberd marvelled at how quickly he had taken control of the situation. "This guy's good," he said to Colin Eaton.

By now, Colin Eaton had ordered the "Local Standby" alert earlier instigated to be upgraded to a "Full Emergency". Airport fire crews were in position along the runway. Local police headquarters at Bridgend and county fire brigade headquarters at Cardiff were alerted. A light aircraft and an RAF Tristar tanker were kept out of the airspace; an incoming passenger aircraft was put into a holding pattern. To all intents and purposes, Cardiff Airport was now closed.

Robert Legg was aware that, at 120mph, he and Alan were going much too fast for a landing approach. To get Alan to slow down without losing height, he asked him to pull out the throttle slightly. "Which one is the throttle?" asked Alan.

Below in the radar room, Colin Eaton could hardly believe his ears. "Good grief," he said to John Hibberd, "if he gets down it will be a miracle."

Robert Legg was shaken, too, but he calmly told Alan how to locate and reduce the throttle. "Ease gently back on the control column now to maintain your altitude," he instructed. Gaydog slowed to 100mph and Legg breathed a sigh of relief.

Robert brought his plane level with Gaydog, a few hundred feet to Alan's left. "I can see you," said Alan. "Thank Christ you're there!" Recalling a scene from the film *Airport 1975*, he expected Robert to position Charlie Echo close to Gaydog, jump on board and scramble into the cockpit. *He'll land it for me*, he thought.

With both planes at 1,000 feet and heading directly for Cardiff's main runway, Legg wondered whether to tell Alan to attempt a landing. "Hang on," he told himself. "He knows the basics now, using the throttle and control stick, but all he's done is make a right turn. Let's not be too hasty." As a complete novice on his first flight, Alan's chances of landing safely were next to nil. His life hung in the balance.

"We're going to fly over the runway first," Robert told Alan.

Suddenly Alan asked Robert if there was anyone who could contact Alison and tell her about Les. More than anything, he wanted to put his arms round his girlfriend.

Aware that Alan was on the brink of panic, Robert soothed, "Yes, we'll get that sorted out for you. Just concentrate on my instructions." Carefully he went on, "We're going to do a left-hand circuit . . . a nice gentle turn to the left about the same sort of rate as we did before . . . and we're going to come all the way around again and bring it down on the runway. Do you understand?"

"Yeah, I understand," said Alan. "But how do you stop it?"

By now, he realized he had to land Gaydog by himself. Confusedly he thought, *Les will be so furious with me if I scratch Gaydog. He loves this plane.*

Robert continued to guide him carefully through the turn: "Hold the aircraft in a gentle bank . . . That's fine. Add a little more power. Pull slightly back on the control column to maintain your height."

"I tell you," said Alan, "I've never been so scared in all my life!"

After another small turn to the right at about 400 feet, Gaydog was positioned to make its final turn to the left and approach the runway. "This time I'm going to attempt to get you down," said Robert. "Just aim for the runway . . . just a gentle bank turn . . . as you've done before."

The runway still seemed very small to Alan—and very hard. He fully expected to crash. *Maybe I can make it if I land on the grass*, he thought.

Robert positioned Charlie Echo behind and 100 feet above Gaydog. He hoped he could bring Alan down low enough, and slow enough, to prevent him being badly hurt if he crashed—as he surely must. Three things were in Alan's favour: the Rallye Minerva is a plane that handles very well at low speeds, there was hardly any wind, and the runway was the biggest in South Wales, capable of taking giant 747s.

When Gaydog was about a mile from the runway, Robert told Alan, "I'd like you to slightly reduce the throttle . . . Come over to the right a little . . . we're aiming for the big tarmac strip to the right of the white and red lights."

This is it, thought Alan as Gaydog floated gradually down to 100 feet. *Either I do this or I die!*

Once Alan was flying over the beginning of the runway, Robert told him: "Pull the throttle all the way towards you now and pull gently back on the control column . . . Hold it there . . . Hold it . . ."

As Alan concentrated on Robert's every word, the runway seemed to rise up and fill the windscreen. Gaydog touched down on the tarmac in a perfect landing.

HIGH FLIER: **Robert Legg receives the Royal Aero Club's silver medal for achievement in aviation from the Duke of York.**

In the radar room, Colin Eaton shouted excitedly: "He's made it!"

When Alan felt the wheels touch the runway he closed his eyes, expecting to crash into parked planes. With no brake on the co-pilot's side, he had no way of stopping Gaydog. But the plane coasted down the runway, veered into the grass and rolled to a halt—virtually unscathed. To the last, as air traffic controller John Hibberd puts it: "Someone up there was clearly looking out for Alan Anderson."

Les Rhoades was pronounced dead on arrival at hospital; an autopsy revealed that he had suffered a massive heart attack.

Alan was treated for shock at the hospital and released. He and Alison subsequently announced their engagement.

Even though Alan swore he would never fly again, in July 1992 he went up in Gaydog—with a pilot—as a final tribute to Les. His nerve recovered, he was determined to get a pilot's licence. In November 1992 he received a Royal Association for Disability and Rehabilitation award as one of the "People of the Year".

Robert Legg, who shrugged off his actions as "all in a day's work", received the Royal Aero Club's silver medal for achievement in aviation.

Swarm!

by Gerry Johnson

As the family explored the Florida swamp,
there was one enemy they had not counted on.

ebbie Jacoby Walker lifted her gaze and smiled. Above the century-old cypress and water oaks of the Florida marsh, eagles glided across the afternoon sky. Here and there she caught sight of blue herons standing silently and still.

Having grown up in Maryland, the 41-year-old mother of two still felt a certain trepidation entering this wild jungle terrain. The steamy realm of alligators and snakes was not her element. But high atop her husband Ben's home-built swamp buggy—a tanklike, open-air machine with six-foot-tall tractor tires— she felt safe.

That late October day in 1995 was the start of hunting season, and 46-year-old Ben had left his nursery business in Naples, Florida, to scout for deer and wild boar. The native Floridian had brought Debbie and their boys, Matthew, four, and Mark, two, along.

Tired from their long day and lulled by the machine's rocking, the boys were now napping in back. Beneath their elevated seats, Ben's two hunting dogs lay quietly in a large cage.

"Shouldn't we head back?" Debbie asked.

"All we've got to do is follow our own tracks, and we'll be back before sunset," Ben assured her.

The swamp buggy became entangled in branches, and Ben climbed onto one of the huge tires to cut them away. A moment later, above the rumble of the idling engine, Debbie heard a high-pitched yelp from the dogs. Then Ben cried out, "Oh, my God."

"What's wrong?" she asked. Ben was clawing at his jeans. Debbie looked down and saw, from Ben's ankles to his thighs, a blanket of vibrating, probing yellow jackets.

Within seconds, thousands of wasps had engulfed the swamp buggy in a cloud of fury. Debbie felt the stiletto jab of scores of tiny stingers.

The boys! She turned to see wasps swarming over her sleeping children. Matthew awoke screaming, helplessly waving his arms. She heard two-year-old Mark cry, "Mommy, make it stop!"

Fighting his way back into his seat, Ben jammed the transmission into reverse, but the gears would not engage. "We have to run," he yelled. "I'll go first. Throw the babies down to me."

Ben leapt blindly into the tall subtropic grass. His right leg landed on something rock-hard and buckled beneath him. A searing pain shot through his body.

"Debbie, wait!" He dragged himself to the rear of the vehicle. "Drop Mark here! The ground's soft."

Debbie hesitated. How could she toss her baby almost 12 feet down? Then the great angry swirl slammed into her from behind. Debbie screamed and dropped Mark as she doubled over in agony.

POISONOUS THREAT

Yellow-jacket wasps live in the ground or in paper-like nests in trees. They forage for discarded foods, especially meat and sweets. By fall a colony has attained its maximum size of up to 5,000 worker yellow jackets. If their nest is disturbed, they will mount an aggressive defense of their colony by swarming and stinging. The venom from a single sting can be life-threatening.

The boy landed in the mud unhurt, and Ben dragged him away from the buggy. Debbie dropped Matthew, then tumbled down after him.

Still locked in their cage, the dogs howled forlornly. Debbie's heart broke. *I can't help them now,* she thought. *I've got to think of my family.* She pulled Matthew away from the buggy.

"We've got to shield the kids," she shouted. She and Ben began brushing the wasps off them and rolling the boys in the mud. But everything seemed vague and hazy. *I've lost my glasses!* Debbie realized. Extremely nearsighted, she needed glasses even to find her way around the house.

Ben glanced at Debbie. Yellow jackets covered her face like a writhing mask. Already her cheeks, forehead and chin were starting to swell—sign of an allergic reaction that could send her into fatal shock.

"Take Mark and move back down the trail, Deb," Ben ordered. "I'll send Matt after you."

Picking up the boy, Debbie stumbled along the buggy tracks as far as she could from the yellow jackets. The swarm finally stopped pursuing her.

"Follow Mom," Ben told Matthew hoarsely. "She'll take care of you."

The frightened four-year-old, still covered with yellow jackets, crawled away. When Debbie saw him coming alone, she realized Ben must be too injured to walk. "Stay here," she told the kids. Head down, arms flailing, she re-entered the yellow storm.

"Try to walk, Ben—I'll help you," she said between gasping breaths. But Debbie couldn't lift the six-foot-one-inch, 220-pound man. "Oh, Ben," she cried, "what are we going to do?" Her speech was beginning to slur.

Ben knew they were in trouble. He was in terrible pain, and Debbie was going into shock—she had been stung before, and reacted to it so badly that she'd had to seek hospital treatment. No one knew where they were, and night was coming on.

"Listen to me, Deb," he said. "You've got to run for help. Leave the babies."

"I can't!" she said.

"They'll slow you down. Go while you still can. Follow the buggy tracks back to the camp we passed."

Seeing her incapacitated husband and hearing her two small boys sobbing, Debbie knew she had no choice. "I love you, Ben. I'll try my best."

Ben watched her stumble out of sight. It seemed impossible she would make it in her condition. But the couple shared a deep Christian faith. He began to pray, asking for help for his family.

Debbie staggered through the muck, trying desperately to keep between the huge tire tracks. Without her glasses, everything was a blur. Her mind was dull, her body lethargic.

The insect venom was doing its heinous, silent work. As anaphylactic shock sets in, the venom allergens first lower blood pressure, reducing oxygen flow to the brain, heart and other vital organs. Then external body tissues, also shortchanged of oxygen, open their

VENOM ROAD: **would they find their way out?**

cellular doors to fluids. These tissues swell, closing the throat and air passages. Some victims die quickly; others suffocate slowly.

Debbie was entering the early stages. And without knowing it, she had wandered off the buggy track.

Phil Pelletier had been looking forward to this hunting trip with his buddies for a long time. Yet the morning's hunt had been disappointing for the 45-year-old county recreation director. There had been plenty of game and his friends were in a festive mood, but something was tugging at him. He elected to stay behind to pack up their camp. He wasn't sure why.

"I'VE GOT TO THINK OF MY CHILDREN." **Debbie Walker and her family by their swamp buggy.**

It was 4.25pm before he headed his truck down the narrow, abandoned railroad bed they used for a road. Within a hundred yards, a figure appeared. It was a woman, staggering and covered with mud, her face grotesquely swollen. *Lord,* he thought, *she's been beaten up bad!*

"Lady, are you all right?"

At the sound of his gentle voice, Debbie began screaming. "My babies are dead! My husband broke his leg . . . attacked by yellow jackets. They were all over us!"

"I'll help you," Pelletier said, trying to calm her. "We'll go look for them."

"I can't," she gasped. "My throat is closing. I need medicine." There was an unnatural look in her eyes, and her skin was a lifeless pale gray.

"I'll take you to Ortona," Pelletier said. "It's five minutes away. There's a store there. We can call for help."

Paramedics met them there and quickly gave Debbie an epinephrine injection. Her condition was listed as priority one: life threatening.

As the paramedics worked, Debbie did not take her eyes off Pelletier, pleading with him to go back and look for her family. A father of two, he could only imagine her anguish.

"Don't worry," he told the half-conscious mother. "I'll find your family."

Sweat trickled down Pelletier's back as he pushed his pickup to nearly 60mph along the railroad bed into the swamp. Debbie had described to him the place where she came out of the woods. Suddenly Pelletier noticed an opening and slammed on the brakes. *Maybe this is the spot,* he thought.

But the pickup dipped low into the mushy, swollen marsh and began sinking. Quickly he backed up onto the railroad bed and drove on.

Fifty feet later, he found another narrow gap. He recalled there were old logging roads snaking through these woods. *That must be the way she walked out.*

Daylight was fading. Pelletier pushed ahead without any sign of a trail. The staccato of fan blades hitting water kept him apprised of how deep his truck had sunk in the soggy terrain. A half-mile passed before a flash of color caught his eye.

He idled the truck and looked again. There, sitting in a shallow water hole, was a little boy! He was facing away, talking to himself. Not wanting to alarm him, Pelletier called from a distance, "I've got your mama!"

At the sound of a voice, the child turned and started to cry. Pelletier was unprepared for the sight. Four-year-old Matthew's neck, arms and legs had swelled to grotesque proportions. His ears stuck straight out from his head. His skin—stretched tight and bloodlessly white—revealed hundreds of crimson-purple stings.

Scooping up the boy, Pelletier gently carried him to the truck. Matthew screamed and wriggled in pain. He began to shake, cold even in the 90 degree weather. Staring blankly, he put his head down. *He's slipping away from me,* thought Pelletier. He had to get the child to a hospital. This was one life he could save.

Heading out, Pelletier tried to avoid water holes. By the third one, his luck ran out. As water covered the pickup's hood, its engine stalled. Picking up Matthew, now limp, Pelletier waded into the hip-deep pond.

Then, across a clearing, he spotted a man. It was Deputy Sheriff Carlin Coleman, who had followed Pelletier's tracks to the spot.

"This boy needs help!" Pelletier called. "The only way we're going to bring the others out is with a swamp buggy." He told Coleman about a friend's buggy at his camp.

The two men had driven only a short distance when they met Fire Chief Dennis Hollingsworth. The three decided Coleman would take the boy on to the store at Ortona, while Pelletier and Hollingsworth went back to the swamp in the borrowed buggy. It was 6.37pm. In an hour, their chances of finding Mark and Ben Walker would be virtually nil.

Back on the trail, Hollingsworth noticed a section of rutted mud. "Hold it," he commanded. "There are two sets of buggy tracks, one big, one small. They cross right here."

"The woman told me her husband has a big buggy," Pelletier said. "If she got mixed up here and followed the small tracks, it would account for her getting to my camp so fast. It was the luckiest thing she could have done."

The two men followed the big ruts to a pond surrounded by thick palmetto grasses. Looking across, Pelletier caught the outline of a head.

Jumping into the pond, Hollingsworth furiously waded through the murky waters. There he saw the bloated, ashen face of Mark Walker. The fire chief choked back tears as he cradled the muddy toddler in his arms. "We'll get you out of here, little buddy," he promised.

He radioed his dispatcher. "We've got him," he said, his voice breaking. "We'll bring him out, then go back in for his daddy." It was agreed that Coleman would come and take the child to the Ortona store.

Ben Walker hadn't moved since Debbie left. He had called to his boys and got no answer, so he feared they had wandered off after their mother and were hopelessly lost. His only relief was that the yellow jackets had lost interest in him. They had targeted the swamp buggy, its engine still rumbling, as their enemy.

Ben was in great pain, drifting toward unconsciousness, when he heard the sound of another buggy. A man's voice rang out: "Ben? You all right? We're coming, Ben."

"Thank you, God," Ben cried. "Thank you."

CHOSEN ONE: Phil Pelletier felt fated to find the Walker family.

Shortly after, hunters went in to retrieve Ben's swamp buggy—and to free his dogs, who survived. The vehicle was moved, but wasps returned to it, even after being burned off. Finally, hunters burned the nest. Most yellow-jacket nests lie beneath the earth, but this one had expanded above ground to include a fallen tree. The nest was apparently disrupted when it was hit by one of the tires on the Walkers' swamp buggy.

At Columbia East Pointe Hospital, Debbie was brought back from the edge of death. Compound fractures in Ben's right knee and upper leg required several operations, but he eventually returned to work. The boys recovered quickly, and no longer have bad dreams. Replacing the family's memories of terror and pain is a heightened awareness of love, an emotion that moves people to acts of spontaneous courage and sacrifice.

Around the Ortona store they still talk about the inexplicable connections—the timely appearances of the right people at the right time; how every seemingly wrong turn ended up being right. They call it a miracle.

The man who refused to die

by Robert Collins and Ian Bickle

He was lying in agony in a silent, frozen wilderness, and nobody knew he was there.

As he slowly came to, lying flat on his back on ice and hard-packed snow, Reinhold Kaletsch felt two warm wet tongues licking his face. His dogs Blondie and Simba were hovering anxiously over him.

Suddenly pain stabbed at his chest, neck, back and stomach. His head ached, his ankle hurt, his right arm felt numb. Then the awful truth flooded over him: *I fell, I'm hurt . . . and alone. Just the dogs and me and a stalled truck in the wilderness. Nobody knows I'm here . . . Nobody will come looking!*

He fought down panic. In his 24 years as a medical doctor, and in a half-dozen years of part-time adventuring all over the world, Kaletsch had coped with many crises. Surely he could get out of this one. He was strong, for a man of 50, and quick-witted. *And I'm alive!* He lay still, steeling himself against the pain and collecting his thoughts.

BEST FRIENDS: **Kaletsch with his dogs, Blondie and Simba.**

He remembered standing high on a frozen hummock to photograph South Bay, on Manitoba's South Indian Lake, 750 kilometres north of Winnipeg. He had shifted his feet for a better position, felt them slip, then the sudden sickening plunge . . . That had been morning. Now, afternoon sunlight was slanting through the scrub pine and spruce. Gingerly, Kaletsch lifted his left arm to read his watch. Four o'clock, and the calendar date read "24." So it was still April 24, 1979. He had been knocked out for six hours.

The doctor in him took charge. *Must not try to get up. Must diagnose.* He moved his feet and, with enormous relief, felt them respond. He wiggled his right hand; like the arm, it felt numb. With his left hand he gently explored his face: congealed blood under his nose, on the left cheek and beside his left ear. That was alarming.

It could be only a bruise, but it could mean internal injury, maybe a concussion, maybe even a skull fracture. *Must move as little as possible.*

With utmost care he shifted position. It didn't hurt much more when he moved than when he lay still. Cautiously he probed the base of his neck. Bad pain. A fractured vertebra? Perhaps. He couldn't reach his back but the pain there and numbness in his limbs suggested a similar fracture. He had seen such injuries in his medical practice and had suffered one himself 28 years before in a motorcycle accident: a "compression" fracture that squeezes the bone rather than shattering it. From his symptoms he could almost pinpoint the affected vertebra. An intensely painful injury because of its proximity to nerves, but, if his diagnosis was correct, not crippling.

He must lie as still as possible for nine or ten days, while the body began repairing itself. He also knew that pain and shock would probably make him black out again in two or three hours. To move was risky; to stay here in the snow was certain death. It was a bitter –10 degrees.

Already his face was frostbitten, and the chill was penetrating his red snowmobile suit and camel's hair overcoat. *It's a wonder I'm not frozen already.* Then his hand felt shallow depressions in the snow on either side of him. The dogs had snuggled close all day and helped to keep him warm. The dogs would help, too, if a bear or wolves came close.

His 1975 Chevy half-ton truck was mired in a snowdrift 90 metres away, its side door hanging open, its tail gate down, just as he had left it that morning. *If I can get inside . . .* Not daring even to get to his knees, Kaletsch inched toward the truck on his belly. His lonely fight for survival had begun.

As he crept through the snow, stopping often to rest, he reflected wryly that if it weren't for the cold weather he wouldn't even *be* here. He would be working the 250-hectare family farm at Sclater near Pine River, in western Manitoba. Only a few days ago he had flown to Winnipeg, on vacation from his lucrative medical practice in Giessen, a city north of Frankfurt in West Germany. After visiting his son, Kai, 16, a student at St John's Ravenscourt School, he took a bus 425 kilometres northwest to the farm. He looked forward with genuine pleasure to a "holiday" far from the stresses of medicine, helping his neighbor clear brush off land that Kaletsch rented to him.

But spring was late and the land was still soggy. To Kaletsch—a stocky five-foot-six, with blond hair, square craggy face and pale lively eyes—this was simply a new opportunity. As a man obsessed with learning and discovery, he instantly decided to drive north as far as his truck would take him.

With boyish enthusiasm he flung supplies for a month into the truck: three sleeping bags, a small tent, hatchet, ax, shovel, handsaw, toboggan, a .30-30 rifle and a .22, two packages of plastic garbage bags, an emergency kit with self-igniting flares, plenty of matches, two tow-ropes and a modicum of medical supplies (painkillers, antibiotics and bandages).

For his dogs, he added a bag of commercial dried meal and 100 kilograms of beef liver in small plastic packages. For himself, he tossed in boxes of crackers, some

FROZEN WILDERNESS

HUDSON BAY

South Indian Lake

Leaf Rapids

CANADA

Winnipeg

Kaletsch had planned to drive 60 kilometres across a rough second-class road from Leaf Rapids to South Bay, and then cross the 80 square kilometres of ice to the Cree Indian village of South Indian Lake. Then, some 30 kilometres from the village, his plans were dramatically halted when he fell and badly injured himself. Alone, except for his two dogs, and with no means of communication, how would he find a way to survive?

apples, cheese, tea, sugar, powdered protein concentrate, several cans of apple juice, a five-gallon plastic container of water, one bottle of whiskey and two packages of prepared meat. He would buy more food along the way as he needed it.

Only his photo equipment was packed with care—a 16-mm movie camera, a 35-mm still camera and an Instamatic. Kaletsch kept elaborate photo records of his travels.

Then he phoned Kai and poured out his plans. "I'll be back on May 24," he promised. "Or I'll phone you at noon that day from wherever I am."

Kai was unconcerned. Over the years his father had journeyed to Australia, Asia, Africa and South America, often piloting his own single-engine aircraft. He never phoned home while he was away. "Bad news travels fast enough," he often said. But he always came home intact, full of stories about his escapades.

Now Kaletsch drove to a neighboring farm to pick up his dogs from Bill and Donna Boyachek, who looked after them while he was in Germany. Blondie, a mongrel with traces of coyote in her lean face and yellow eyes, had wandered half frozen into Kaletsch's farmyard one November night in 1977. He had befriended and tamed her, but she was still a creature of the forest, able to dart like a shadow through brush where a man could barely walk. Simba, her rollicking year-old son, had the look of a Saint Bernard from his anonymous father. Now, while the pair leaped on Kaletsch, yelping their love and excitement, the Boyacheks tucked a loaf of bread and a dozen eggs into his bedroll as a surprise.

Speeding north, Kaletsch reviewed his route. He'd take conventional highways to Swan River, The Pas, the nickel-mining town of Thompson, and Leaf Rapids near the roof of settled Manitoba, a 900-kilometre drive, and then have another 60 kilometres east on a rough second-class road to frozen South Bay.

There his real adventure would begin: a drive across the 80 square kilometres of ice to the Cree Indian village of South Indian Lake. After that Kaletsch would play it by ear, following the makeshift winter roads carved by northerners' trucks and snowmobiles through the bush and over the ice. Where he couldn't drive, he would get out and explore.

Falling, Falling . . .

It took him nearly an hour to drag himself to the truck, the dogs snuffling and whimpering beside him. The tail gate was in two parts: the bottom folded down; the top folded up and it was still shut. *Thank God I left the bottom open!* He hoisted himself carefully inside and wriggled forward onto a ready-made bed under the aluminium roof that covered the back of the truck. *And thanks to that Mountie too!*

It had seemed such an insignificant incident at the time. Only yesterday, halfway between The Pas and Thompson, a Royal Canadian Mounted Police officer had stopped him for a routine check.

"May I see your driver's license, please?"

"I'm sorry, it's in a suitcase in the back with all my other stuff," Kaletsch said. "I'll get it."

The Mountie glanced at the mess, asked Kaletsch about his destination and said pleasantly, "Never mind now, but when you stop tonight I suggest you rearrange your gear so everything's handy."

Very late that night he pulled off the road south of Leaf Rapids and by the light of an unmanned telephone relay station sorted out the jumble. He arranged the towropes into a kind of mattress on the metal floor, made a neat bed of sleeping bags on top.

Only this morning he had crossed the bay without incident and reached the village. There the locals warned him that the northern ice route was unreliable. Manitoba Hydro had dammed portions of the mighty Churchill River system and had built a diversion channel that changed the water flow and was affecting spring breakup.

Unperturbed, Kaletsch turned southeast and started over the ice along the eastern shoreline of South Bay. It was cold, sunny and dazzling white. The bay seemed infinite, as though Kaletsch were the only human on earth. He turned the dogs loose and drove slowly as they pranced alongside; he photographed their antics, called them back and pushed on.

Suddenly, some 30 kilometres from South Indian Lake, the ice gave a thunderous crack. Startled, he spun the truck toward shore. In the distance huge drifts reached out from the land like fingers, threatening to block his passage. Kaletsch spotted a clear path and gunned the motor. The screaming Chevy gripped the bank, ploughed through heavy snow and then stalled.

The tail pipe was broken; otherwise the truck seemed intact. He shoveled a path back to the ice, planning to roar out in reverse and try his luck again, this time staying closer to shore.

Noticing a hummock about six metres high, he decided to survey his route. He grabbed a camera and scaled the slippery mound. The view of sunlit trees and snowdrift patterns was beguiling. He began to snap pictures. Then he was falling, falling . . .

Now, huddled among the sleeping bags, Kaletsch knew he was facing days of blackout, fever and pain. But his medical knowledge also told him they would pass, and that strengthened his will and his hope.

Liquids, I'll need liquids. He tugged the water jug, apple juice and can opener within reach. *Remember the dogs.* He nudged two packages of frozen liver out the back of the truck. Blondie and Simba would tear them open. They could also find shelter in the open cab if they wanted it. The lower tail gate hung open but there was nothing he could do about that. Exhausted, hurting badly, Kaletsch felt himself slipping into unconsciousness.

The next three days were a discordant blur of sleeping, waking, perspiring, shivering. He dreamed, fought pain and tried to remain still. He stubbornly refused the urge to take painkillers. *I must not deaden my wits.* In each waking period he forced down a few sips of water and juice. When the water jug and juice cans froze during the second night (although he had no way of knowing it at the time, the temperature went down to −20 degrees), he dragged them into bed until his body heat thawed them. He could urinate on the floor without drenching his bedding because the rope mattress left enough clearance.

By the fourth day the fever had passed but the pain was as sharp as ever. In another five or six days he would try to get up. In the interim he would plan the next steps to survival. This would also help keep him awake by day, so he could sleep better through the long miserable nights. Planning was one of his great skills and pleasures; he'd been doing it all his life.

For most of his adult years, Kaletsch had been a man in a hurry. Perhaps it was rooted in his youth. His early life had been comfortable. His father, an engineer, had a good job with the German government as a roads superintendent in the Giessen region. Then World War II turned everything upside down; toward the end, as Hitler's armies were backed to the wall, children and old men were rushed into the ranks. At 15, Kaletsch was assigned to an antiaircraft battery. One day, home on leave, he helped save his family house when incendiary bombs set fire to the roof.

In postwar Germany the competition for advancement was fierce, but the young Kaletsch was equal to the challenge. When he applied for medical school, he was accepted on the basis of his excellent high-school grades. When he graduated in 1955, his professor chose him over older, more experienced doctors to form part of a new medical team in the town of Tübingen.

Kaletsch also showed considerable talent for invention. He devised a pump that worked off automobile exhaust to inflate tires or campers' air mattresses. As an intern, he created canvas slings for the operating table, to support patients' legs during gynecological surgery. The idea was immediately put to use in the hospital where he worked.

In the mid-1960s he mocked up a sleek cigar-shaped aircraft with no propellers or wings. It was designed to be kept aloft with vanes, each in the teardrop shape of an airfoil, rotating around the fuselage. Kaletsch maintained that it would be more stable and efficient than conventional aircraft, and aerodynamics experts at the Berlin University of Technology acknowledged that it was feasible. But Kaletsch had no resources to produce it.

He finally hit pay dirt with an improved process for making pleasure boats: a method of injecting synthetic resin between layers of fiber to produce an uncommonly strong fiber glass. He became the principal owner of a factory to build the boats, and in 1966 was featured in a German magazine in a series on "Germany's young millionaires." There, in the photographs, was a prosperous, portly young Kaletsch with his pretty, dark-haired wife, Margrit, a pedigreed dog, and a speedboat skimming across a lake with its manufacturer at the helm.

By the early 1970s he realized that in his "obsession with things that *had* to be done," he hadn't had a holiday in 22 years. He took flying lessons, earned a private pilot's license, and discovered the seductive pleasures of soloing—trusting his life to his own skill and judgment.

It was a narcotic; Kaletsch couldn't get enough. He began his adventuring with a short flight through northern Europe. Then, a trip to Spain; another across bleak Baluchistan in West Pakistan; two lone flights across the Sahara. He hunted big game in Africa, rode a motorbike through Liberia and flew to Australia. Wherever he went, people wondered at a man gambling his life on a single engine. Kaletsch liked to reply, "I never worry about the motor. If you can take care of it, why should it quit?"

But he always braced for the possibility of a forced landing in a remote area, and his constant state of mental preparedness served him well now.

A Farewell Message

The truck was turning into an ice-box. Its open end pointed north and caught the full blast of winds whooping off the bay. Moisture from his body, breath and urine formed a frozen crust on the metal interior. His sleeping bag was an icy cocoon. As soon as the ten days were up he would move out and pitch the tent. He planned and pictured each step in his head: how he would wrestle the tent out, find a sheltered spot, make a fire, melt snow, have a hot drink.

From where he was lying, Kaletsch watched a squirrel frolic up and down a tree. It was a welcome diversion. From its chattering and the occasional frustrated barks, he guessed it was teasing the dogs. Sometimes he heard Blondie and Simba up front in the cab, but mostly they were away, perhaps foraging around in the bush.

At first, during his conscious periods, the pain was constant. But gradually the pain-free periods grew longer. During them he sometimes ate a raw egg, frozen but tasty, and a piece of bread. Always he sipped juice and water. Once a day he now allowed himself a swallow of whiskey. These little breaks cheered him. He was slowly improving and might eventually fend for himself—which was essential, because it would be weeks before a search would be launched. Even then the searchers would not know where to look.

Kaletsch still felt sure he would get out, but he knew his situation was desperate. Although a Christian, he did not pray. To beg small favors of God went against his beliefs. *I am in the hands of God*, he told himself. *But I must do the best I can to survive on my own.*

By the seventh day he could shift about in his cramped quarters for ten minutes at a time without much pain. During one of those breaks he propped up the movie camera, set the timer and photographed himself. Then he flopped back in triumph. One of his schemes was working! Earlier he had tried to write but his hand was still too clumsy. So, he had decided to make a photographic diary. If the unthinkable happened, if he did not get out, this would be a farewell message for Kai and his other son, Ralf, 12.

On the eighth day his water and juice ran out. Now he *had* to move. He was glad. Every night the temperature nose-dived and the truck was unbearable.

Gently he eased himself out into a crisp sunny morning. He leaned against the truck, weak and shaky after eight days on his back, and still feeling pain. Blondie and Simba went wild. Their mournful howls of the past week changed to raucous barks! The boss was back! They raced in giddy circles and leaped on him with slavering tongues until Kaletsch feared for his injured back.

After a rest, he looked around for a camp spot. Still capering like puppies, the dogs disappeared. Kaletsch dragged out the tent, rested again, and prepared to tug it into the nearest clump of trees. The dogs reappeared, then darted away. Were they trying to lead him? Shuffling slowly, he tracked them through a thin screen of spruce.

They were waiting, tails wagging, in a small cup-shaped clearing, evidently their favorite hideout. One side of it was in full sunshine and almost free of snow—a prime campsite. Working and resting over a couple of hours he moved the small tent there and raised it. Then he filled an empty juice can with snow, set it atop another empty can fueled with twigs and gasoline, melted the snow and cooked some rice—his first hot meal in more than a week.

The temperature still hung around –10 degrees, and Kaletsch spent three miserable nights in his summer-weight tent. Paradoxically, he was becoming obsessed by the fear of rain. It was now May 5. Spring was surely near. Suppose he and the tent were drenched in a quick rain, followed by a quick freeze? He'd die before he could dry out. Yet he dreaded even more the thought of returning to the deep freeze of his truck. He longed to sleep warm and dry beside a fire.

Moreover, Kaletsch had never before been so inactive for so long. He watched small gray birds flutter in to steal scraps of dog meal, went on short walks during his pain-free periods, and talked to the dogs, who beamed at him with loving eyes and lolling tongues, and sometimes made him laugh. Kaletsch had buried bags of liver in different places in the snow for safekeeping, but the dogs regularly dug them up. Once, catching Blondie with what seemed to be meat smears on her nose, he boxed her ears. Then he discovered it was merely soot. Blondie sulked at the injustice of his act. From then on, she would suddenly become uncommonly attentive, sticking to her master like plaster for minutes on end. At those times, Kaletsch later discovered, Simba was raiding the meat cache!

But boredom was gnawing at him. He decided to take care of it and his housing problems in one swoop. He would build a hut.

Others in his predicament might have settled for branches piled up in the form of a crude lean-to, but Kaletsch, the inventor, would settle for nothing less than walls and a roof of proper logs. Methodically he scouted the surrounding timber, always wearing sunglasses or reading glasses to protect his eyes. *If a branch should blind me, I'm finished.*

Most of the trees were mere sticks— three to four metres high, and up to ten centimetres in diameter—but they had to be felled and cut up. He rehearsed the motions of handsaw versus ax, and decided the saw would cause him less pain. Slowly he sawed down a few trees each day, cut them (plus any deadfall that he could find) into two-metre and one-metre lengths, lopped off brittle branches with the

SAFE HAVEN: **the dogs led Kaletsch to the clearing where he raised his tent.**

hatchet and tugged small loads to his site aboard the toboggan. His pain-free periods now recurred every hour or so and lasted 30 to 45 minutes.

At the site, Kaletsch meticulously notched the ends of each log and rolled it into place up a ramp of hard-packed snow. Once he'd laid a solid base, he used thinner, lighter logs for the walls. As the hut grew higher, he slid each piece up a makeshift ramp of two skinny poles.

From time to time he filmed his progress. At night, exhausted but happy, he slept well despite the cold and periods of pain.

Slowly the shelter took shape, two metres long by one metre wide with an entrance in front. By working about five of the 15 hours of daylight and another half hour by the light of his campfire, he raised the structure about 20 centimetres a day. When the walls were chest-high, he shoveled mounds of snow around the outer perimeter and stood on them to finish the roof: a layer of brush, another of garbage bags, a final layer of brush, all atop a back-sloping pole frame. A garbage bag served as a screen across the doorway. He finished on May 12, and that night a wet snow fell. Kaletsch, however, was dry inside his new home. The achievement gave his spirits an enormous lift. But Kaletsch was not one to dwell on past triumphs. What next?

It was 18 days since his accident. More and more he thought about Kai and the promised phone call of May 24, only 12 days away. He thought also of the farm, the first piece of property he had truly loved in all his restless life.

He had first glimpsed the Pine River region on one of his aerial odysseys—a solo flight from the eastern United States to Alaska—and had admired that part of Manitoba, where boreal forest verges on rolling plains. Kaletsch had been looking for a country where his sons might build their future. He felt Europe was becoming too crowded for them, and his marriage had broken up. Manitoba had trees, water and the luxury of space. A man could hunt, camp, grow crops, live off the land in such a place. *If freedom survives anywhere it will be here*, Kaletsch told himself.

A year later an advertisement in a German newspaper offered a farm with buildings for sale at Sclater. He bought it sight unseen as a jointly owned property with his mother and sons.

Now, huddled in his log hut in the middle of nowhere, the peripatetic doctor—who had never before even *wanted* to holiday twice in the same place—longed to return to his fields, his cattle, his home.

Into the Unknown

His hut had one serious flaw. The first night that Kaletsch built a small fire inside, poorly vented through a roof hole, the acrid smoke almost drove him out. He set his mind to the problem; maybe he could build a stove. Next day, on a short hike in hitherto unexplored bush, he stumbled onto a small, circular, sheet-metal drum, with a lid on top and a hole for a pipe—a portable stove of a type that's used by campers, trappers and hunters. Somebody had thrown it away—its bottom was rusted out—but Kaletsch jubilantly rolled it home. *"Heute Abend werden wir es warm haben!"* ("We'll be warm tonight!") he cried to the dogs, who barked agreeably in the spirit of the occasion.

Kaletsch cut the ends out of some empty juice cans and fitted them together into a stovepipe. The contraption worked. The dogs enjoyed it as much as he did, snuggling with him into the hut at night, jockeying for the best position.

Typically, Kaletsch was soon restless again. To boost his spirits, he tried shaving his ragged beard in the truck's side-view mirror, but his face was too sore from frostbite. He tested his body daily with longer walks in the bush. One morning, fog engulfed him and he walked in circles for an hour. From then on Kaletsch always carried his compass.

"WE'LL BE WARM TONIGHT." Kaletsch puts the finishing touches to his stove.

He ate sparingly each day from the dwindling supply: a small ration of cheese, crackers and protein concentrate. Sometimes he boiled beef livers, drank the broth, ate a little meat and gave the rest to Blondie and Simba.

Occasionally a bush plane flew over South Bay, to and from South Indian Lake where the residents had a government contract to supply fish. Three times Kaletsch lit smoky gasoline fires, but to no avail. No one saw him because no one was looking. He had not been reported missing—and would not be—for at least ten more days.

Sometimes he felt strangely ambivalent about leaving his refuge. Except on flights over deserts he had never felt such inner peace, such total communion with nature. But soon Kai would become worried; besides, Kaletsch could not hold out much longer without more food. Yet he was in no condition to hunt or trap, nor did he *want* to kill any of the few small animals and birds around him. It seemed a violation.

Since his truck's battery was dead and the ice unable to bear the weight of a heavy vehicle, there was no hope of driving out. More and more he thought of walking. But walk where? South Indian Lake village was perhaps 30 kilometres away, a hard trip across weakening ice with no shelter in case of a spring storm. His map showed what seemed to be a hydro line about 25 kilometres distant. "If we go slow and easy we can reach it," he told the dogs. "Then maybe I could set fire to a hydro pole and bring somebody." He had been lucky so far, Kaletsch mused.

He loaded the toboggan with what he felt were essentials: sleeping bags, the tent, a change of shoes and socks, his cameras, the flares, left-over tea, rice, crackers and dried dog food. He left the rifles behind; they were excess weight. In the unlikely event that he met a bear or wolf, he hoped the dogs would divert it.

Early on May 17 he ate the last frozen egg and the last beef liver. His film of the past weeks went into the hut, sealed in plastic. *If I don't get out, maybe somebody will find it and give it to my boys.*

Then he hitched Blondie and Simba to the toboggan with a make-shift harness of scarves and spare bootlaces, and gave then an affectionate pat. Without them, none of this would be possible. They had never pulled a toboggan before but willingly stepped into the harness when he led the way. He looked back at the hut one last time, and then the three of them headed out into the unknown.

"Go Get 'em!"

It was slow, painful going. The spring thaw had begun and there was water everywhere, but it was warmer. Every hour or so they stopped to rest and by noon had to stop for the day. Kaletsch pitched the tent, took pictures and changed his boots and socks. He had begun the outing with two pairs of good boots, heeding the bush pilots' adage: "Always wear the boots you would like to walk home in." He wore paratrooper's high leather boots by day. At camp he wore the spares, with leather uppers and heavy rubber soles. If his marching footgear weren't dry by evening, he took the boots into bed with him.

With temperatures around –5 degrees overnight, the trail froze solid. Kaletsch was on the move in predawn light shortly after 5am. A frozen creek provided easier walking until the thaw stopped him again. On the third morning, spring arrived with a vengeance. He detoured briefly off the winding creek bed; when he picked it up again it had turned into bubbling water. Now he and the dogs had to labor through bush and swamp, twisting and turning, adding many extra kilometres.

Their meager food supply was nearly gone. Kaletsch drank water from open pools, and kept up his fluid intake by scooping mouthfuls of snow every few minutes.

The weary dogs were struggling now to keep the toboggan moving. Once it jammed in a deadfall. Kaletsch finally freed it with the hatchet. Then he tossed away extra sleeping bags and blankets, and his spare boots, to lighten the load. He had stripped himself to less than the essentials. If bad weather came, his chances would be nil. But surely the hydro line was near?

On the fifth day they broke into an open space. *We've made it!* he thought. Then he looked around. There was *no* power line, only an open cut in the bush, perhaps *intended* for a power line. For the first time in his long ordeal, Kaletsch felt defeated. He slumped to the ground, and the dogs dropped panting beside him.

After a while he made camp, shared the last scraps of food with the dogs, and summoned up his hope. If the map was not misleading, this open cut would take him northwest to the road he had traveled from Leaf Rapids to South Bay, in what seemed a lifetime ago. There, surely, someone would find him.

He filmed himself one more time and stowed camera and film in the bush. On the sixth morning he started again: walk, rest, walk, rest. His pain had receded; fatigue was his enemy now. Through that day and the seventh, he and the dogs trudged in fits and starts, stumbling into gullies cut by water runoff, reaching down to their last dregs of strength. Kaletsch guessed they had now walked nearly 30 meandering kilometres in what had looked like an easy journey on the map.

On May 24, the eighth morning of the walk, they came abruptly to a wide stream. This, as it turned out, was a diversion channel, part of the hydro project but not shown on Kaletsch's outdated map. On the other side of the water—his heart leaped!—were buildings. It seemed to be an abandoned construction camp. But surely there would be shelter, maybe food, maybe some means of communication?

Then he looked at the channel again. It was at least 100 metres wide, very deep and with a swift current—a challenge for a strong swimmer, impossible for a man whose strength was spent. His brain went doggedly back to work. Somewhere in the bush—was it only yesterday?—he had passed a few empty oil drums. Maybe he could haul them back on the toboggan, lash them to logs somehow, build a raft.

It would take at least a day to go back . . . another day to return . . . another to build the raft. He looked at Blondie and Simba, drooping beside him. Did they or he have the strength? None of them had eaten in two days.

It was now 10am. Soon Kai would be expecting his call. Kaletsch stood numbly beside the channel. His luck seemed to have run out. Then, in disbelief at first, he heard the sputter of a motor. A helicopter swooped over the horizon. Frantically he fumbled for a flare and fired it. No reaction. Another flare. No response. *My God, I've lost them!* Kaletsch started back into the bush for the old oil drums when he heard the helicopter again. He fired more flares and turned back to the water's edge.

The helicopter was landing on the opposite shore. It unloaded three men and flew away. Kaletsch waved and screamed. Still they seemed to not hear. *The dogs! If he could make the dogs bark . . .*

"Blondie! Simba! Go get 'em!' he yelled hoarsely. The dogs, catching his excitement, barked furiously. Across the water the men turned. Then they began to launch a rubber dinghy.

A Sad Duty

In fact, the Manitoba Hydro crew from Thompson, 128 kilometres south, *had* already noticed Kaletsch. As they flew in for one of their infrequent trips to meter the current flow in the diversion channel, pilot Jack Beaman of Custom Helicopters said, "There's a guy waving his hands." That in itself was not unusual. Lone trappers sometimes wave at passing aircraft out of sheer friendliness.

But after the landing, the Hydro men saw the flares and heard the shouts and barks. The man obviously needed help. When they beached the dinghy in front of him, Kaletsch stood dazed. Then he stammered, "I've been four weeks in the bush!"

As he told his story in bits and pieces, the others listened with mingled astonishment and skepticism. There had been no report of a missing man. Yet Kaletsch seemed to be on the level.

"His clothes were hanging loosely on him," Hydro employee John Willis recalled later. "And he was really scruffy-looking and walking stiffly. He'd been there a long time, all right. He probably wouldn't have made it without the dogs."

"Do I smell bad?" Kaletsch blurted. "I have not had a bath for a month."

The others grinned, shrugged, shook their heads. Suddenly Kaletsch looked at his watch. It was almost noon. "I have to phone, it's very important!"

So Beaman, who was back now with the helicopter, flew him and the dogs across to South Indian Lake. Kaletsch called his son, proud that he was "right on time." In fact he was an hour later than promised; he had forgotten that Canada had moved ahead to daylight saving time.

"Kai, I was lost in the bush but I'm all right," he shouted over the line. "So whatever you hear about me, don't worry. I'll call you as soon as I get into a hospital for a checkup." Then Beaman flew the trio across South Bay to the end of the road, where a taxi picked them up.

At Leaf Rapids, Kaletsch, as single-minded as ever, shunned medical attention. "If they had put me in hospital who would have looked after the dogs?" he said later. "Blondie and Simba stayed with me all those weeks when they could have run away to some settlement. They helped me get out. Now I had to get them home."

No plane or bus out of Leaf Rapids would take the dogs. Kaletsch saw a sign on a bulletin board: "Car for sale, body rusty, engine good, $300." The owner, who happened to be a local doctor, accepted a check. Kaletsch was on the road that afternoon and in Pine River 24 hours later.

While the Boyacheks cared for his dogs, he checked into Swan River Valley Hospital, 80 kilometres away. There Kaletsch's injuries were diagnosed as a compression fracture of the seventh thoracic vertebra (in the middle of the back) and a severely sprained neck. Kaletsch had lost 30 pounds but otherwise had come through remarkably well.

During a week in hospital he had a call from Boyachek.

"That Blondie, she's gone kind of wild," the farmer said. "She's leading packs of dogs around in the bush. I don't know what they might do. I'm going to have to chain her."

"OK," Kaletsch agreed. "Maybe she'll calm down in a few days."

But she did not. The weeks in the wilderness had turned her "wild" again. If allowed to run loose, she would continue to lead the neighborhood dogs in packs and perhaps kill cattle and wildlife. Yet Kaletsch could not bear to chain her for the rest of her life. It would be worse than death. Nor did he want a vet to put her to sleep. Kaletsch regards a bullet through the head as the quickest and most humane death for an animal.

"I would not let someone else do it," he says. "She was my friend, she had helped save my life. I did not want her to be suspicious or frightened for one minute."

So, after leaving hospital, he sadly carried out what he felt was his final obligation to the dog he loved. He gave her a good meal and while she was absorbed in eating it, he shot her.

Back in Germany, Kaletsch gradually recovered his vigor. That summer Kai went over to South Bay, found the hut and brought back the film, cameras, rifle and a sleeping bag. The following winter, with the help of men from South Indian Lake, Kaletsch hauled the truck out of the bush.

His fascination for the area that almost killed him sometimes puzzles even Kaletsch. "Up there," he says "heaven and hell are both so close."

Whitewater
nightmare

by Kathy Cook

Three young adventurers thirsted for the ultimate challenge. Few had ever done it—several had died trying.

Snow melting in the midday sun trickled down from the peak of Mount Quehuisha, 5,500 metres above sea level, deep in the Andes Mountains of Peru. Colin Angus, 27, a lean, boyish-looking Canadian with blond hair and blue eyes, squatted down and caught the water in a small bottle as it dripped from a jutting rock. His head throbbed from the lack of oxygen in the thin air, and he ached from three weeks of uphill hiking. "The source of the Amazon River, in my hands," he marvelled, raising the bottle and taking a sip.

It was September 29, 1999. Just ten months before, Angus had decided to undertake a daring—some would say foolhardy—expedition: to raft down the world's mightiest river, the Amazon, from its source in the headwaters of the Apurímac River, through some 600 kilometres of whitewater, to its end in the Atlantic almost 7,000 kilometres later. He knew of no one who had rafted its length before, though he'd heard that several had died trying.

A university dropout from Vancouver Island, Angus had spent some five years cruising the islands of the South Pacific, funding his way with odd jobs. The Amazon venture would be the ultimate challenge. And it would have to be done on a shoestring.

Angus estimated that the adventure would require three people, take six months and cost $5,000 per person, including airfare, the price of a four-metre inflatable raft, supplies and food. He found his two team members in Ben Kozel, 26, an Australian conservationist who had travelled with Angus through Europe one summer, and Scott Borthwick, 23, a South African computer student with whom Angus had worked as a construction labourer in London.

Arriving in Peru in early September, the men stored their heavy gear and raft in the city of Cuzco and took a bus to Camaná on the coast. There they dipped their feet in the Pacific. While forming their plans, they had decided to cross South America from the west coast to the east, on foot and by raft. The first leg would be a 250-kilometre hike, mostly through desert, to the Continental Divide.

Carrying 30-kilogram backpacks, they set off. Behind schedule, trying to reach the Apurímac before the rainy season made its waters too treacherous to run, they took a shortcut through an uninhabited desert pass.

A 70-kilometre slog under a relentless tropical sun left them exhausted. At the end of the second day and out of water, they finally reached an algae-filled pond crawling with mosquito larvae. They slaked their thirst and wearily made camp.

Crossing the Continental Divide two weeks later, the group set up base in a snow-covered livestock shelter at the foot of Mount Quehuisha—one of the most distant sources of the Amazon—and next day climbed to its summit.

Pages 134–35. INTO THE STORM: Scott Borthwick, somewhere between Iquitos and Manaus.

TAKE A BREAK: **Colin Angus (left) and Scott Borthwick pause in the Andean canyons.**

"Now, let's go get the raft," Angus said thankfully as he stowed his sample of Amazon headwater in his backpack. After another six days of hiking, they reached the mountain village of Pilpinto. Here, the Apurímac was deep enough for rafting. They took a bus to Cuzco, some 50 kilometres away, collected their raft and gear, and returned, ready for the main event.

The Apurímac is the Amazon's most distant tributary and is accepted as one of its chief sources. Dropping more than 4,000 metres over 600 kilometres, it has cut a gorge that for kilometres at a time is more than 2,000 metres deep. It is one of the most dangerous whitewater rivers in the world.

On October 6, loaded with backpacks, gear and red rubber raft, the trio made their way to its shore. They pumped up the raft, slipped into wet suits and put on life jackets and helmets. A dozen natives watched, whispering among themselves.

"They look like they're waiting for us to commit suicide," Angus laughed.

A gnarled man with missing teeth stepped forward, introducing himself as the village chief. "The river is not too bad here," he said in Spanish. "But farther down, it becomes very dangerous."

Kozel, who understood Spanish best, translated. By now they were tired of all the warnings they'd received, both here and at home. They had studied the river and read every book they could on technique. They believed they could run it.

"We'll be careful," Kozel said. At six foot four and 195 pounds, he towered over the tiny elder. "Thank you for the warning."

The chief stared deeply into Kozel's eyes. "If you continue, you will die," he said, turning away.

The group waved goodbye to the unsmiling villagers and pushed off. "Yee-ha!" Borthwick hollered as the raft splashed through the first set of rapids. *God, it's good to be on the water,* Angus thought. Dozens of children ran along the bank, calling excitedly after them.

Although explorers and geographers in the 20th century have been keen to find the source of the Amazon, few have ever attempted to raft its entire length, largely because of the danger and isolation of the Apurímac. Bordering the river, high in the Andes, is the birthplace of one the most ruthless terrorist organizations in modern South America, the Shining Path guerrillas.

Leaving Pilpinto, the Apurímac wound gently between looming 6,000-metre-high mountains. Aside from wildflowers and moss, there was no sign of life in the rock towering above the banks. That night, 40 kilometres along, the trio camped on a white-sand beach, the sky a vast expanse of stars.

On the second day, the Apurímac gained volume as it twisted sharply down the mountains. Huge boulders spiked out of the river. In some places the rocks formed sieves that, aided by the powerful current, could suck a body underwater and keep it there. Before each set of rapids, the men paddled ashore and scouted ahead to pick the safest route.

Less than two months earlier, Borthwick and Kozel had arrived in Canmore, Alberta, to train with Angus in the whitewater rivers of the Rockies. Both were novice rafters, and Angus, their teacher, had taken up rafting only a few months before. Now, on the Apurímac, they were learning to be a team in earnest, practising techniques they had only read about. For each rapid, they changed positions so all had equal time steering in the stern.

In the afternoon they paddled to shore at the start of some rough water. Angus and Borthwick walked over the rocks to scout ahead. "Looks like these rapids end in a waterfall," Borthwick said. If everything went well, however, they could navigate through the 2 ½-metre drop.

With Angus steering, they headed into the rapids. *We're not far enough over,* Angus thought. "Paddle!" he yelled. But the raft, having veered sideways in the rapids, now

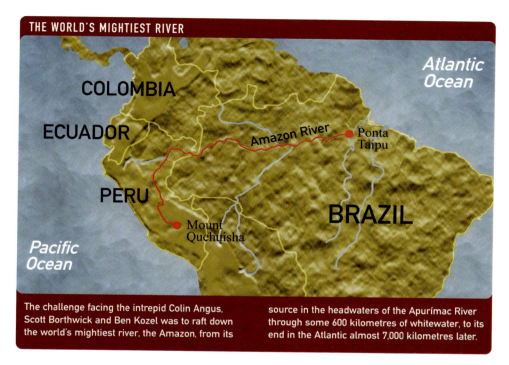

THE WORLD'S MIGHTIEST RIVER

COLOMBIA

ECUADOR

Amazon River — Ponta Taipu

PERU

Mount Quehuisha

BRAZIL

Atlantic Ocean

Pacific Ocean

The challenge facing the intrepid Colin Angus, Scott Borthwick and Ben Kozel was to raft down the world's mightiest river, the Amazon, from its source in the headwaters of the Apurímac River through some 600 kilometres of whitewater, to its end in the Atlantic almost 7,000 kilometres later.

cascaded over the waterfall and flipped. Kozel and Borthwick were thrown into the water, and Angus smashed onto a boulder. Bruised but otherwise unhurt, he rolled into the current and followed the raft downstream. He caught up to it and all three men were able to get back in. Such a bad start boded ill for the bigger tests ahead.

Camped by a sand dune after three days of whitewater, Borthwick cooked chili over an open fire while Kozel wrote in his journal. Angus gazed at the stars, having regained any confidence lost at the waterfall. "Hey, isn't everything absolutely perfect?" he said.

Kozel, too, was awestruck by the rugged beauty of the river. But his exhilaration after a few scares was tempered by a sense of foreboding.

Back on the river the next morning, the group soon saw more rapids in the distance. They climbed to a ledge to get a better view, only to gaze down on a maelstrom of water barrelling between two-storey boulders.

"Wow, this is a Class Five-plus rapid," Angus said. Class V rapids are considered extremely difficult for expert rafters and represent about the limit of man's ability to navigate whitewater.

"We can do it," Borthwick said enthusiastically.

"OK, we'll follow that line down by the left," Kozel said. It was his turn to steer.

They paddled into the first drop, and the rushing current immediately swung the raft sideways into a boulder, lifting the stern over a metre into the air. Kozel was thrown overboard. Despite his life jacket, a strong undertow yanked him under and pulled him downstream.

Angus and Borthwick shifted their weight around the raft to keep it from flipping. Suddenly Kozel surfaced in front of them, but before Borthwick could grab him, the current slammed Kozel against the rock wall.

A searing pain ripped through Kozel's side. Again he was pulled under, then dragged along the bottom. *I'm not going to survive this time*, he thought.

Seeing a two-metre waterfall ahead, Angus and Borthwick secured their feet in the rope at the base of the raft. They slid over the falls stern first, landing right side up in the foam, with both men still inside.

"Paddle!" Angus screamed. *This is a keeper hole*, he thought, glancing at the churning whirlpool trying to suck them in. The raft was lifting on its right side, about to flip. The two men paddled hard but couldn't break out.

Submerged beneath them, Kozel fought the churning hole's grip. He was bashed into rocks and pulled in every direction, and had no idea which way was up.

Finally outpowering the hole, Angus and Borthwick looked upriver for Kozel but saw nothing. Then, again, he surfaced in front of them. Borthwick could now pull him up. "You OK?" he asked.

"No!" Kozel gasped, shocked and amazed that he had survived.

That evening Kozel sat apart, nursing deep bruises and cuts. Traumatized, he gazed silently out over the river. It would be a while before his sense of humour came back.

After four more days on the water, the formidable Acobamba Abyss lay ahead. "Do you think it's doable now?" Kozel asked as they sat by a campfire.

He had read about the abyss, a 25-kilometre section of river bound by canyon walls hundreds of metres high, where the sun streamed in for only minutes each day. Scouting ahead was impossible.

"No way. The river is too high," Angus replied.

On October 15, they reached the entrance. The decision to portage around the abyss was unanimous. With gear in tow, they climbed the 2,000-metre-high mountainside and followed a road strewn with small villages. In a local store, they stocked up with rice, beans, sardines, herbs and spices. Hiring a local man with two horses and a mule to help them with their gear, they stumbled down a zigzag trail to continue their journey on the river below the abyss.

Six hundred kilometres after entering the whitewater in Pilpinto, the three men finally rafted out of the mountains. The roar of the rapids and the steep canyon walls gave way to a gentle current and rolling rain-forest hills.

It was now mid-November and they were still in Peru, with less than one tenth of their journey completed.

The Apurímac drained into the Ene River, which in turn entered the meandering Tambo River. Ferns and exotic flowering plants lined the shores, and tree limbs stretched 10 metres out over the river. Their wetsuits now stored away, the three men wore shorts, T-shirts and sun hats.

They tethered their paddles to the sides of the raft, turning them into oars so that one person instead of three could propel them through the calmer waters. Attracted to the sound, pink dolphins surfaced near the raft. Monkeys perched in trees called out in alarm as they passed, and brightly coloured tropical birds flew from treetop to treetop.

Life on the raft became a cozy routine. They waved to local fishermen passing in dugout canoes. When they ventured ashore to buy food, they were surrounded by excited, barefoot children.

In late November, Kozel spotted farmers on shore walking with rifles over their shoulders. A helicopter armed with missiles passed overhead. When they docked to buy supplies, a dozen stern-faced Peruvian men carrying bows and arrows, rifles and machetes surrounded them.

"What are you doing here?" a bare-chested elder asked. Kozel explained.

The locals eyed them with distrust. After a long silence, the elder said, "It's not safe for you here. There are terrorists in the jungle."

FLAT WATER, AT LAST: **Colin Angus takes a turn at the oars.**

By now, 50 armed men had circled them. Their travel literature had said that the threat of the Shining Path guerrillas was over. Peruvian military reports stated that the leaders had all been caught and the rebels disbanded. *I guess no one told these people the Shining Path aren't around anymore*, Angus thought.

They eased their way out of the circle and rowed away.

Two days later as Kozel rowed and the others dozed, he saw five longhaired men in rags step out of a camouflaged thatched hut. "Check these guys out," Kozel said apprehensively, waking Angus and Borthwick. Two of the men, holding shotguns, pointed to the bank below, demanding they come ashore.

"Hello," Angus greeted them, pretending not to understand. Kozel and Borthwick waved casually.

"Stop!" the leader yelled angrily.

"Row faster, Ben," Angus said, still smiling. When the raft was clearly not about to come ashore, one of the men lifted his gun and fired.

Borthwick and Angus ducked. With no more room on the raft floor to hide, Kozel bent his head and rowed furiously. A second shot rang out. It missed.

Kozel considered jumping overboard, but the river turned just ahead. Borthwick raised his head. "There might be more of them waiting at the bend," he said.

"Or they may have a motorboat," Angus replied, eyeing a dugout canoe on the opposite bank. Defenceless, they rowed on in tense silence.

Two hours downriver, they saw a small village on the right. The Peruvian flag flew from a hill. As they rowed past, a gunshot rang out. "Not again!" said Borthwick. Running to the shore, yelling, were dozens of armed men in khaki. Angus rowed harder. The soldiers climbed into a motorboat.

"They're coming for us!" Kozel yelled. Angus stopped rowing.

When the boat was within 50 metres of the raft, six men stood up, aimed their rifles and opened fire above the trio's heads. Terrified, Angus jumped into the water, followed by Borthwick and Kozel. Hiding behind the raft, they raised their arms in the air, but the firing continued. Angus peeked around the side of the raft.

The commander of the group angrily aimed at his head. "Swim to shore!" he barked at them. Kozel spotted the insignia on his breast pocket: Peruvian Army. On shore, they were questioned and reprimanded. "You passed a military checkpoint," the commander said. The army was still battling Shining Path guerrillas who lived in the surrounding jungle and terrorized local villagers—despite what the travel pamphlets and military reports said.

"Do you realize the danger you're in?" the commander asked sternly, drawing his finger across his throat. "You're stupid to be here."

The Shining Path were known for murdering civilians, tourists and anyone associated with the government. This part of the jungle was their turf. The commander told them to sleep in the barracks that night. "You'll be safer."

At 4.30 the next morning, taking the commander's advice to travel early when the rebels were likely, sleeping off hangovers, they rafted onward, voices hushed and eyes scanning the shore. They camped without building fires.

Three days later they reached Atalaya, Peru. They were out of rebel territory.

By the end of November they were in the heart of the wet jungle. Camping along the wooded shore, they suffered mosquitoes, sand flies, spiders and large, unknown tropical bugs. White moths, attracted by their fire, filled the air like snow and landed in their food.

One evening a loud splash came from the edge of their campsite. Borthwick shone his flashlight, and a set of crocodile eyes glowed back at them from the water.

With images of malarial fever haunting them, they decided to row in shifts around the clock, cooking, washing and sleeping onboard. This way they made 120 kilometres a day, and on December 5 they rowed into a remote section of lower Colombia. Two days later they entered Brazil.

Now they were in the rain forest. Three times a day clouds covered the tropical sun and thunder showers pelted down on them. As soon as it stopped raining, a hot mugginess took over. Saturated banks periodically gave way, sending trees and large sections of earth crashing into the river.

Although they washed daily, their clothes, torn and always wet, rotted with mould. A peculiar red welt developed on Kozel's foot. Within a week the infection spread, leaving hundreds of open sores over the soles of his feet. Walking became an agony. Soon the same sores developed on Angus's feet. Without access to antibiotics, they hoped the mysterious infection would heal on its own. For weeks they kept their feet out of the water and in the sun.

By New Year's Day they had reached Manaus, a city of 1.5 million. There the Negro River merges with the Amazon. But they were still 1,450 kilometres from the Atlantic. Ocean-size swells batted the raft around, and torrential downpours, with high winds and lightning, struck daily.

Some days later the men in the raft could no longer see the far shore and were now several hundred kilometres from the Atlantic. Nearing the sea, they shared the river with ocean liners.

One foggy night as Angus rowed, a ship approached without external lights. They listened intently as the sound of the engines grew louder, echoing off the water. Borthwick and Kozel frantically waved their flashlights. Suddenly, seconds away, the ship's massive bulk loomed over them.

"It's going to hit us!" Borthwick yelled. Angus rowed furiously. The ship passed six metres from the raft, the huge wake rocking them in the water.

"That was a little too close," Angus breathed as the vessel slipped back into the fog.

On February 8 a heavy ocean storm hit them. Three-metre waves crashed over the trees lining the shore. Unable to dock, the men tied up to a fishing stake in the water and curled up on the floor under a plastic cover, trying to sleep as rain pounded down and waves crashed over the raft.

At 4am, feeling seasick, Borthwick looked out. "Hey guys, take a look." The black water glowed green with phosphorescent algae blown in by the storm.

Angus grabbed a cup and tried some water. "It's salty!" he said.

Two hours later they stood on shore, soaked, shivering, seasick and wretchedly exhausted. They studied their tourist map but couldn't figure out where they were.

Angus approached a fisherman fixing his net by a lighthouse. "Is this Ponta Taipu?" he asked in Portuguese. The fisherman nodded.

The three looked at one other, wide smiles splitting their faces as they embraced wildly.

"We did it!" Angus shouted. Ponta Taipu was where the Amazon met the Atlantic.

Angus brought out three bottles of cheap champagne, bought a week earlier with their dwindling dollars. They popped the corks, spraying the raft and one another. "Although I'm a little tired of you both, I love you guys," Angus smiled, swigging his champagne.

They tied their hand-sewn flags of Canada, Australia and South Africa to their paddles and took pictures of themselves standing by the raft in their moment of triumph. They had beaten the Amazon.

THE VICTORS: **Colin Angus (left). Scott Borthwick and Ben Kozel beat the world's mightiest river.**

Leopard attack!

by John Dyson

It was man against beast. And for
Paul Connolly the odds weren't good.

Rosemarie Honman woke at four in the morning to the loud noise of her five big dogs yapping and fighting. At the back door of her house in Victoria Falls, Zimbabwe, she yelled at them to shut up, then went to the kennel and threw their water bowl over them.

Three ran from the kennel and she dragged a fourth into the open. The last dog, Scruff, seemed to be making a strange throaty noise and wouldn't budge, so she left him. At dawn Scruff emerged, his ears and paws bleeding. Yet the strange, rumbling growl continued inside the kennel.

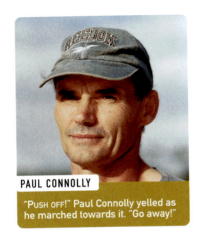

PAUL CONNOLLY

"Push off!" Paul Connolly yelled as he marched towards it. "Go away!"

Honman called her gardener, who shone a flashlight into the dark enclosure. Two blazing eyes, bright as fireworks, glowed in the beam. "It's a bloody leopard!" Honman shouted.

Retreating to the house, she telephoned her neighbour Fanie Pretorius, a retired big-game hunter and safari guide. He grabbed a shotgun and called Steven Zvinongoza, chief warden of the area's national park; the two men then hurried to the Honman home.

Pretorius knew leopards almost never attacked humans, but if this animal had been cornered and taunted by dogs it would be frightened—and dangerous.

From the safety of the kitchen doorway they lobbed stones at the kennel, three yards away. Spitting and snarling, the leopard slunk out into the daylight and charged. The two men jumped inside the house and slammed the door in the leopard's face. It thudded into the door, then dropped to the ground and crept away through the trees.

"We should shoot it because it will attack people," Pretorius said.

"Let it be," Zvinongoza replied. "It will go back to the wild if we leave it alone."

Honman quickly telephoned her neighbours to warn them of the danger. But she didn't call Paul and Marie Connolly, whose big garden was just over the wall. The family, she thought, was not at home.

In fact, that Friday morning, July 30, 1998, Paul Connolly had just returned from a solo kayak expedition on the Congo River. The oldest of his four daughters was away at boarding school, and Marie had taken the youngest to visit her parents in Belgium. Their two other girls had left for school. Every door of the family's big thatched house was flung wide to catch the cool morning air.

Though trained as a lawyer, Connolly, 45, had pioneered white-water rafting trips for tourists on the Zambezi River in Zimbabwe. Now he ran canoe safaris and expeditions to remote parts of Africa. Dressed as usual in denim bush-shirt and shorts, a green baseball cap pulled low over his dark brows and suntanned face, he was vigorous, agile and—at a shade under six feet tall, weighing 165 pounds— superbly fit.

Shortly after 9am, he was sitting in his office, detached from the main house, having a cup of coffee with Marilyn Ndlovu. A neighbour, she had stopped by with her daughter Violet, age three. Suddenly they heard the housekeeper screaming in the backyard. Connolly jumped up and raced out of the door.

"Boss, get the gun!" yelled Tanyara Ngwenya, the gardener. "Leopard! Leopard!"

"Where?" Connolly demanded. Ngwenya pointed towards the back of the house. In the shadows, Connolly saw a handsome young female leopard, at least two-and-a-half feet high at the shoulder and well over six feet long from its nose to the end of its twitching tail.

On tough, daily training runs along bush roads, Connolly had often met dangerous wild animals face to face. His first instinct was to run straight at them, yelling loudly and waving; once he had even stopped a charging lioness in her tracks. At other times nimble footwork had saved him from charging buffalo, elephants and even warthogs.

Crouching low, the leopard was 20 yards away and slinking past the bedroom windows, pausing to peer curiously into each one. Connolly marched boldly towards it. "Push off!" he yelled. "Go away!"

POWERFUL PREDATOR

Leopards are solitary creatures who seldom attack humans, but the female that attacked Paul Connolly had become frightened and dangerous following her encounter with five large dogs. More likely to hunt nocturnally, when its piercing eyes see best, a leopard will stalk, chase and then pounce on its prey. It inflicts the most damage with its large fore paws, which enclose sharp, retractable, one-inch claws. But it is the four canine teeth, approximately two inches long, that are used for killing.

For an instant, man and cat stared at each other in the bright sunlight. Then, a yellowy blur of lightning, the leopard shot across the yard straight at Connolly. Even as he braced himself for the hit, Connolly had a quick-flash thought: *How incredibly beautiful this animal is!*

In one last mighty spring, the leopard flew at his throat. With no time to duck or dodge, Connolly threw up his left arm to protect his face. Sharp teeth punctured his hand and wrist and a massive weight crashed into his chest.

Twisting to absorb the impact, Connolly shot his arm straight out from the shoulder. Fangs clamped on his wrist, the leopard stretched upward, its back legs on the ground and its front claws thrashing the air. Tanyara Ngwenya bravely darted in from behind, grabbed the leopard's tail and pulled with all his strength.

Connolly glimpsed little Violet Ndlovu standing nearby. "Get the child!" he yelled. "Run!" With a scream, Violet's mother grabbed her daughter and raced indoors.

Connolly felt a surge of confidence. The leopard's weight was about 100 pounds, and holding it up was no problem. *I can sort this out*, he thought. Then his foot slipped on the courtyard tiles. Man and leopard fell sideways and came down on the ground facing each other, Connolly's left hand still in its jaws. The leopard's ears were pinned flat, its yellow eyes blazing. From deep down in its belly came loud grunts. The gardener sprang away and fled inside.

Connolly grabbed the soft folds of the animal's throat with his right hand and squeezed with his full strength, trying to crush its windpipe. But the leopard was all muscle, with anger seething at its core. One hand alone wasn't enough.

So with a huge effort, Connolly slithered up onto his knees and, half-crouching over the leopard, finally dragged his hand from its jaws. Now he could lock both hands round the leopard's throat.

In a fury, the animal drew in its back legs and struck upward at Connolly's arching body, kicking repeatedly and fast, its extended claws shredding Connolly's shirt. Knowing he was close to being disembowelled, Connolly let go and sprang to his feet.

The door was just a couple of paces away. Connolly crept slowly towards it, his gaze locked on the leopard's eyes. Suddenly the animal attacked him again. Connolly barely had time to lift his right arm in defence before the leopard's teeth sank into his wrist.

Leaning back to keep his face and throat out of range, Connolly found the

SAFE AS HOUSES . . . **or was he?**

148

strength to rain desperate one-handed punches on the leopard's nose. The animal half-closed its eyes and shook its head. Clearly, the punches hurt.

Abruptly the leopard let go. Connolly jumped across the threshold into the kitchen and slammed the door. With all the kitchen windows and doors shut he figured he was safe. His arms were bleeding and the pain was agonising. Wild-animal wounds, he knew, were invariably infected and must be quickly cleansed. As he moved to the kitchen sink, he glanced out of the big window.

The leopard was in a half-crouch, looking up. As soon as it spotted him the big cat hurled itself at the window.

The leopard's left paw hit the window first, followed by its head. As the glass exploded, the animal landed in the kitchen's stainless-steel sink. It slashed out at Connolly's face with both front paws.

HANDSOME RUG: **Connolly and his big cat.**

Clenching his right fist and drawing back his arm, Connolly delivered a haymaker punch to the leopard's nose. The animal reeled back but quickly rebounded, lashing out again.

Face to face, man and cat slugged it out. With both fists, Connolly threw blows at its face as if hammering a punchbag. Blood flew from his wound and the leopard's vivid face-markings blurred in his eyes.

The leopard tried to block his furious assault, blood spraying from a cut in its right paw. Dazed, confused and off-balance, it struggled desperately to fight out of its corner.

For 20 long seconds the deadly boxing match continued. Connolly felt his energy flag, but saw the leopard begin to cringe. Connolly punched harder and faster.

The big cat now retreated until it was balancing on the window sill. Connolly leaned over the sink and gave it one last, hard punch that became a kind of push. The animal dropped to the ground outside.

Connolly shouted to the women to stay in the TV room where they were hiding and ran to the bathroom where he bathed his arms in hot water. Suddenly he heard the double blast of a shotgun. Drawn by the screams from Connolly's yard, Fanie Pretorius and park warden Steven Zvinongoza had rushed to the scene.

Paul Connolly's lacerated arms required 37 stitches, but he is philosophical about the encounter. "Things like this are bound to happen," he says. "It's the price we pay for being able to enjoy the enchantment of Africa."

The leopard's skin is now a handsome rug in his hallway.

Hobart
TASMANIA

Race for his life

Southern Ocean

South
Pole

ANTARCTICA

Rescue
Call

Goss's
Route

by Rudolph Chelminski

He was the only one close enough to
save his friend. Pete Goss would have
to sail back into the face of the storm.

n the icy reaches of the Southern Ocean between Australia and Antarctica, Christmas night, 1996, brought a sudden, violent storm. Aboard *Aqua Quorum*, a 50-foot racing yacht, the barometer dropped like a stone.

Frantically, 35-year-old Pete Goss lowered sail, leaving up only the storm jib, a triangular scrap of canvas in the bow. Now the sea smoked white with spume, heaving and writhing under shrieking winds, as *Aqua Quorum* bounced through waves higher than a three-storey house.

Goss was one of 15 sailors entered in the Vendée Globe, a singlehanded, round-the-world race. He had left France nearly two months before, sailed south past Africa's Cape of Good Hope and was now in the empty seas southwest of Australia. From there he would cross the Pacific, round Cape Horn, then head back up the Atlantic.

On the wall above his instrument panel Goss had taped snapshots of his family back in England: his wife, Tracey, and their three kids—Alexander, Olivia and Eliot. As he glanced at their faces, a chill ran down his spine. *What if I don't make it?*

As if to answer him, *Aqua Quorum* plunged down a wave, the cabin growing dark as the seas buried her. Bailing water from the cabin in the midst of the fury, Goss heard a bleep from the laptop computer on his chart table. It was an emergency call from the Australian Maritime Rescue Coordination Center: a boat named *Algimouss* had sent a mayday.

He hadn't recognized the name as a Vendée Globe boat. Minutes later the computer bleeped again and spat out a fax from race headquarters: "Hi, Pete. Raphaël is in trouble. Do you think you can help?"

Raphaël Dinelli and Pete Goss might have been brothers, so similar were their stories. Professional sailors since their early years, they were penniless outsiders in a rich man's race. Dinelli, at 28 the youngest of those racing, was piloting *Algimouss*, an aging, second-hand boat.

Goss, a former Royal Marine commando, was a veteran of the shoestring approach. In one transatlantic race his boat was so primitive that he navigated by following jetliners' vapor trails all the way to America. He had spent ten years planning and raising money for the Vendée.

But *Aqua Quorum*, like other boats in the race, was outfitted with state-of-the-art electronics. It carried the satellite-based Global Positioning System (GPS) navigating gear, which locates a boat with pinpoint accuracy, and Argos emergency beacons, whose SOS signals can be tracked to within about 150 yards.

As the race progressed, Dinelli and Goss got acquainted by radio with the help of a fellow competitor as interpreter—Goss spoke no French, and Dinelli's English was rudimentary. Gradually they became friends.

HELL AND HIGH WATER: **Pete Goss was in radio contact with his storm-tossed rival, Raphaël Dinelli.**

But now Raphaël Dinelli was in deep, deep trouble. A massive wall of water had piled up behind him, seething and hissing. Up *Algimouss* rose, angling her bow ever more steeply until it seemed as if she'd pitch over forward. Then down she dived, skidding sideways as he vainly struggled to cope with terrible forces at the stern. "Too fast," Dinelli said aloud in alarm. "Too fast!"

With a thunderous crash the monstrous wall of water flipped *Algimouss* on its back, propelling Dinelli against the cabin roof in a shower of provisions, papers and instruments.

With its mast and rigging underwater, *Algimouss* couldn't right herself. The mast's top half had snapped off and become impaled in the upside-down deck.

Buffeted by the waves, the mast crunched open a larger and larger hole. *Algimouss* was slowly gutting herself.

"Hell's teeth," Goss muttered. Dinelli's position, as faxed from race headquarters, was 160 nautical miles *upwind*. He would have to sail back into the face of the storm, through the worst seas he'd ever seen.

He banged out a message: was anyone closer to Dinelli? The answer was negative, and at 1190 nautical miles from the Australian coast, Dinelli was out of helicopter range. Goss was the only hope. He paused. With a wife and three children, did he have the right to take the risk? He knew what his answer had to be.

Goss crawled through the door of his cabin and put the helm hard over. At once *Aqua Quorum* was slapped down by the titanic power of the wind. *I'm never going to make it*, he thought. But the boat righted herself and thudded off into the gale.

Dinelli yanked his red survival suit over warm arctic clothes, grabbed his Argos radio beacons and tied them around his neck. With the three central compartments of *Algimouss* waist-deep in freezing water, all he could do now was wait. At least watertight compartments fore and aft kept her afloat for the moment. But how long could that last?

For three hours the yacht lay upside-down with Dinelli stuck inside. Then the broken mast worked itself free, and the boat righted herself. Scrambling out onto the deck, he found nothing left.

Dinelli now began to contemplate death not as an abstract notion but as a force eager to embrace him. With the deck awash in water, he clambered to the roof of *Algimouss*'s cabin, held fast by his safety harness against being swept overboard. All through the afternoon he rode *Algimouss* like a circus rider, knees bent, leaning into the wind and the waves.

CHALLENGING THE STORM

AUSTRALIA

Hobart
TASMANIA

Goss & Dinelli

Goss Continues

Southern Ocean

Rescue Site

Rescue Call

South + Pole

ANTARCTICA

Goss's Route

Dinelli's position, as faxed through from race headquarters, was 160 nautical miles upwind. Goss would have to sail back into the face of the storm, through the worst seas he'd ever seen.

Then, as darkness settled in, he bargained with his boat. "We've got a pact," he said. "You don't give up, and I won't give up. OK?"

DON'T PRAY, BAIL: Goss battles to stay afloat.

Hour after hour Pete Goss tacked against the storm. Progress was maddeningly slow.

Finally, cold and exhausted, he set the autopilot, crawled below and fell asleep. But he was jerked awake by a thunderous crash and fireworks.

An aerosol bottle of oil had lodged between terminals of *Aqua Quorum*'s generator, causing a short circuit and a shower of sparks. Frantically he yanked the bottle free. Sleep forgotten, he went back on deck, where the wind had eased enough for him to set the mainsail.

At 2am Flight Lieutenant Ian Whyte, captain of the Royal Australian Air Force Orion plane designated Rescue 251, was awakened by a call. There had been a mayday in the Southern Ocean. Within three hours of confirmation, his four-engined turboprop was airborne. His job: to locate the stranded boat, and if Dinelli was still alive, drop an air-sea rescue kit, then find Goss and guide him toward *Algimouss*.

Late in the afternoon of December 26, more than 1000 nautical miles from the Australian coast, the aircraft picked up signals from an Argos beacon. Whyte descended through the clouds. Throttling back at 600 feet, he and his copilot, Nicholas Platts, scanned the horizon.

Dinelli heard the hum of an aircraft. He straightened up from his surfer's crouch and saw a gray plane. Through salt-crusted eyes he watched as four containers dropped from the plane's belly. Inflating as they fell, two rubber life rafts hit the water and drifted toward his stricken boat. The life rafts were attached by nylon cord to the other containers, which held emergency supplies.

Grabbing the first raft, Dinelli fell into it and cast off. Moments later *Algimouss* disappeared under the waves. She had kept her side of the pact to the end.

Dinelli, unable to rise, curled up at the bottom of the life raft. Every time a wave jostled the raft, he cried out in pain, his body racked with cramps. Stunned by the cold and exhaustion, he shivered through the night, waiting for the Antarctic dawn.

Pete Goss was on deck sewing up a ripped sail when a big gray aircraft swept overhead. A flight crewman from Rescue 251 radioed that they'd dropped Dinelli a life raft.

"I've had a bit of damage," Goss informed them, "but I've managed to fix it. Merry Christmas."

The plane swung back to *Algimouss* and dropped three hand-held radios in special boxes. Attached to each was a message banner: "Pete Goss ten hours in the south. Rescue tomorrow." With fuel running low, the aircraft then headed to Australia.

That night Goss stayed on deck, where the wind plunged the wind-chill factor to minus 22 degrees Fahrenheit. But before dawn a new position update showed that he was only six miles from Dinelli. He fired off flares and blasts of a foghorn. Nothing. He couldn't shake off the thought that had been torturing him: even if he did find the raft, would it hold a dead sailor?

"Come on, Raphaël. You've got to help yourself!"

FOAMING MAD: "Aqua Quorum" battles through a raging sea, its monstrous waves whipped up by gale-force winds.

Inside his life raft Dinelli was shivering so hard he couldn't control his chattering teeth. *Don't sleep,* he told himself. *Pete's coming.*

Dinelli thought of his childhood near Bordeaux, France, his happy-go-lucky youth as a surfboard champion, the warm years with his girlfriend, Virginie, and their 18-month-old daughter, Philippine. He should be married. He would ask Virginie—if he lived.

At dawn Goss still saw no sign of Dinelli and called the Australian air force. A reply came instantly: "We should be with you in four minutes." A second rescue plane had taken off during the night and was only a few miles away. "We've located the survivor," Flight Lieutenant Warren Hutchinson radioed. "We'll lead you to him."

Goss was only half an hour from his target. "Watch me," Hutchinson radioed Goss. "I'll flash our landing lights when we're on top of Dinelli."

At last Goss saw a speck of orange and brought *Aqua Quorum* alongside the raft.

GOSS AND DINELLI

"YOU'RE NOT GOING TO CROAK ON ME NOW." Pete Goss and Raphaël Dinelli won the only race that counts.

Dinelli stood, and Goss heaved him over the railing onto *Aqua Quorum*'s deck.

"You're not going to croak on me now," Goss said. Carrying the Frenchman to his cabin, he stripped off the man's clothes, pulled on dry thermal clothing and hustled him into a sleeping bag. Then he poured him hot tea. Dinelli sipped gratefully, then drifted off to sleep.

Back on the radio, Goss told the crew of the circling plane that he would head for Hobart on the Australian island of Tasmania. "Thanks very much for your help," he signed off. "You guys have been great."

Standing at the bow of *Aqua Quorum*, Goss waved and prepared to raise sail. No matter what happened next in the Vendée, he knew he'd already won the most important race.

After depositing Dinelli in Hobart, Goss went on to finish the Vendée Globe in fifth place in March 1997. That June, President Jacques Chirac presented Goss with France's most prestigious award, the Légion d'honneur. And on August 30, Raphaël and Virginie were married, with Pete Goss as their best man.

Two months later Goss's boat was scudding across the ocean in a race from France to Colombia. This time it carried a two-man crew: Pete Goss and Raphaël Dinelli.

Slap shot!

by Kathy Cook

As Trent McCleary skated off the ice, he knew he was hurt. What he didn't know was that he was already dying.

Trent McCleary stepped out of his hotel in downtown Montreal eagerly anticipating that afternoon's game against the Philadelphia Flyers. Breathing in the cold winter air, the 27-year-old forward for the Montreal Canadiens set off to walk the five blocks to the Molson Centre. The walk would give him time to himself, time to focus.

During his four seasons with the Canadiens, McCleary had been back and forth between the minors and the NHL. But he'd always played with heart and just a month earlier had been called back up to play with the Canadiens. He was playing well and, at 180 pounds on a six-foot frame, he was in top shape.

At the Molson Centre, McCleary checked the day's lineup—he'd be playing right wing—and dressed alongside his teammates. Nearby, the team's chief physician, Dr David Mulder, 62, a former head of surgery at The Montreal General Hospital, chatted with fellow team physician Dr Vincent Lacroix.

After an up-and-down season, the Canadiens had won four of their last six games and were fighting for a play-off spot. For today's game, January 29, 2000, some 21,000 fans were on hand, including McCleary's fiancée, Tammy Klassen, 28; another 700,000-plus across North America watched on television.

By the second period, the game was tied 2-2. As the puck came off the boards in the Canadiens' end, McCleary saw Flyers' defenceman Chris Therien arching back to take a slap shot at the net. Hoping to block the shot, McCleary dived to the ice in front of Therien.

BADGE OF COURAGE: **The Canadiens' logo**

As he fell, McCleary watched the puck. *It's going to hit my shins, he thought.* But the angle wasn't what he expected. At 140 kilometres an hour, the puck slammed into his Adam's apple, shattering his larynx.

Mulder jumped to his feet behind the Canadiens' bench.

Facedown on the ice, McCleary grabbed at his throat, shocked at the pain, tasting blood. He badly needed to breathe deeply after his exertions but could draw in only a trickle of air.

Growing faint, McCleary jumped up and headed for the bench. *Maybe it's my mouth guard*, he thought, spitting it out. *My neck strap?* He flung his helmet off. But McCleary's smashed throat had swollen shut.

Following the game on both radio and television back home in Swift Current, Saskatchewan, McCleary's mother, Leah, had seen her son get hit. "This kid's in trouble," radio commentator Pierre Maguire told listeners. Leah began to pray.

Reaching Mulder at the bench, McCleary pointed inside his mouth. Veins bulged from his blue face and neck. He tried to speak but no sound came out. *It's his larynx,* Mulder knew instantly. *We might have only minutes.*

McCleary, now semiconscious, collapsed into Mulder's arms. Born in Saskatchewan, the doctor still owned a farm near McCleary's hometown, and the two had become friends when McCleary first joined the team. "I've got you, Trent," Mulder reassured him. "Don't worry."

Mulder and a trainer dragged McCleary to the dressing-room clinic, where, joined by Lacroix, they laid him on his back on a table. Struggling to force air through smashed bones and swelling tissue, McCleary thrashed in panic.

Tammy Klassen hadn't seen the accident, but when she saw Trent being helped off the ice, she hurried to the wives' room to wait anxiously for word of his condition.

ICEMAN COMETH: **Trent warms up.**

Mulder knew he needed to open a passage to McCleary's lungs. "We'll do an endotracheal intubation!" he shouted. "Trent, work with us. Don't fight us!"

McCleary relaxed, but the staff members restraining his arms and legs held on.

Lacroix ripped the wrapper off a plastic tube and opened McCleary's mouth. The injured man coughed, splattering blood everywhere. Blood dripped steadily over the table and onto the floor, and drained from the player's nose.

When trainer Graham Rynbend momentarily relaxed his hold on McCleary's arm, the desperate man, suffocating and filled with adrenaline, threw him across the room and clawed at his throat. Rynbend clambered to his feet and pulled McCleary's arm down again. McCleary's eyes bulged, his face purple.

Just then Dr David Fleiszer, Mulder's good friend and a senior trauma surgeon at the Montreal General, appeared. He'd been watching the game with his wife from their regular seats. "Can I help?"

"Absolutely," Mulder said as he suctioned a steady flow of blood from McCleary's mouth. "We're in deep trouble."

"We know Trent's parents listen to the games," Pierre Maguire said over the radio. "Mr and Mrs McCleary, we'll keep you posted." Leah called her husband, Ken, who was away at an old-timers hockey tournament.

"Trent's in trouble," she told him.

"No, it hit his collarbone," said Ken, who had been watching. "He skated off the ice."

"But the announcers think he's in trouble."

"I think he's OK," Ken reassured her, "but call when you hear anything." The moment she hung up, the phone rang.

"What's going on with Trent, Mom?" her daughter Shannon asked.

"I don't know."

Air, unable to escape from McCleary's lungs, was now leaking into his neck tissue, forming thousands of bubbles. His neck puffed grotesquely to twice its size, and his chest swelled. He looked like a bullfrog.

Holding the intubation tube, Fleiszer peered into McCleary's mouth. *I could do more harm pushing the tube down*, he thought, afraid he might stuff tissue farther into the airway.

Instead, Fleiszer grabbed the largest needle on the tray and stuck it into McCleary's throat just above the breastbone. Air hissed from the needle's open end. "We've got access," Fleiszer said.

They attached an air bag to the needle and, through the pinhole opening, pushed oxygen in. But McCleary's throat continued to swell. Fleiszer pushed the needle in farther, but eventually lost the airway.

"Either we do a tracheotomy or leave for the hospital now," said Mulder. With McCleary's thrashing, the swelling and the shattered bones, it would be almost impossible to perform the procedure in the clinic. But the trip to the hospital would take at least seven minutes, and it would be too bumpy to operate en route. Either way, McCleary could die. Somebody had to decide now.

Mulder's mind rushed back 12 years. He had been watching his son's hockey game when suddenly a slap shot shattered the goaltender's larynx. Mulder rushed down to the ice to help. The boy turned black and began convulsing on the ice. Mulder tried a jaw thrust and the airway opened a little. After rushing to the hospital with the boy, Mulder performed a tracheotomy, saving his life.

"Let's do a jaw thrust," Mulder decided. Standing behind McCleary, he pulled the player's jaw forcefully towards him and upward. The jaw being attached with cartilage to the larynx, the movement pulled the shattered bones closer together, reducing the effect of the fracture.

McCleary gasped for air through the tiny opening. Mulder covered his face with an air mask, and Fleiszer squeezed the attached air bag each time he saw McCleary try to breathe. Oxygen trickled into the injured man's lungs. His haze lifted, and he looked around.

Still it felt as if he was breathing through a straw. Panicking, he fought to free himself, gasping deliriously.

"That's our try. Let's go!" Mulder said. Ambulance attendants strapped McCleary to a stretcher for the trip to the hospital as he lapsed back into semiconsciousness.

"Give him 100 percent oxygen," Mulder told an ambulance attendant as the vehicle screamed through Montreal's busy streets. Rarely was more than 50 percent given by mask, but Mulder hoped to reduce any brain damage.

Holding McCleary's head in the jaw thrust, Mulder's arms trembled with fatigue. McCleary's neck muscles were now resisting the position. *I don't know if I can do the tracheotomy with tired hands*, he thought. "Can you relieve me?" Mulder asked.

Fleiszer, who had been holding the mask against McCleary's face and squeezing the air bag, traded places with Mulder. Both knew that pushing air into McCleary's lungs could cause them to explode, but that was reparable; brain damage wasn't. "Trent? We're almost there," Fleiszer whispered in his ear.

Then McCleary lost consciousness, and the doctors exchanged a long glance. Death or brain damage were becoming more likely every second.

"We're not stopping at emergency!" Mulder told the two attendants as they pulled the stretcher out at the Montreal General. They had perhaps seconds before McCleary went into cardiac arrest.

The four ran through the ER to the elevators, ignoring the nurses' calls. By the time they reached an eighth-floor operating room, 17 minutes had passed since the accident.

Luckily, doctors and nurses had been alerted to McCleary's impending arrival. Dr Michel Germain, the anesthetist on duty, was administering anesthetic to a patient with a broken leg. "Dr Germain! The Canadiens player is here!" a nurse shouted. "They want you to intubate."

Germain headed for the elevators, and when the doors opened, McCleary lay before him, swollen, almost black and drenched in blood. *Is he dead?* Germain checked for a pulse—160 beats a minute. His blood pressure had surged to 260. *If he wasn't an athlete, he'd already be in cardiac arrest*, Germain thought.

At the Molson Centre, Tammy was still waiting for news when she heard a TV announcer say Trent had been rushed to the hospital. She ran into the hallway, where trainers and medical staff stood ashen faced. Several had tears in their eyes. "What's going on?" she demanded, crying.

"I'll drive you to the hospital, Tammy," said Arron Asham, a teammate who wasn't playing that day.

Germain opened McCleary's mouth and inserted his laryngoscope to look for the airway. "All I can see is blood," he said. He suctioned it, but more flowed into its place instantly.

Mulder and Fleiszer watched tensely. "If you can't get through, I'll have to do a tracheotomy now," Mulder said.

"I'll try," said Germain. "There's nothing to lose."

Gently he pushed the tubelike instrument against the mass of tissue. McCleary coughed, and Germain caught a glimpse of the opening. Then he had the tube past the larynx. "I'm in!"

He quickly connected the tube to a machine that measures levels of poisonous carbon dioxide—the needle shot off the scale. *He's nearly dead*, thought Germain.

But the team ventilated McCleary, releasing the carbon dioxide and returning oxygen to his brain and organs, and within a few minutes his vital signs had stabilized. Germain anesthetized him.

Now that McCleary was stable, a proper tracheotomy could be performed. Mulder cut across McCleary's neck, below his Adam's apple and, with Fleiszer assisting, inserted a tube directly into his trachea. The other end of the tube was attached to a respirator.

Suddenly Germain noticed the carbon-dioxide levels increasing again; McCleary was suffocating.

Mulder tapped McCleary's chest and the right side echoed: The lung had exploded. And air in the chest cavity had caused the left lung to close. Mulder quickly made a small cut between McCleary's ribs and stuck in a tube. Air hissed out.

"He's ventilating again," Germain said.

Half an hour later, Mulder stepped out of the operating room and found Tammy waiting. "It was close," he told her, "but he's alive."

Then Mulder called Trent's mother.

"Has he got brain damage?" she asked.

"It's too early to tell," he replied. "We'll know more when he wakes up."

A few hours later McCleary awoke to the buzz of voices. Someone shone a light in his eyes. "His right eye won't dilate," he heard. *It hasn't since I took a stick in the eye five years ago*, McCleary thought. He knew the doctors suspected brain damage. They left the room.

Desperate to reassure them, McCleary struggled to get the small clamlike heart monitor off his fingertip but was hampered by the medication he'd been given to stop him from grabbing his throat when he awoke. Sweating from the exertion, his heart pounding, he finally managed to flick the monitor off.

The alarm sounded and a nurse ran in. Seeing he was awake, she called Tammy in.

Trent smiled weakly. "I love you," was all Tammy could manage as she struggled not to break down.

The next morning Canadiens' general manager Réjean Houle visited—after arranging for McCleary's relieved parents to fly to Montreal. "Trent, the team's really worried," said Houle. "You've got a lot of friends here."

Unable to speak, McCleary motioned for some paper. "Doing great, everyone," he wrote to his team. "Battle hard. I'll be listening. Go Habs Go—Trent."

Trent McCleary took seven months to recover and reported back to the Canadiens' training camp in the fall of 2000.

In McCleary's first game of the new season, Mulder stood by watching him closely. But the player had lost 20 percent of his airway and couldn't recover from exertion quickly enough. At the end of the game, Mulder regretfully took away his friend's medical certification, and the next day McCleary announced his retirement.

Today McCleary lives in Swift Current with his wife, Tammy, and is a scout for the Canadiens. He's also a spokesperson for the Intensive Care Foundation of Canada and, along with San Jose Sharks player Patrick Marleau, has opened a sports and recreation foundation to encourage Saskatchewan youths to participate in sports.

Teammates for life: **Trent and Tammy.**

164

The sand's
eating me alive!

by John Dyson

After a dozen steps on the moonlit beach,
Terry Howlett began to feel himself sinking.

The air was tangy with mud and brine as the train rattled into the Lancashire town of Carnforth. Terry Howlett took a deep, invigorating breath as he stepped on to the platform, glad to be back.

It was a breezy Saturday evening in August 1996, and Howlett had travelled here from his home in Darlington, County Durham, with a lot on his mind.

After buying a meal, he headed off to his favourite spot—the eerie wilderness of shifting sandbanks, muddy channels and racing tides of Morecambe Bay.

He'd first discovered this lonely place while on leave from the Navy in 1988 and had returned often. Its haunting magic never failed to lift his spirits.

A long causeway jutted for more than a mile into the bay's flat and desolate shore. Howlett walked towards the sea, feeling the tranquillity of the marshes gathering him in, as he wrestled with his thoughts.

A painful football injury had brought his naval career as a weapons technician to an end. After three knee operations, he could no longer go to sea and had to resign. No quitter, Howlett had willingly taken on a string of casual jobs, but none had led to anything.

Now his knee was healed and, as he approached his thirtieth birthday, he was anxious to get on with his life. Above all, he told himself, he needed to get more qualifications—*If I keep going, I could get through to college.*

EERIE LANDSCAPE: the causeway jutted more than a mile into Morecombe Bay's flat and desolate shore.

Coming to the end of the causeway, Terry wandered on to the beach. In the moonlight, he could make out the channel of a river some 200 yards broad. The tide was well out, leaving an expanse of rippled sand dotted with pools. Thinking that he'd be able to walk for hours on the salt-grasses beyond, he continued on.

But after a dozen steps he felt himself sinking into the soft sand. Windmilling his arms to keep his balance, he tried to leap free, but he only sank deeper. In seconds he was up to his knees in a man-hungry pudding of cold, oozing jelly. *Quicksand.*

Howlett was stunned. There had been nothing on the surface to suggest it was soft or dangerous. As local people well knew, the swirling of river or tidal currents sometimes digs out isolated hollows which fill with a porridge-like sediment. Only an expert eye can detect these melgraves, as they are called, and they have a voracious appetite. Shrimp-fishermen's horses, motorbikes, even dump trucks have been swallowed.

Howlett had read that farmers who got stuck in quicksand while rounding up sheep would spreadeagle themselves to distribute their weight. But it was too late for that. The sand was already climbing up his thighs. *My God, it's eating me alive!*

Fear gripped Howlett, and he yelled for help. Nobody heard. He had an awful vision of himself choking to death as his nose and throat filled with sand. *I'll disappear and nobody will ever know what happened to me.*

The clammy sand nuzzled up to his crotch, seeped inside his trousers and crawled over his belly. One more inch . . . another inch . . .

Hardly daring to breathe, he sank to his waist—then stopped. He tried wriggling his toes, but his feet seemed cast in concrete. Although Howlett's body was immobile, his brain was spinning. And, suddenly, he was electrified by a frightening thought. *When will the tide come in again?*

Thinking back, he remembered that the tide had been going out when he reached the beach, which meant it wouldn't be back for another nine or ten hours. *I've got a chance after all, he thought.*

Cupping his fingers, he began to scoop away the sand around his waist that was holding him prisoner. But as fast as he dug, the muck oozed back into place. After an hour his fingers were numb and sore, his legs raging with cramps.

Then he heard a roar like a waterfall. Moments later a vicious rain-squall struck. Drenched in seconds, Terry buried his face in his hands and bowed his head. Gripped in jaws of sand, he had nowhere to run.

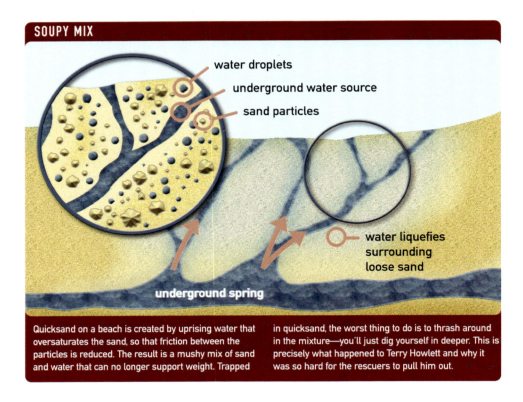

SOUPY MIX

water droplets

underground water source

sand particles

water liquefies surrounding loose sand

underground spring

Quicksand on a beach is created by uprising water that oversaturates the sand, so that friction between the particles is reduced. The result is a mushy mix of sand and water that can no longer support weight. Trapped in quicksand, the worst thing to do is to thrash around in the mixture—you'll just dig yourself in deeper. This is precisely what happened to Terry Howlett and why it was so hard for the rescuers to pull him out.

The storm rattled through the night. At the crack of dawn, Tony Gardner, 54, got up to check his sheep and stepped out to a glorious morning.

A grey-bearded stonemason from Yorkshire, Gardner spent weekends on the small hill farm that had been in his family for generations.

The sky was clear and sunny, the air cool and still. His boots were swishing through the grass when suddenly he heard something and paused to listen. Was somebody shouting?

Far below, Gardner saw a herd of cows being taken in for milking. *The farmer's calling his stock*, he thought.

An hour later, returning home, Gardner heard the same sound. Puzzled, he called his wife Frances to come and listen. "It's got a rhythm to it, sounds like 'help-me, help-me'," she said. Driving along the road, the Gardners saw no climber trapped on the rocks, no road accident. "It must be coming from the shore," Gardner told his wife. He dialled 999.

Minutes later, police constable Ian Nickson met the Gardners at the beach and the three of them set off towards the cries at a run. After a mile Gardner paused. "Where are you?" he yelled.

"Over here!" a hoarse voice replied.

Gardner blinked and stared. Incredibly, somebody was out there, buried to the waist in sand.

"Right, I've got you!" Gardner called, running along the beach.

"You're OK, lad, we've found you now," he said, when he reached Terry. "How on earth did you get here?"

For nine hours Howlett had scratched vainly at the sand, pausing only to hug himself to preserve body heat. Since dawn he'd been shouting for help, his energy flagging as he grew more and more desperate. Incredibly, his cries had been heard one and a half miles away.

Nickson arrived on the scene moments later. "Don't worry, son, we'll have you out in a jiffy," he said cheerfully. Howlett slumped with a feeling of relief as Nickson radioed police headquarters.

Gripping Howlett beneath the armpits, the policeman and farmer pulled firmly upwards. But Howlett's body wouldn't budge.

"We're stretching him in two," Nickson said finally. He radioed headquarters again. "We can't get the trapped man out. Request coastguard, the fire brigade and an ambulance."

Their biggest enemy now, Gardner realized, was not the quicksand but the sea. Tides in the bay were fierce, some days the sea-level rose by more than 20 feet in a very short time. He glanced at the policeman. "You'd best check the tide."

On his radio, Nickson was advised to expect high tide at 7.38. It was already 7.30. "We're all right, the tide's nearly full," he said.

STUCK FAST: despite the rescuers' frantic attempts, the quicksand refused to release Terry.

But Gardner was suspicious. He gazed out towards the bay. *If the tide's full*, he wondered, *where's the water?*

Leading Frances by the elbow until they were out of Howlett's earshot, he whispered, "My bet is there's still a tide to come up the channel."

Hauntingly deserted through the night, the area was now bustling with rescuers. Firemen ferried air-bottles, ropes, ladders and rescue gear from their trucks. Local fire chief Bob Gleeson, called in to supervise the rescue, stood back on high ground with the Gardners.

Paramedics in green overalls arrived. Tall, with a blonde ponytail, Sue Williamson, 38, had two red blankets tucked under one arm and carried a bag filled with emergency equipment. John Dockray, the fire station commander, introduced her. "This is Terry Howlett and we'll have him out in a few minutes," he said.

"It's Sunday morning," Sue teased smilingly. "You should be in church, not stuck down a hole!"

Terry's wan smile triggered in Williamson a childhood memory of finding a seabird covered with oil on the beach. The stricken gull had looked at her with the same bright and trusting eyes as she'd carried it tenderly to a refuge. Her heart went out to him.

As the firemen tried to lift Howlett up, he grimaced, then yelled with pain. "My legs!" he gasped.

Dockray looked on with concern. Mud and sand rescues cropped up several times a year on Morecambe Bay, but the victims were seldom more than shin deep. The usual technique was to sit them down on a board to take the weight off their legs, then work on lifting their feet. This one was different. *The lad's in deep*, he worried.

Something else troubled Dockray. He had the same thought as Gardner. *If it was high tide, where was the water?* He radioed fireman Barry Maguire to double-check tide times. "High water's 8.38, John," Maguire answered, knowing it was summer and an extra hour had to be added.

Dockray checked his watch. It was 7.50 and the water would come licking up the river channel any minute. He told his men and the mood of relaxed cheerfulness abruptly changed.

On their minds was the memory of a similar incident. In 1980 a teenage boy was trapped on his trail-bike in soft mud. Frantic efforts to dig him out failed. As the water rose, the mask of a breathing set was fitted over his face, but he tore it off and drowned before the firemen's eyes.

With grim determination, the rescue team redoubled their efforts. Using a sand lance, a four-foot steel tube attached by rubber hose to an air cylinder, firemen blasted air through the tube in an attempt to loosen the quicksand's grip. But the jets of air only drove the suspended water out of the sand, making it even harder.

HELPING HANDS: Terry Howlett (front row centre) will never forget those who saved his life.

Up the beach, Chief Gleeson weighed the options. A mechanical digger would sink. Getting firehoses to jet the sand out of the hole would take too much time.

It might already be too late. A tongue of frothy water was now sweeping into the river channel at the speed of a wave running up a beach. When Howlett saw Sue Williamson glance over her shoulder and in a frenzy renew her attack on the muck, he understood. He felt sorry for the rescuers. These were good people trying so hard to get him out. *If they have to watch me drown, it'll be really tough on them*, he thought.

In moments the in-rushing water bubbled round his waist and poured over his rescuers' legs. Its speed was frightening.

Watching the desperate scene, Gleeson calculated that the water was rising at about two inches a minute.

Fireman Steve Darby approached. "We're not getting him out—we've got to get a breathing set on him."

Gleeson hadn't broached this earlier in case Howlett was spooked. Like the boy who'd died in the mud, he might panic at the idea of going underwater. Steve Darby was already starting to take off his uniform. His plan was to don a breathing set and sit beside Howlett under the water.

Lugging a coiled hose over his shoulder, auxiliary coastguard Tom Hayhurst, 56, and his team of seven carried pipes and hoses along the beach to what looked like

171

BOB GLEESON

"You've got five minutes." said Fire Chief Gleeson. "My men are in danger."

SUE WILLIAMSON

"You should be in church." joked paramedic Sue Williamson, "not stuck in a hole."

a football scrum of wet and half-dressed people out in the water.

They began setting up a high-pressure water jet that would blast away the mud trapping Howlett. Again and again, the team had to stop to extricate each other as they sank down into the wet sand.

Water was now swirling around Howlett's chest. He steeled himself to remain calm. *I'm so scared—but I won't think about it.* Even as he made himself smile, he could feel the cold wetness licking around his ribs.

While Hayhurst's men tried to help the firemen, on shore Gleeson told Dockray. "John, it's getting dangerous for the men. You've got five minutes, then I'm ordering them out."

Howlett bent his head back and upwards as the water swirled beneath his chin. Working knee-deep in water next to him, one of the paramedics pushed the nozzle down the side of the trapped man's leg and the power jet began pushing the sand aside.

Froth and muddy water bubbled around Terry's face, making him cough. His bad knee was agony. To blot out the pain and fear he thought of his mother and his gran. He loved them both dearly and dreaded to think of their anguish as they were told of his death.

But suddenly the sand round his feet shifted. "I can move my toes!" Howlett cried, spitting water. As the firemen strained to heave him upwards, his right leg pulled clear. A cheer went up.

"Don't you dare put that foot down!" Dockray yelled, then, "Keep pulling lads," as the rescuers grabbed Howlett by the arms and shoulders for one mighty last-ditch effort.

Howlett screamed with pain. Then a great shout went up. "He's out!" A cradle of helping hands carried the exhausted man up the beach and he was laid in a nest of coats and blankets. Down on the shore, the tide, three to four feet deep now, swept over the spot where he'd been trapped.

Flown by helicopter to hospital suffering severe hypothermia, Terry was released the next day. His ordeal, he says, was a reminder of how precious life is. "You think you're totally alone, without hope, then someone reaches out to help you. It's made me believe in myself again, and in my future."

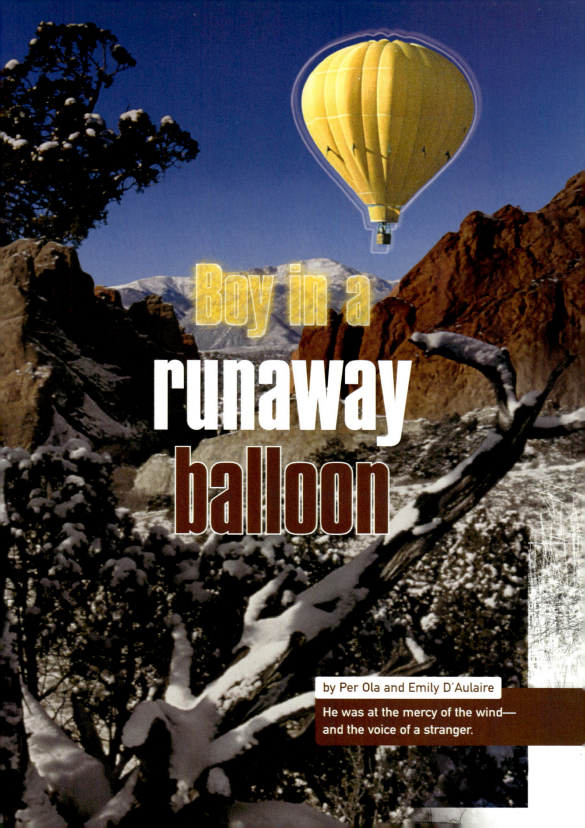

Boy in a runaway balloon

by Per Ola and Emily D'Aulaire

He was at the mercy of the wind—
and the voice of a stranger.

Eleven-year-old Alex Nicholos was excited. Not only was it a sparkling winter morning that Sunday, January 7, 1990, in Colorado Springs—it was also the day that Alex, his nine-year-old sister and their parents were going to help their friend Tex Houston launch his hot-air balloon.

A half-mile away, Dave Hollenbaugh, 60, rubbed the sleep from his eyes. He had been fighting the flu for weeks and felt miserable. He wanted to stay in bed, but he, too, had promised to help Houston with his balloon, aptly named The Yellow Rose of Tex's.

Hollenbaugh and the Nicholos family arrived at the launch field shortly after sunrise. Houston, a portly, genial man, was already there, along with five other balloonists and their crews.

Alex and his father, George Nicholos, hauled on the crown line attached to the top of the balloon's 75-foot-high envelope. The boy's mother, Linda, and sister, Stephanie, held open the mouth of the balloon for the inflation process. Houston climbed into the wicker basket and lit the powerful propane burner to heat the air inside the balloon. Two other ground-crew members, Shawn Tayloe and Debbie Prosise, held the basket down.

Before long The Yellow Rose towered as high as an eight-story building. Alex all but danced with excitement. Anything mechanical fascinated him, especially things that flew.

His curiosity about how things work was important, because Alex had a minor brain dysfunction called Attention Deficit Disorder (ADD). As a result, though bright, the fifth-grader was a slow book-learner. He did best when things were demonstrated. Typical of ADD children, Alex was impulsive, easily distracted, and his moods and emotions could swing widely.

Hollenbaugh was the opposite: calm, methodical, unemotional. An Air Force pilot for 24 years, he had served in Vietnam. In 1973, he suffered decompression sickness in a plane that lost its pressurization system. Even though he fully recovered, he was eliminated from flight status. Hollenbaugh retired from the military

GROUND CREW: Tex Houston readies his balloon.

FULL BLOOM: **The Yellow Rose inflated.**

and later earned his balloon pilot's license and qualified as an instructor.

Now with The Yellow Rose poised for flight, Hollenbaugh heard Houston call out to Alex, "Hey, want a ride?" The delighted boy clambered into the wicker basket and donned a crash helmet. Moments later, the bright yellow balloon lifted off into the cobalt sky, following the breeze and five other balloons.

George, Linda and Stephanie climbed into the rear seat of Houston's van. Shawn took the wheel. Debbie sat in the center seat, map in hand, with Hollenbaugh to her right, where he could keep the balloon in sight through the windshield and the side window. He held a CB microphone, ready, if the need arose, to talk with Houston.

Watching his family grow smaller beneath him, Alex gasped in awe. Soon he began to bombard Houston with questions: "How do you heat the balloon? How does the radio work? What are you doing now?"

Houston answered every question carefully. Alex watched as Houston pulled the lanyard attached to the burner valve, releasing a roar of propane flame into the mouth of the balloon to make it rise after each slight "downhill" coast.

Between "burns," Houston pointed out the flight instruments: the fuel gauges; the variometer that showed whether the balloon was rising or falling, and how fast; a temperature gauge that indicated when it was time to turn the burner on or off. What fascinated Alex most was the CB radio.

A half-hour into the flight, Houston noticed the breeze increasing. The other balloons, two miles ahead, had begun their descent. He spotted a flat area, the last suitable site before a wooded expanse called the Black Forest, and radioed Hollenbaugh that he planned to land.

"Squat down," Houston warned Alex. "We may be in for a bumpy landing." Alex hunkered low, holding on to the inside wall of the basket and closing his eyes. Then, unexpectedly, he heard the throaty roar of the burner and felt the balloon rise abruptly.

Houston had aborted the landing. Below the basket, directly in its line of travel, was a barbed-wire fence. Ahead of that, blocking their route, was an electric power line.

UP AND AWAY: "I really can fly this thing," Alex told himself proudly.

In the chase vehicle, Hollenbaugh was becoming concerned. The winds had picked up to a brisk 15 miles per hour. *Why hadn't Houston set the balloon down?* he wondered. He switched on the CB. "Yellow Rose, what are your intentions?"

"I see a flat space on the far side of the forest," Houston replied. "I'll land there."

Twenty feet from the snow-covered ground, the balloon's basket disappeared from Hollenbaugh's view as it went behind a knoll. The upper half of the balloon tilted forward, an indication that the craft had hit and was dragging. Then the balloon straightened itself and shot skyward. *Tex really botched that one,* Hollenbaugh thought.

The moment The Yellow Rose touched down, the basket pitched forward so sharply that its upper edge plowed into the snow. The result was a sudden jolting motion that threw Houston forward, catapulting him out of the basket. He grabbed for Alex but missed.

Crouched in a corner of the basket with his eyes still closed, Alex didn't realize what was happening at first. "Boy, that was a close one," he said, looking around. But Tex Houston was gone!

"There's Tex!" Shawn shouted. "He's down!" Hollenbaugh looked toward the site of the aborted landing. Houston was limping over the rise, waving his arms. *Where was Alex?* Just then the radio crackled to life with Alex's high-pitched frightened voice. "Help me," Alex pleaded. "I'm scared!" Hollenbaugh looked up at the balloon racing silently through the sky. *The boy is up there alone!*

Houston, in emotional shock, reached the van. "I'm sorry," he kept muttering. "I'm so sorry."

Alex's mother and sister began sobbing, and his father tried to comfort them, fighting back his own terror. Hollenbaugh knew he had to keep himself and everyone else calm. He reached for the radio. "It's all right, Alex," he assured the frightened youngster. "You're the pilot now, and I'm going to teach you how to land the balloon."

What's the minimum the boy needs to know to fly the balloon? Hollenbaugh knew that if he overloaded Alex with information, the boy would not be able to follow instructions.

Hollenbaugh told Alex how to work the blast valve that shoots a 12-foot flame into the balloon's envelope. He decided not to mention the vent line, which also controls altitude by temporarily dumping hot air. Alex might confuse it with the rip line, which if pulled, could send the balloon plummeting. Alex would need the rip line when he landed, though, so Hollenbaugh told him where it was and not to touch it yet.

From the speeding van, Hollenbaugh couldn't tell whether The Yellow Rose was going up or down, so he explained to Alex how to read the variometer. "What's the needle doing now?" Hollenbaugh asked repeatedly.

Alex felt enormous relief when he heard the man's quiet voice over the CB. He sounded so reassuring, so personal, that it was more like talking to a friend than to a stranger. *He doesn't sound worried,* Alex thought. *Maybe I'll be OK.*

But whenever the balloon sank, the boy would panic. "I'm falling!" he'd yell into the mike. "What if I crash?" Then he'd pull the lanyard that turned on the burner to propel the balloon skyward.

Hollenbaugh worried that Alex would add too much heat and send The Yellow Rose too high, where strong winds could quickly carry the boy beyond CB-radio range. If that happened, Alex would have no hope. "We won't let you fall, I promise," Hollenbaugh radioed Alex. "Please don't use the burner until I tell you."

Once he realized that he could follow Hollenbaugh's instructions, Alex felt more secure. He liked reading the instruments and reporting back. *I really can fly this thing,* Alex told himself proudly.

GROUNDED: **Alex Nicholos (left) stands proudly with Dave Hollenbaugh.**

The chase van soon met up with a car carrying Rollie Elkins, one of the other balloonists who had landed earlier. Elkins had been Houston's instructor and knew The Yellow Rose intimately. He jumped in the van to assist Hollenbaugh.

The terrain was more open now, range land with fewer trees and rocks. "Alex," Hollenbaugh spoke firmly into the radio. "I need you to bring the balloon down closer to the ground so I can help you land."

Hollenbaugh told Alex how to handle the burns. "Now, burn—one, two . . . stop. You're doing fine, Alex. Burn—one, two . . ." Slowly, smoothly, The Yellow Rose descended from 2000 to 200 feet, then sailed majestically 90 feet above a farmhouse, just clearing a power line.

The balloon crossed the road in front of them at 50 feet. "Alex, reach up and grab the rip line I told you about, sit on the bottom of the basket and pull, pull, pull . . ." Hollenbaugh saw the balloon start to deflate and sink more rapidly. "Pull, pull, pull!"

The basket hit the ground, bounced once, dragged along the ground a short distance, then settled on its side, the envelope collapsing. When all was still, the uninjured boy was found pulling on the rope, making certain that The Yellow Rose was grounded for good. Amazingly, after 90 minutes alone in the air, covering some 35 miles, the fifth-grader had brought the balloon down in a textbook high-wind landing.

Through the ordeal, Hollenbaugh's voice had been so easygoing that Alex never fully realized the danger he faced. When his parents swept him in their arms, crying, he was surprised. "Gee, I'm sorry I got everybody so frightened," he said.

Hollenbaugh sat in the van, unable to move. Then he broke down. "Thank you, God, oh, thank you," he murmured, tears streaming down his face.

When Linda Nicholos brought Alex over to thank him, the boy stared at the man as if perplexed. "You sounded a lot younger," Alex said.

Hollenbaugh smiled wanly. "Believe me, Alex, before we started all this, I was."

The next day in school Alex's solo ballooning feat was announced on the intercom, and all his teachers praised his courage. He proudly displayed the balloon pilot's wings that Tex Houston had taken off his own chest and given to him.

"I got through that balloon ride," Alex says. "I can get through anything."

The National Aeronautic Association awarded Hollenbaugh its Certificate of Honor for safety. He is the first balloonist to receive it for this achievement. "It was the longest, toughest flight of my life," Hollenbaugh says, "and I never left the ground."

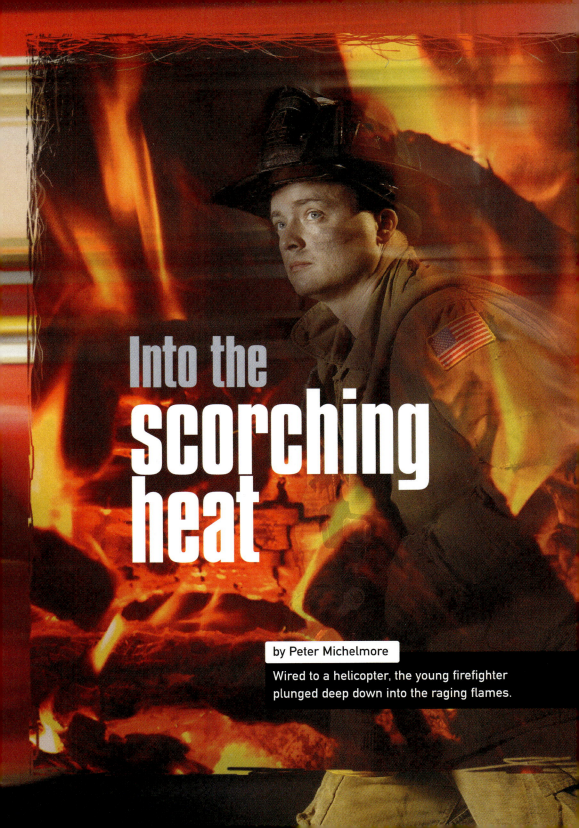

Into the
scorching
heat

by Peter Michelmore

Wired to a helicopter, the young firefighter plunged deep down into the raging flames.

From the cab of a crane towering 220 feet in the air, Ivers Sims surveyed the old Fulton cotton mill below him. The red-brick, five-story building in Atlanta was being converted into loft apartments. Inside, each level of the cavernous structure had been stripped to bare wooden floors and concrete support posts, and on the roof workers were removing the old tar paper.

Suddenly Sims spotted a plume of white smoke billowing through a three-foot hole in the roof and saw workers dashing about feeding hoses into the opening. Sims, a 49-year-old veteran construction worker, was not perturbed. Thumbing a key on his walkie-talkie, he called superintendent Keith Almand and said calmly, "Y'all got a fire on top of the building."

Minutes later, at 2.40pm on that cool, sunny Monday of April 12, 1999, firefighter Matt Moseley, 30, pounded up the metal stairs to the mill's fourth level with other members of Rescue Squad 4 and several engine-company firefighters. Floorboards ingrained with oil were ablaze across one section of the floor. Ladders and powerful hoses were expected on the scene at any moment. But at the rear of the floor Moseley saw a downdraft of fire flare through the ceiling. "It's breaking through from the fifth floor," he yelled.

Running up the stairs with a lieutenant, Moseley's group reached the top floor and stopped dead. A cloud of black smoke surged toward them. Behind it they saw a rolling ball of fire. The men ran back to the fourth floor as a firestorm shook the building.

Up on the crane tower, Sims saw fire racing across the roof and heard over his radio someone yelling: "Everyone out! Clear the building!" Sims's only route to safety was down a ladder inside the crane's steel tower. He was about to go for it when he heard a huge whoosh and saw an explosion of fire at the crane's base. Flames enveloped the ladder, and Sims felt a blast of heat through the cab windows.

He desperately looked for an escape. Then he heard Almand on his radio, "Hang in there, Ivers. We'll send a helicopter for you."

"OK," Sims replied, struggling to keep his voice steady.

Inside the mill the stairs clattered with the boots of a dozen firefighters running for their lives. Fueled by a stiff northwesterly wind blowing in through wooden window frames, the fire roared from floor to floor, a giant orange wave chasing the men down.

Nearing the ground level, Moseley saw a parapet wall to his right collapse and hot bricks skid across the burning floor. Pieces of metal, glowing red, pelted down from above, while black smoke turned day into night. Moseley thought briefly that he was going to die—then he noticed an open doorway to the outside. Gasping for breath, he and a pack of other firefighters dashed through as the inside of the building imploded.

Embers were now shooting onto the rooftops of nearby houses. Moseley's squad went door to door ordering residents to leave. Ten minutes into the evacuation, one squad member happened to glance up at the crane. His eyes followed the flames upward as they leapt toward the cab. To his astonishment he saw a man edging his way along the horizontal arm—called the counter deck—extending from the rear of the cab. Although Keith Almand had called for a helicopter, Moseley had not yet heard about a man on the crane.

When Moseley checked out the situation, he saw it was impossible to reach Sims by ladder. And when he realized that the rescue would have to be made by air, an adrenaline rush made Moseley's mouth dry. Rescue had been a calling for him since he was ten years old and crawled into a storm drain to save a puppy trapped inside. He'd planned to become a doctor, but a paramedic class in college turned him to firefighting and rescue.

From the time Moseley answered his first call, he was enthralled by the action and danger. "We train for the big one, a major-league rescue," he told friends. "If it happens, we're ready to take care of it." He knew that his confident words would now be put to a supreme test.

Driven from his cab directly above the fire, Sims walked along the shorter, 50-foot arm of the crane to the concrete counterweights that balanced the hoist. The heat was so intense, it scorched the soles of his work boots. He could hardly bear it.

The concrete slabs were a better insulator, so he hoisted himself onto them and lay down on his stomach. "The crane's not going to stand much longer," he gasped into his radio.

Raising his head, he saw a helicopter approach and hover about 70 feet above his perch, then wheel away. Soon about half a dozen choppers from various TV and radio stations, Life Flight and the Atlanta Police Department were circling. He wondered why they weren't coming for him. Then he realized it was just too perilous. The choppers were buffeted by waves of heat so intense it made the arm rock up and down. And a steel cable, running from the base of the concrete counter-weights to the top of the tower, might snag the rotors if the choppers came too close.

"How much longer is it going to take?" he asked into his radio.

"We're working on it," Almand replied. But just then Sims was jarred by an explosion behind him. He turned to see the cab in flames and the windows shattered. Between the cab and his perch, the steel was blackened by the broiling heat.

Moseley knew that time was running out; this kind of blaze could reach 2000 degrees F, enough to collapse the crane. The only option was a rope rescue. He took a moment to visualize himself swinging on a rope from a hovering helicopter and scooping the man to safety. Then, dashing to his truck, he strapped on a full-body harness and reported to his captain, "I'm ready to try a rappel."

HANG IN THERE: **Moseley begins his descent.**

At 3.45pm a sleek black-and-white LongRanger helicopter from the Georgia Department of Natural Resources set down on a grassy knoll some 100 yards west of the burning mill. The rear doors were off and a heavy rope-ring was strapped to the craft's underbelly. It was rigged to lower a rescue basket.

Moseley shook his head, "A basket won't work," he told the crew. "We don't know the man's condition. If he panics, jumps for the basket and misses, it'll be over."

Instead, Moseley climbed aboard with a spare harness. "Let me get to him on a rope and hook him to this," he said to pilot Boyd Clines. A former Army chopper pilot, Clines had inserted and recovered many Special Forces teams behind enemy lines during the Vietnam War. He knew how chancy and dangerous a rope rescue was. "OK," he told the firefighter. "If you want to take the ride, let's go."

The helicopter crew chief, Larry Rogers, attached an 80-foot length of one-inch woven polyester rope to a hook and snaked out the line on the grass. "C'mon," he said, signaling Moseley. Puzzled, Moseley got out and the crew chief handed him the free end of the rope. "Hook it on," he instructed. Only then did it dawn on Moseley that he'd be making the entire ride at rope's end. He attached the rope to his harness with a steel carabiner while Rogers reboarded the chopper. Then, as the helicopter slowly ascended, straight up, Moseley walked underneath to take up the slack in the rope. A tug at his chest and he was airborne.

Soaring above houses and rail tracks, he saw columns of smoke all around the mill. Hundreds of feet away, he could feel the heat. It was like bee stings on his face. *If he flies over the mill, I'm roasted,* Moseley thought, turning his face into the collar of his jacket.

Almand's voice rang out over Sims's radio, "They're coming to get you!" But Sims was already sitting up, his gaze fixed on the man swinging toward him at the end of a rope. Immediately he understood the plan and dared to hope. "This will work OK," he told himself, "if only there's time."

Below, throngs of people lined neighborhood streets to watch. Office workers in downtown Atlanta crowded windows, their eyes shifting back and forth between the man waiting on the crane and the man risking his life for him.

Moseley was at 300 feet, circling around the fire, coming into the crane upwind. Within earshot of Sims now, he called, "Don't touch me. I'll come to you."

Rope trick: "Down a little . . ."

. . . "That's good, hold it . . ."

Up above, Clines's gaze did not move from the horizon. With practiced touch he flew the chopper through the turbulence with hardly a jolt to the man dangling below. Meanwhile, crew chief Rogers, strapped to a seat and leaning out a back door, was the pilot's eyes. "We're on top of him," he said into his headset. "Down a little . . . lower . . . that's good . . . hold it."

Moseley was a foot too high on the first pass. Swinging in, thrusting out his boot, he tried to hook the cable that ran from the concrete counterweights to the tower. He missed by inches. As he came back in, he turned himself 180 degrees, saw the cable within reach, and made a grab for it.

His gloved fingers closed on the wire, and he pulled himself in until he got his feet on the arm. Sims was barely ten feet away, sitting on a slab, his legs over the side. "Be careful," he said. "The metal's hot."

Looking down from the chopper, Rogers reported in an even voice, "He's on the crane." Then he gave a sharp intake of breath. "But he's still hooked up to the rope."

Clines felt a stab of alarm. They'd expected the firefighter to unhook the line once he got on the crane, then reconnect after fastening Sims into the harness. Man and machine were bound together.

Clines had to keep the chopper hovering with just enough slack in the rope to allow Moseley to work while the firestorm buffeted them about. If they hit the cable or the boom, they'd all die. "Forward a little," Rogers said in a steely voice, helping Clines keep the rope at precisely the right tension. "Not too much . . . lookin' good."

The two men in the chopper were so engrossed that neither noticed that the Plexiglas floor panels at the helicopter's nose were beginning to warp.

On the arm, Moseley saw concern in Sims's eyes. To ease the tension he asked his name and made a joke about coming up to get him off work early. Sims had no reply. His single thought was to stay calm and do his part for this man. Then Moseley said crisply, "I've got to put a harness on you. Just sit there and let me do the work."

With quick, sure movements, he laced the harness straps between Sims's legs, across his chest and up under his

. . . "We got 'em! Bring 'em up!"

arms. "Try to pull it higher," he said. Wordlessly Sims made the adjustment, and Moseley then hooked the harness to the rope. "We're off," he said softly, signaling to the helicopter with a raised thumb.

"We've got 'em," Rogers told his pilot. "Bring 'em up."

As their boots left the crane, Moseley wrapped his arms and legs around Sims for the ride back to the knoll. It was 4.03pm. Sims had been trapped for about 90 searing minutes.

A roar rose from the crowd below, and men pounded the air with their fists as the two figures swung away from the crane on what looked like a spider's thread. Television commentators spoke in hushed tones, not finding words to describe what they had seen.

Moseley himself felt exultant. He chatted to Sims about the great view, and reported a traffic jam. Then, at the knoll, Clines set them down as gently as a cup on a saucer.

Medics swarmed over and carried Sims off on a stretcher. Moseley's hands began trembling as his adrenaline drained. He felt his tongue swollen in his mouth and asked for water. Sims was examined at the Atlanta Medical Center and found to be in good condition, his blood pressure a solid 120/80.

In an emotional reunion at a mayoral ceremony honoring the uncommon heroism of the rescuers two days later, Sims took Moseley's hand in his own. He pictured again his last-minute, midair encounter with Moseley above the inferno, and a simple prayer formed in his heart: *Thank God for your courage, Matt.*

LIVES ENTWINED: **Moseley (left) and Sims.**

185

He's down there
somewhere!

by Tim Bouquet

As he groped through the acrid black water for the nine-year-old, Bob Edwards knew time was running out.

Towards the end of the long hot summer afternoon, the water in the canal was dark and docile. Nine-year-old Tony Wicks and his friend Joshua Soper, six, sneaked past the keep-out signs and a British Waterways office, to a slipway down to the canal.

They walked along the side of the canal—a section of the River Don, winding through Doncaster's former industrial heartland—and on to a pontoon jutting 150 feet into the water. It was deserted. The boys stripped off and dangled their feet in the water, then began larking about.

Suddenly Tony slipped on the slats and fell in. "Tony, get out!" shrieked Joshua as his friend hit the canal. In seconds, bubbles stopped coming to the surface and the water was still again.

Bob Edwards gazed out at the canal through the windows of the British Waterways office. Nothing stirred. A brisk 57-year-old former police superintendent with a straight-backed military stance, Edwards had been a British Waterways patrol inspector for six years, responsible for safety and security on 470 miles of rivers and canals stretching from north Yorkshire to Lincolnshire and Leicestershire.

Increasingly concerned at the number of children throwing themselves off bridges or hurling rocks on to pleasure boats, Edwards had called in on Chris Davidson, supervisor for the 23 miles of waterways from Doncaster to Sheffield, to discuss how they could stop the young hooligans.

He glanced at his watch: 4.45pm. Normally Davidson closed the office at 4.30. But on that Tuesday, August 8, 1995, Edwards was waiting for a call from a colleague.

"I wish he'd ring soon, then we could both get home," sighed Edwards.

There was a knock on the office door. On the step stood a small boy. "Yes, young man, what can I do for you?"

"My friend Tony," blurted Joshua Soper, pointing at the canal. "He's fallen in the water! He's gone down and he hasn't come up. He can't swim!"

Edwards raced to the canalside office car park. "Stay here," he told Joshua.

He climbed down the steel ladder on to the pontoon, and spotted a dark object floating about 200 yards away. *A body!* Sprinting along the jetty, he then realized: *It's a piece of driftwood.*

Quickly he retraced his steps, scanning both sides of the jetty. The water lapped peacefully beneath his feet. He could see nothing.

"Where did you last see Tony?" he shouted up to Joshua. "River side or moorings side?"

The boy shrugged. He wasn't sure. *Maybe this is a hoax*, thought Edwards. It wouldn't be the first time a boy had staged a diversion to draw people out of the office so that another could nip in and steal something.

Then, next to a pile of clothes by the canal wall, he saw a pair of kids' trainers. Clearly it was no hoax. "I'm going in," he shouted to Davidson. "Get help!" Davidson rushed back to his office and dialled 999: "We need a diving team and oxygen. Pronto!"

KEEP OUT: they took no notice.

At that moment 34-year-old Nadine Wicks, Tony's mother, was with her sisters, accompanying their terminally ill mother to a hospice. She had left Tony playing with Joshua, knowing his mother Debbie was around.

As they drove past the run-down council estate where Nadine lived, less than a mile from the canal, a sickening feeling suddenly seized the pit of her stomach. "You've got to stop," Nadine told her sisters. "I must get home! Something's wrong!"

Out on the pontoon, at the point where Joshua thought he might have last seen Tony, Bob Edwards peered into the oily black water. *There's not a lot of current*, he thought. *He shouldn't have gone too far.*

Time was critical. If someone is unconscious in the water, permanent brain damage occurs at around three minutes. In six minutes, most people are dead. "How long ago did Tony fall in?" Bob called to Joshua. The boy had no idea. *Tony might already be dead*, thought Edwards grimly.

He'd spent hundreds of hours competing for the Nottinghamshire Police Life-Saving Team. He knew that if a victim was to stand any chance of survival, the rescuer must stay calm. If he just plunged in, he could gash his head on debris beneath the surface.

He stripped to his underpants. *This time*, he told himself as he lowered his body into the water, *it's for real*.

Nadine Wicks rushed next door to Debbie Soper's flat. "Where's Tony?"

"Gone somewhere with Joshua."

Tony, an asthmatic, didn't usually wander off without telling anyone where he was going. Her mind blank with fear, Nadine ran to her flat.

Bob Edwards arched his wiry five-foot-ten-inch frame and dived into the darkness. About eight feet down, his fingers touched the canal bed.

He flattened his hands and began moving his palms systematically in a zigzag motion. He moved cautiously, wary of cutting or snaring himself on rusting junk and other rubbish. But he could feel only thick, treacly mud.

Twenty seconds later he shot back to the surface, gulped air, swam forward five feet and dived again. He stretched as far as he could. Still nothing.

Seven or eight times Edwards plunged in, fingertipping his way 40 feet alongside the pontoon. There was no sign of Tony. *He must be down there somewhere. Maybe I am searching the wrong place*, he thought.

He was fit for his age but, after two and a half minutes in the water, he was tiring. *I've got to change tactic*, he realized. *If I dive feet first instead of head first, I'll only have to come up two feet for air. And by searching with my feet I can cover a wider area.*

Back on the bottom, he kept himself upright by moving his arms in a lateral breaststroke motion and started to circle his feet over the canal bed. He swallowed some of the dank black water. It stung his throat and tasted revolting. His toes touched nothing but sticky mud. His second feet-first dive yielded nothing, either. He dived for the third time. By now Edwards had spent almost three minutes working his way along parallel to the pontoon. As he swung his left leg round one more time, his foot banged into something about six feet out from the side. It felt like a bundle. He prodded it again. Though hard, it had some give in it. *It's him! It's got to be Tony!*

Edwards's lungs were aching, and he was running desperately short of air. He had to make a split-second decision: *Do I go back up to the surface, or do I rescue him now?*

Even though Tony must have been under the water about eight minutes, Edwards realized it wasn't the moment to take a risk.

He shot back to the surface, gulped for air and dived one last time. Seconds later he grabbed an arm and dragged a limp Tony Wicks to the surface. "I've found him!" Edwards yelled. "He's not breathing!" Chris Davidson ran back to his office, cancelled the divers and called for specialist paramedics.

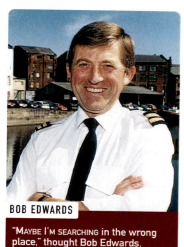

BOB EDWARDS

"Maybe I'm searching in the wrong place," thought Bob Edwards.

Treading water, with Tony's head cradled in the crook of his left arm, Edwards felt halfway up the boy's neck for his carotid pulse and pressed gently for five seconds. Nothing.

The boy's eyes were open. Steely grey, they bulged out of his face. Edwards blew on them in the hope the eyelids would flicker. No reaction.

He's got to be dead, thought Edwards. Tony's skin was clammy and paper-white. The only colour in him was his ginger crew-cut hair.

Tilting Tony's head back with his right hand to ensure a clear airway to his lungs, Edwards began mouth-to-mouth resuscitation, all the while manoeuvring himself and the boy nearer the pontoon. He managed to hook his left arm round one of the supporting posts, but was still treading water.

LUCKY LADS: **Joshua (left) and Tony.**

Then his toes felt something metallic. Edwards put his feet down flat and found he was standing on a submerged supermarket trolley.

Now that he had something to take his weight, he held Tony's shoulders out of the water, tilted his head back and placed his mouth over the boy's to continue resuscitation.

Slowly, colour returned to Tony's skin. Three minutes after being plucked from the canal bed, a noise came from the boy's mouth. But his body remained limp, his eyes blind. Still Edwards refused to give up.

"How is he?" bellowed a voice. Looking up, Edwards saw a fireman kneeling on the pontoon. He felt the boy's neck again. This time there was no mistaking the tell-tale sensation under his fingers: *A pulse!* He called out: "He's alive! I'm sure he's alive!" The fireman reached down for Tony.

"Have you got oxygen?" Edwards asked. The fireman nodded. "Get that first," Edwards told him. "I'll carry on with the resuscitation. We've got to keep this going—I don't want to lose him now!"

As the oxygen arrived, Edwards passed the still unconscious Tony up on to the pontoon. The fireman placed the boy in the recovery position. Thick black water and vomit trickled from Tony's mouth. But when the oxygen mask was put on him he coughed and spluttered, obviously breathing, albeit erratically.

Moments later an ambulance crew was on the scene. Paramedics wrapped Tony in blankets and strapped him to a stretcher for the four-minute dash to Doncaster Royal Infirmary.

Just ten minutes had passed since Joshua knocked on the office door.

As he picked up his clothes, Edwards had a new fear. *Tony must have been under that water for at least eight minutes,* he reasoned. *If he lives, what sort of state is he going to be in?* In his police days, he had pulled a suicide from a gas oven. He had saved her life but she was left with permanent brain damage.

In her flat, Nadine Wicks decided she would go and look for Tony. But where?

"Mrs Wicks?" Two police officers were standing at her door with Joshua, who was sobbing. "Will you come with us? Tony's been fished out of the canal. He's in the Infirmary."

In the resuscitation room, Tony lay wrapped in a blanket as doctors desperately tried to warm him up. He was still unconscious and his veins collapsed at the first prick of a rehydration needle.

Thanks to Edwards, he was still breathing. The shock of his hot body hitting cold water had thrown him into a sort of suspended animation or "dive reflex", where the pulse falls dramatically and blood is redirected from the skin and intestines to heart muscle and brain. Babies can survive this way under water for up to an hour, but the medical team at Doncaster Royal Infirmary had never heard of it happening in a child Tony's age.

So many doctors and nurses were swarming around Tony that Nadine could not get near her son. He looked so small, submerged under tubes and dials.

"Has he been baptised?" a nurse asked her. "Would you like a priest?"

Next morning Bob Edwards was driving to his office in Leeds when his mobile phone rang. It was a local radio station.

Tony Wicks had just regained consciousness, they told him. "Do you know how he is?" asked Edwards, dreading the reply.

"Oh, he's fine. He's sitting up in bed and asking for his breakfast."

When Edwards walked into the ward later that day, he discovered that Tony had suffered no ill effects beyond a sore throat from a tube the doctors had inserted.

Nadine rushed over and grabbed his hand. "I just can't believe you risked your life to save my Tony," she sobbed. "I don't know how to thank you."

"There's one way you can thank me, young man," smiled Edwards, perching by Tony's bed. "Promise me you'll take some swimming lessons!"

For saving Tony Wicks's life, Bob Edwards won awards from the Royal Humane Society, and a British Gold Hero Award from the Association of Retired Persons.

Tony Wicks has learnt to swim.

Attacked by pit bulls!

by Jim Hutchison

They were crazed by blood lust and they turned a quiet residential street into a highway of horror.

Glen Nikkel was looking forward to a Christmas break as he drove his pickup down 128th Street in Surrey, British Columbia, on the sunny afternoon of Friday, December 18, 1998. Having just wound up his last construction job before the holidays, the 43-year-old was taking his wife, Kim, a red-haired, slender 42-year-old, to get her car at a repair shop.

Ahead, on her right, Kim spotted pit bulls barking furiously on the front lawn of a house, its front door wide open. Knowing city bylaws forbade such dogs being loose, she said: "Where's the owner? Those dogs are going crazy." The couple had no idea that on their left, they'd just passed Allan Lavallee, sitting in his car tending the pit bulls' first victim.

At 1.15pm Lavallee, a slim 33-year-old ironworker, had been driving his sedan along 128th Street when he saw an elderly man lying in the busy road fending off the attacking dogs. Screeching to a halt, Lavallee leaned on the horn. The startled dogs released their victim.

Before they ran back to their owner's driveway, Lavallee glimpsed the spine-chilling look of wild animals disturbed from a kill. The larger dog, a white male with black markings and a head the size of a basketball, was the biggest pit bull he'd ever seen. Its mother, black with white feet and powerful, stocky shoulders, was no less intimidating.

From her house nearby, Joan Dupre, 49, had seen Lavallee help the badly mauled man into his car. She ran to call 9-1-1. Lavallee, meanwhile, kept the man talking for fear he'd slip into shock. Blood seeped from gaping wounds on his hands and arms.

As the Nikkels drove past the barking dogs, Kim froze. A fit, petite woman power walking along the sidewalk was headed straight for them. A fence alongside the driveway blocked the walker's view, and with her portable radio on, she was oblivious to the danger ahead. As they approached the stoplight, Kim glanced in the side-view mirror. "Stop the truck!" she yelled. "Those dogs are attacking that woman!"

Glen jammed on the brakes, but with traffic backing up behind them, they had no room to turn around. "Go around the block," Kim ordered. "Quick!"

Glen floored the accelerator.

Danielle Ovenden, 39, barely got her arms up before the snarling animals were on her. One leaped at her chest as the other went for her legs. Their quarry brought to ground, each dog locked powerful jaws on a leg, dragging Ovenden up the driveway like predators hauling prey into their lair. Shaking her small body like a rag doll, they sank their fangs deeper, and Ovenden felt them crunch into her bones.

Her cries snapped Lavallee's head around to see the dogs attacking her across the street. With his injured passenger still sitting beside him, he threw the car into gear and skidded into a U-turn.

Mounting the curb, he charged the dogs, slamming on the brakes at the last second and revving the engine till it howled. The dogs dropped Ovenden in a bloody heap and bounded through the front door of their owner's house.

Just then, the Nikkels lurched to a stop behind him. Trained in first aid, Kim ran to Ovenden and knelt beside her. "Can you move?" she asked.

"The dogs!" Ovenden gasped, her eyes flitting about in terror. Kim was shocked at the amount of blood flowing from more than a dozen wounds. Monstrous, sharklike bites had ripped apart so much flesh, Kim didn't know where to begin applying pressure to stem the bleeding. She wanted to get Ovenden to the safety of the truck but feared she would die if she was moved.

"Just hang on," Kim pleaded as she saw Glen rummaging through the cab of his truck for a hammer, a wrench—anything to protect the women. He cursed himself for having cleaned out his toolbox earlier.

Lavallee, meanwhile, had spotted the dogs at the living-room window in the owner's house. Jumping from his car, he raced to shut the front door, but before he could reach it, they charged. Spinning around, he ran for his life, just making it to his car as they snapped at his heels.

Kim now heard deep-throated snarls. Fighting the urge to run, she looked up. Teeth bared, the pit bulls were eyeing the two women on the ground, their slavering jaws dripping red. *They've tasted blood and want more*, she shivered.

"Don't move," Kim whispered to Ovenden. She looked for Glen. He'd found a three-metre-long extension cord with heavy, yellow plug ends to use as a weapon. Coiled into loops, it wasn't much, but there was nothing else.

From across the street, Kim heard a shout. Joan Dupre, unaware the dogs had attacked again, stood on the sidewalk signalling to Lavallee, parked in the driveway alongside Kim. "I called 9-1-1," she yelled.

Instantly, the dogs homed in on her and bolted across the road. Dupre's eyes widened in fear as they galloped towards her, their claws clattering on the roadway. Knowing she would never make it to her door, she ran behind the neighbour's hedge, hoping that if the pit bulls couldn't see her, she might escape.

They ran her down from behind, the smaller dog plunging its teeth into her left thigh, pitching her on her stomach. Then, the larger dog snapped its jaws over her face, ripping her left nostril open and sinking another fang deep into her left eye socket, filling it with blood. Kicking and screaming, Dupre begged for help.

Glen sprinted towards her, the extension cord in his right hand. Rounding the hedge, he went for the dog with Dupre's head in its jaws. "Get away!" he bellowed.

Swinging the cord like a medieval flail, he whipped it across the animal's back. It flinched but didn't let go. He lashed again, landing a blow to the skull. This time the maddened animal dropped Dupre's head and lunged for Glen.

Sidestepping, he swung the cord again, catching the dog on the side of the head. Snarling, it drew back and tried to circle behind him. Glen knew that if he took his eyes off the dog for a second, it would be on him, but the other dog was still tearing at Dupre's legs. Keeping his back from the circling animal, he moved close to Dupre and whipped the cord down. Whistling through the air, it smacked into the pit bull's spine. The dog let go with a yelp and retreated.

The dogs now began stalking Glen from both sides. *Don't let them get behind you,* he told himself. Standing over Dupre, he whipped the cord around in front of him, like a cowboy with a lasso.

Suddenly, as if at a signal, the dogs wheeled and raced off around the hedge. Fear gripped Glen as he realized where they were headed. "Kim!" he bawled. "Get in the truck. They're coming back!"

He was in an agonizing predicament. His instinct was to run to protect Kim, but if the dogs came back for Dupre, another attack would surely kill her. He had to trust that Kim would make it to the truck. Grabbing Dupre under the arms, he dragged her to her front door.

Kim, holding Ovenden in her arms, heard Glen's warning as the dogs ran towards them, sending a dozen bystanders scrambling for their vehicles. Now she, too, faced an awful decision. If she left Ovenden, the movement would surely bring the dogs back to finish her off. If she stayed, they would get her, too.

At that instant, Ovenden's eyes rolled back and she slumped down, unconscious. *As long as she keeps still, the dogs will leave her alone,* Kim thought. Taking a deep breath, she dived for the open passenger door of the truck. Slamming it shut, she broke down, shaking with fear. From the truck's window, she was thankful to see the dogs paid no attention to the motionless woman. In the driveway, Lavallee was shouting and blowing his horn to distract them.

A moment later, Kim cried out in terror. Ovenden was stirring. "Don't move!" she shouted. "Lie still!"

Semiconscious, Ovenden sat up. Kim screamed as the pit bulls pounced. The female went for Ovenden's head, ripping her left ear off. The male tore her open along her upper spine. In a frenzy, they savaged her body. "Somebody help her!" Kim sobbed. Then she saw her husband flash by.

Adrenaline pumping, Glen waded in. "Get off her!" he bellowed, bringing the cord whipping down. The plug ends cracked hard onto the male's back. Yelping, it dropped Ovenden's head.

Swinging at the other dog, Glen flayed it across the haunches. It too, let go,

THE SERIAL ATTACKS

Dog owner's house

Carport

128th Street

Dupre's house

1. The male and female dogs run across to victim **1**, then back to their yard.

2. Both dogs attack victim **2** (Ovenden).

3. The dogs then go across the street to attack victim **3** (Dupre).

4. They return to victim **2**.

5. The male dog jumps the fence and hides.

6. The female dog is killed near the carport.

backing out of range. The pair darted around him, probing for an opening.

In terrible pain, Ovenden clung to the fence as Glen stood between her and the snarling dogs. "Stay with me," she pleaded.

"I won't leave you," he promised. The pit bulls edged closer. Glen raised the cord, ready to strike.

I've got to give him cover, Lavallee thought from his car. Backing across the lawn, he now moved in at right angles to the dogs. "I'm coming in!" he shouted, aiming for the dogs and hoping to crush them against the fence. They were too fast. Running around the front end, they went berserk, trying to sink their teeth into his right bumper and tires.

Grateful Lavallee was shielding Ovenden and him, Glen flicked his eyes back and forth trying to anticipate the direction from which the next attack would come. It had been 15 minutes since Dupre's 9-1-1 call. It seemed a lot longer.

As the dogs ran for the rear of the car, Lavallee slammed into reverse, cutting them off. They spun and ran for the front again. Frantically, he lurched forward, barely managing to head them off. Suddenly a pickup truck roared across the lawn. Another driver had realized what Lavallee was doing. The width of the two vehicles now filled the driveway, making it harder for the dogs to get around them. Each time they tried an end run, the cars roared back and forth to intercept.

Lights flashing, a police car pulled up. Royal Canadian Mounted Policeman Constable Brent Kelly saw Ovenden in a pool of blood and headed for the barking dogs.

An off-duty firefighter passing by ran to Glen as he knelt by Ovenden. "I've got her," he said.

"DON'T MOVE! LIE STILL!" shouted Kim Nikkel (far right), now reunited with (from left) Allan Lavallee, Joan Dupre, Danielle Ovenden, and her husband Glen.

"All right," Glen replied, following Kelly, cord at the ready. *He doesn't know what he's walking into,* Glen thought.

"Draw your gun!" Kim yelled to the policeman. "The dogs will attack as soon as they see you."

The officer took out his semiautomatic and moved up beside Lavallee's car. Spotting him, the dogs charged. Taking aim at the galloping female, Kelly fired and missed. He then took aim at the male but missed him, too. Sensing it was now the hunted, the animal turned tail and leapt the fence. The female, however, lunged.

Kelly fired again. The dog, hit in the chest, hurtled backward and lay still. To Kelly's disbelief, it suddenly rolled over and came to life, charging at him again. He fired once more. This time the female stayed down.

As the three victims were rushed to hospital, Glen put his arm around Kim. His overalls were blood-spattered and his hands shook as he threw the electrical cord into the truck. "Let's get out of here," he said.

Constable Kelly entered the dog-owner's house and found a third pit bull in a laundry room. The male was later found hiding three blocks away, cowering in a hedge. It was euthanized that day.

Danielle Ovenden needed more than 300 stitches and months of painful reconstructive surgery. Joan Dupre received 260 stitches to her face, right arm and legs, and was off work for a month.

On June 5, 2000, Governor-General Adrienne Clarkson presented Glen Nikkel with the Medal of Bravery for saving the lives of Ovenden and Dupre. Dupre and Lavallee were also recognized for providing assistance to others in a selfless manner.

Bus plunge into
the raging river

by Richard Shears

Clinging to the wreckage, the three watched in terror as the waters continued to rise.

Jack Rogers could barely see through the windscreen of his bus. Heavy rain fell steadily as he drove toward the Hastings River, which flows near Mount Seaview in New South Wales. Usually placid, the river had been transformed into a thundering, 60-metre wide torrent by days of rain. Darkened by tonnes of silt, the water rolled and seethed; branches and trees sped by in the flood. Rogers' mission was to cross the turbulent river using a narrow bridge now hidden beneath flood waters.

The 54-year-old bus driver didn't want to make the trip. But with the tour bus a day behind schedule, Rogers felt under pressure to go on. He finally decided to make the crossing, but without passengers.

"I'm not going to risk any lives," he said. Suzanne Evers, a tour hostess in her twenties, and Oscar Buckingham, an American tourist, volunteered to accompany him on that April afternoon.

At the river's edge, Rogers strained to see the outline of the bridge one metre below the surface. There were no side rails to guide him. As he eased the bus into the roiling water, the torrent instantly surged up against its sides. But the eight massive wheels held firm. *So far, so good*, he thought. Then, halfway across, the front of the bus reared up and the whole vehicle began to tilt. Rogers's gut tightened with fear. "We're losing it!" he yelled. In chilling slow-motion, the bus began to roll slowly onto its side.

The three clung to their seats as bags cascaded down from the luggage racks. Then the bus rolled upright and began to float nose-first downstream. Rogers turned the steering wheel and stamped uselessly on the brake pedal. Suddenly, there was a loud thump. *We've hit bottom*, Rogers thought. The door sprang open, and water gushed in.

Evers and Buckingham yelled in fear as water swirled round their legs. "Let's get out of here!" Rogers shouted. "We'll be safer on top!" He pushed open an

DECEPTIVE CALM: the mouth of the Hastings River.

overhead hatch, and the three scrambled onto the roof. They crouched there, clutching the open hatchway.

The bus was jammed against submerged rocks, 40 metres from the river bank. With the front two-thirds filling with water, the vehicle shuddered repeatedly from the flood's force. "We're still moving!" Rogers told his shivering companions. "We could roll at any time."

"Please help!" a voice on the phone said to Sergeant Brian Smith at the Wauchope police station. "People are trapped in a bus in the river by the bridge at Seaview!"

Smith dashed to his car. When he reached Mount Seaview, some 50 kilometres away, he was astonished by what he saw: the bridge had disappeared beneath the torrent. Forty metres downstream, a bus rocked like a whale stranded in surf, with three people clinging to the top. The water appeared to be rising.

Smith helped staff members from a nearby tourist lodge and the local fire brigade attach two lines to a small aluminium dinghy and guide it towards the victims. As the boat floated close by him, Rogers climbed inside the bus, kicked out a window and grabbed three life jackets from the dinghy. Then he tied one of the lines to a seat mounting. Donning the life jackets, the three crawled through the window. As they climbed into the dinghy, it began to list violently. *God help us*, Rogers thought, *we're going over!* The boat flipped and hurled its passengers into the maelstrom.

As Rogers sank, he felt the dinghy's line tighten round his lower body. Kicking frantically, he strained to reach the surface. Just as his head cleared the water, however, a massive weight smashed down on it. He felt his head explode with pain. Looking up, he saw a flash of silver. The dinghy! He was caught in a deathtrap: the boat's line had snared his lower body while its hull was keeping him underwater.

His chest hurt, and water kept filling his lungs. *I can't hold on much longer*, Rogers thought. Suddenly the dinghy shifted slightly, leaving a clear space above him. *Air!* He kicked powerfully, broke through to the surface and inhaled, coughing and spitting out mouthfuls of water. With one hand, he seized the static line to shore; with the other, he untangled the boat line from his body. He struggled to keep his head above water, but the current was so strong it formed a plume that cascaded over his face.

Gasping, Rogers dragged himself along the line towards the bus. He was able to hook his feet under a ridge of metal below the vehicle's side panels. Lifting his head out of the swirling water, he grabbed hold of the bus.

Sergeant Smith had watched with horror as the boat overturned. He attached a safety line and leaped into the water, moving hand over hand along the static rope towards the dinghy. Battered by the current, he was pulled under repeatedly.

It's no use, I'll have to go back, he thought.

He saw Evers thrashing her way along a line that was tethered to the boat. She clung to it, but was continually swamped by the water.

The rescuers on the bank waded into a shallower part of the river and gripped each other's arms to form a human chain.

"Let go!" Smith yelled over the roar of the river. "We'll catch you!" The woman released the line and shot downstream. The last man in the chain reached out and pulled her in to safety.

Forty metres downstream from the bridge, one of the lines had caught Buckingham round the hips. He managed to wedge a foot between submerged rocks and keep his head above water. *I must get him out of there*, Smith thought. Again he dived into the icy water and swam furiously about ten metres to a partly submerged tree near Buckingham. "Let go!" he shouted, thinking that Buckingham would be washed downstream to calmer waters and rescued. But with the rope wound tightly round him, Buckingham could not move at all. Smith urged him again and again, but Buckingham didn't budge.

After ten minutes, Smith battled his way back to the bank. Soon after, he collapsed to the ground in agonising pain. A paramedic ran forward to examine him. "He needs a hospital—fast!"

Suddenly there was a loud snap as the rope trapping Buckingham broke and he was swept downstream. The rescuers ran down the river bank and plucked him from the calmer water. He was numb with cold, but still alive.

Still clinging to the bus, Rogers was exhausted and shivering furiously. He knew that, in his weakened state, he would drown if he let go. Even if he managed to hang on, the rising waters might roll the bus on top of him. *How long does it take to drown?* he wondered.

Images of his wife Alice and their eight children spun through his mind. Although he loved the independence of his job, Rogers regretted the precious moments of their childhood that he had missed while on the road. Now, three of his kids had their own children. *I want to see my grandchildren grow. I can't give up,* he thought.

Rogers knew he had to move from the side of the bus, where the full force of the current was sapping his dwindling energy. Digging his fingernails into the rubber window seals, he made his way towards the front of the bus. Holding the side mirror, Rogers reached round to one of the windscreen wipers.

Then suddenly he remembered the small, fold-down step used for window cleaning. Probing with his toes below the windscreen, he found the release button, pushed it and opened the step. With solid metal beneath his foot, he was able to pull half his body out of the water. Rogers pressed himself against the windscreen and clutched a wiper as the water continued to swirl all around him.

On the river bank, Ray Richards, a store owner and member of the State Emergency Service (SES), was pondering how to rescue Rogers. It seemed there was no alternative but to use a flying fox. The "fox" was a seat suspended by pulleys from an overhead rope, much like the device sailors use to transfer men between ships. But the volunteers had not used it in this type of situation. "We'll just have to do the best we can," Richard said.

Then he turned to volunteer Shane Hughes, one of the crew's most experienced members, and said, "I want you to go across on the fox and bring him back." At 163 centimetres and 73 kilos, Hughes was also the smallest member of the team— and the least likely to pull the rope down into the water.

"No problem," Hughes replied. But he had reservations. He wasn't a strong swimmer, and the river was moving at breakneck speed. *Keep calm and you'll be OK,* he said to himself.

As darkness fell, the rescuers illuminated the scene with floodlights. They tied one end of their thickest rope to a tree and the other to a bulldozer, which was then driven across the bridge to the opposite bank, stretching the rope over the bus. The fox hung from it, with a second line leading from the chair to groups of men on either side of the river. Hughes climbed into the chair. "Haul!" Richards barked into a walkie-talkie.

With each tug of the rope, Hughes sank closer to the water. Soon his feet were dipping into the waves. When the water reached his chest, he screamed, "Get me out of here!"

At that moment, a surge of water swept over Hughes. With a rush of panic, he realised the rope harness held him captive underwater. *What are they doing back there?* His lungs demanded air. Instead, a rush of water filled his mouth, and he began to choke. Seconds later, he felt a sudden tug and he surfaced. Hauled back to the bank, he gasped, "I need more height—there's too much sag in the rope!"

Again the crew sent Hughes out over the river, and again they were forced to haul him back. "I am that guy's only chance," Hughes said to himself. For nine years, he had spent every Wednesday evening with the other volunteers, training for emergencies like this one. *Trust the team.* It was the slogan of this close-knit group and it would mean nothing if he backed out. *I must try again*, he thought.

They propped the line higher with a ladder. This time there would be no turning back. *Trust the team*, Hughes told himself as the chair dipped into the water. Sinking beneath the surface, Hughes shut his eyes and held his breath. *C'mon! C'mon!* he silently urged his mates. Then a roaring sound filled his ears, and moments later he surfaced near the rear of the bus. The crew pulled the flying fox hard against the bus, raising Hughes above the raging water.

He could feel the bus shifting in the current. Pulling out a hammer he had stuffed into his shorts, Hughes smashed a rear side window. Shards of glass cut into his hands, but he ignored the streaming blood. *I've made it!* he thought. As he lowered himself into the bus, he could just make out the form of Rogers through the fogged-up windscreen.

Rogers, who had been clinging to the bus for more than three hours, was dazed and disorientated by his prolonged exposure to cold. Peering through the windscreen, he saw a figure approach him, arms covered with blood. "Hang on just a few more minutes, mate!" Hughes shouted, snapping Rogers out of his stupor. Hughes knocked out the windscreen, grabbed Rogers's wrist and hauled him inside.

Hughes's radio crackled to life: "The only way out is the way you went in." But the driver shook his head. "I can't do it," he said. "I can't go back in the water."

Rain continued to fall. The river was still rising and the pressure on the bus was building by the minute. "It's rocking more," Hughes told the rescuers on the bank.

"Knock out some more windows so you can get out if it goes over," came the reply. Hughes steadied himself and managed to punch out five of the windows, all the while trying to keep Rogers calm.

Finally, after more than an hour, Hughes turned to Rogers. "We don't have a choice, mate," he said, helping the bus driver into the fox.

As the rescuers pulled Rogers across the water, he felt the chest-high torrent try to rip him from the chair. His heart pounded wildly as the water closed round his shoulders. *Please God, let me see Alice and the kids again.*

"Give it all you've got!" Richards yelled to the men heaving furiously on the rope. For agonizing seconds there was nothing but churning water. Then Rogers broke clear, and the rescuers hauled him to shore. "Thank God," Rogers said weakly.

Sitting in the bus, Hughes watched as the rescuers sent the chair back. Overwhelmed with fatigue, he gazed at his injured hands and wondered how much blood he'd lost. An image of his wife Leane, and their baby daughter Alex, drifted into his mind. *Don't let them down!* When the chair approached, Hughes climbed in and yelled, "Pull!"

The torrent rose quickly above his waist. Water punched into his chest like a first. *Trust the team*, he thought. His lungs ached and his heart was pounding. Finally, strong hands pulled him to safety as his legs gave way beneath him. Richard knelt beside him and smiled. "I knew that you'd make it," he said. "Never doubted it for a minute."

Hughes and Rogers were taken to Wauchope Hospital, where they were treated for hypothermia and cuts. Also there was Brian Smith, who had suffered physical exhaustion. All three recovered fully from the ordeal. Hughes and Smith were later given commendations for bravery. Hughes spends every spare moment with his family. "I really treasure them now," he says. "I know how quickly we can lose each other."

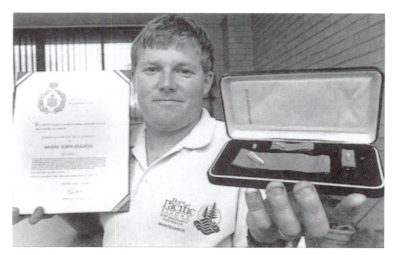

"DON'T LET THEM DOWN." Shane Hughes with his bravery award.

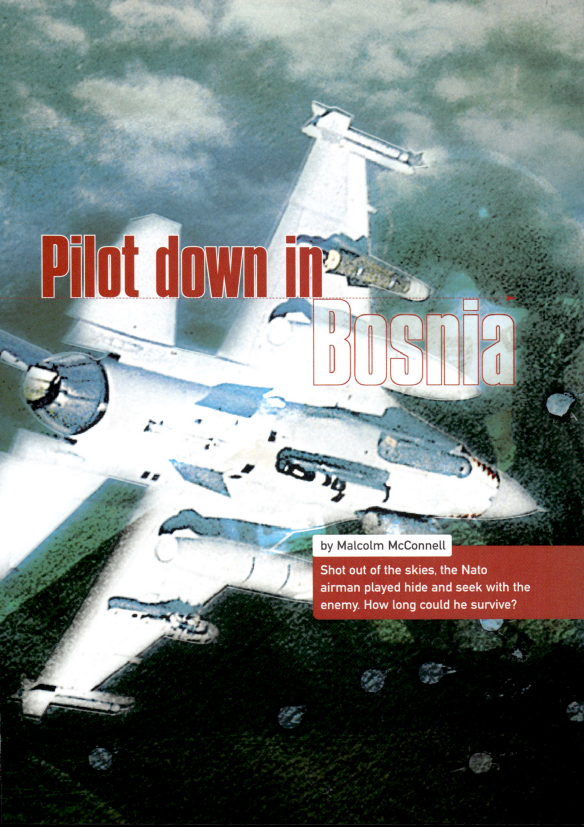

Pilot down in Bosnia

by Malcolm McConnell

Shot out of the skies, the Nato airman played hide and seek with the enemy. How long could he survive?

Captain Scott O'Grady carefully eased his F-16C fighter close beside the one piloted by his flight leader, Captain Bob Wright. Through cloud breaks, they saw the green mountains of Bosnia far below. Their mission that afternoon of June 2, 1995, was a routine combat air patrol, policing a Nato "No Fly Zone". For months no Bosnian Serb plane had challenged Nato fighters in this sector, and intelligence had reported the zone free of surface-to-air missiles (SAMs).

Suddenly O'Grady and Wright were jarred by the buzz and amber flash of their cockpit missile-warning instruments. "Missile in the air!" Wright called urgently.

Seconds later two supersonic SA-6 SAMs ripped through the clouds, exhaust plumes trailing. Wright and O'Grady threw their aircraft into evasive manoeuvres. One missile slashed harmlessly past Wright's plane. The other scored a direct hit on the belly of O'Grady's fighter. Horrified, Wright watched the wings crumple and a fireball blossom around the cockpit. Then O'Grady's jet, canopy intact, disappeared into the clouds.

"Basher 52 took a direct hit—he's down," Wright radioed.

"Any parachute?"

"Negative."

Flames seared O'Grady's neck and licked under his helmet visor, singeing his eyebrows, as his F-16 tore through the cloud bank. The 29-year-old pilot could smell his hair burning. *Eject!* O'Grady's left hand groped for the yellow ejection-seat handle between his knees. *Let it work*, he prayed. Seconds later, O'Grady heard the reassuring twang of his opening chute. He felt his heart pounding as he floated into clear sky. *I can't believe I'm alive.* Hanging beneath him on a tether, his survival pack whipped in the wind.

O'Grady was relieved to see that the winds were pushing him towards a brushy field and away from the orange-tiled roofs of the town of Bosanski Petrovac, a Bosnian Serb stronghold. He noticed hills rising to a green plateau about two miles to the southeast. Then his stomach wrenched as he saw men in uniform pointing at him from a military lorry. When he landed in a clearing near by, O'Grady jumped up, unsnapped his parachute and shed his helmet. He needed a hiding-place *now*.

Snatching his survival pack, O'Grady stumbled through the brush and, like a rabbit, burrowed into thick foliage, forcing himself deeper with his knees and elbows until he was completely covered. He heard men calling to each other. *They know I'm here.* Face thrust into the earth, O'Grady tried to conceal his neck and ears with his green flight gloves. He heard boots thumping close by. O'Grady lay absolutely still. *At least they don't have dogs,* he thought. *At least Wright saw me eject.*

More than 5,000 miles away in Skokie, Illinois, Stacy O'Grady stood on a ladder, helping to decorate the gym of the school where she was a teacher. "Ms O'Grady,"

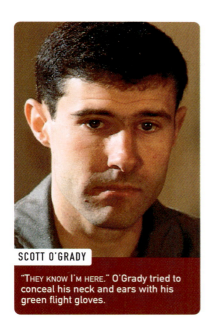

SCOTT O'GRADY

"THEY KNOW I'M HERE." O'Grady tried to conceal his neck and ears with his green flight gloves.

a pupil interrupted, "your mother's on the phone." *Why would Mom be calling?* Stacy wondered. *Scott!* Her mother's call from Seattle confirmed her fears: her brother's plane had been hit; no one knew where Scott was.

Stacy left school immediately and packed a bag to join her father, Dr Bill O'Grady, a radiologist, at his home in Alexandria, Virginia. All she could think of was the time she and her mother had proudly pinned gold lieutenant's insignia on Scott. He had been so happy that day. It capped a youth devoted to adventure: sky diving, gliding, bob-sleighing. Stacy couldn't believe that Scott had not survived.

On board the amphibious-helicopter ship USS *Kearsarge*, 20 miles off the Balkan coast in the northern Adriatic, Colonel Martin Berndt assembled members of the 24th Marine Expeditionary Unit, who were specially trained in combat search and rescue. Intelligence reports now confirmed that the ambush of the two F-16s had been a clever deception. The Bosnian Serbs knew that if the SA-6 mobile missiles had tried to track O'Grady and Wright directly, the cockpit instruments in the F-16s would have detected the radar immediately.

Instead, they had relied on civilian radars across the border in the Serb Republic. The information was processed at an air-defence centre in Belgrade, then transmitted by land-line to three mobile SA-6 missile vehicles in the mountains near Bihac. Only at the last instant did SA-6 operators launch the missiles and then turn on their radar—giving the young pilots virtually no warning.

Berndt tapped the large tactical wall map of northern Bosnia. Normally helicopter rescues were conducted under cover of darkness, with the pilots wearing night-vision goggles. But goggles could not detect the power lines that snaked across the valleys. To avoid SAMs, the rescue team might have to risk flying in daylight, threading their way along valleys, but that would expose them to anti-aircraft guns and shoulder-fired missiles.

Berndt looked at Major Bill Tarbutton, 43, who would command the rescue aircraft, and Lieutenant-Colonel Chris Gunther, also 43, who would lead the rescue team on the ground. "Right now," he told them, "the big questions are: is O'Grady alive and, if so, where is he?"

Rifle fire cracked near Scott O'Grady's hiding-place, and bullets whipped through nearby brush. Instinctively, he thrust his face deeper into the earth. They were shooting to kill. O'Grady prayed, trying to focus all his concentration on the familiar words, *Our Father, who art in heaven . . .* Out of the corner of his eye, he could see shadows six feet away. Weapons rattled against branches as the soldiers made their way through the brush, probing with rifle muzzles. *Holy Mary, Mother of God, pray for us sinners . . .* Soon the rifles cracked from further away.

Finally the sun passed below the western mountains. O'Grady heard the irritating high-pitched whine of gnats and mosquitoes as they hovered about him. But he forced himself to continue lying motionless, his mouth dry from terror and thirst. When darkness fell, he could risk moving. He was determined to reach that plateau away from the road and the town—the best place for pick-up by a rescue helicopter.

For two days the Marines on board the *Kearsarge* had been on one-hour alert—but there was still no word of O'Grady's fate. Bosnian Serb television had shown the wreckage of his plane and announced that he had been captured. Major Tarbutton was sceptical. "If the Serbs had O'Grady," he said, "they'd show him on TV . . ."

O'Grady estimated that he had covered less than a mile in three nights. But he'd worked by the book, moving only at night and finding secure hiding-places well before dawn.

He thought about his survival equipment. In his waistcoat, the evasion map, radio, and smoke and signal flares were vital—so was the Global Positioning

F-16C FIGHTING FALCON

The F-16C fighter was a major participant in Operation Determined Force—the 1995 peace-keeping operations over Bosnia. The plane is renowned for its versatility and reliability.

System (GPS) receiver. This palm-sized set processed signals from navigation satellites, giving him an accurate ground position and providing precise coordinates for rescue forces. A separate survival pack contained a spare radio and batteries, a first-aid kit and more flares. He also had a green foil thermal blanket, camouflage netting and face paint to help conceal him, and plastic bags and a sponge to catch and store rain for drinking water.

So far, hunger hadn't been a problem—but thirst was. That afternoon O'Grady had drunk the last of his eight, four-ounce pouches of water. His evasion map showed the nearest stream was on the other side of Bosanski Petrovac, in the other direction from where he was heading.

Now, as dawn approached, he found another hiding-place and draped his thermal blanket and camouflage net over himself. He then turned on his survival radio and sent a brief coded signal. As sunrise filled the valley, he tried to sleep. *They're not going to capture me,* he vowed.

Television sets were left on round the clock in Bill O'Grady's home. Sitting in the living room, Stacy O'Grady slipped into a shell of emotional numbness, mindlessly flipping through the TV channels, searching in vain for any sign of hope.

Stacy, Scott and their younger brother Paul had all grown up in Spokane in Washington State. From childhood experiences, Stacy knew that beneath his easy smile and soft-spoken charm, Scott O'Grady had a tough core.

Stacy chuckled involuntarily, remembering the day a school bully had cornered her. Scott was smaller and lighter, but he had seized the larger boy with a ferocious grip and glared so fiercely that the bully fled in panic.

It was the afternoon of June 6, four days into his ordeal. Half dozing, O'Grady felt a cow nuzzling between his boots. By now his mouth was almost swollen shut from thirst, his eyes hurt, and his skin was badly wrinkled. He knew his dehydration was severe.

Later that night thunder cracked, followed by a downpour. He opened two plastic bags to catch water, then drank greedily. The night grew colder. He shivered, his soaked flight-suit a chilling weight on his body. Since there was not much chance anyone would be out on a night like this, he'd risk moving faster towards the high ground.

O'Grady reached the plateau before dawn. He found a secure holding point, then set out to locate a landing zone for a rescue helicopter. The only open spot near by was rocky, narrow and sloping, with a crude fence blocking the far end. He read the display on his GPS set and noted his position on the map.

O'Grady hid again when daylight came but managed to sleep only fitfully. Hunger was nagging him. He noticed brown ants moving through the weeds near his elbow. He tried to scoop a handful, but caught only a few. They crunched in his mouth with a lemony tang—not much nourishment, but they moistened his tongue.

After sunset, his thirst returned with a vengeance. O'Grady had finished the rainwater, so he pulled off his wet boots and squeezed a few drops of water from his wool socks into a plastic bag. It was rancid, but drinkable. He dozed off in the hours of early darkness.

He was awakened after midnight on June 8 by heavy anti-aircraft guns firing near by. O'Grady took a compass bearing on the sound. Seconds later he heard a low-flying jet. It had to be a Nato reconnaissance plane looking for him. O'Grady stood cautiously, switched his survival radio to bleeper, and pressed the transmit button. Both the Nato search planes and the Bosnian Serbs would hear the transmission. He had to wait and see who would find him first.

Just after 1.30am on June 8, Captain T. O. Hanford and his wingman, Captain Vaughn Littlejohn, were flying high above the dark mountains. After a report of a "possible bleeper", Hanford was trying to contact O'Grady. For the next 40 minutes he called on the rescue channel. But there was no reply. At 2.07am, with fuel low, Hanford tried O'Grady one last time. "Basher 52, this is Basher 11."

O'Grady's heart raced as he heard Hanford's voice. "Basher 11," he called. "Help!"

Hanford had to verify that the weak voice was O'Grady's. "Basher 52, what was your squadron in Korea?" Hanford asked.

"Juvats," O'Grady replied.

"Copy that," Hanford said, trying to keep his emotions in check. "You're alive. Good to hear your voice." For the next ten minutes Hanford circled as O'Grady used a voice code to reveal his coordinates. Then Hanford told O'Grady he'd be picked up "mañana".

"No," O'Grady replied. "I have to get out tonight."

Hanford reported back to his controllers, then to O'Grady. "You will be rescued, but you have to be prepared to signal in visual range." He added: "If you have an emergency, Basher 52, I will be monitoring this channel."

In Virginia, the phone rang at 12.48am. Another reporter, Bill O'Grady thought, groaning, as he pulled himself awake. It was Scott's wing commander, Colonel Charles Wald. "He's alive. And we're going to get him . . ."

In the pastel dawn, the flight deck of the Kearsarge throbbed with the beat of helicopter rotors. There were four choppers in a trail formation: Super Stallion helicopters Dash One and Dash Two, and two smaller Cobra gunships to guard the flanks. Far above them were two Harrier jets, launched from the Kearsarge. Across the northern Adriatic, Nato warplanes were assembling a protective umbrella for the Marine rescue effort. At 5.43am, they received the command to cross the Balkan coast.

They flew fast and low—no higher than 500 feet—to evade radar. Ahead, the mountains rose in a dark wall, silhouetted by the sunrise. In Dash One, Tarbutton saw that the valleys were choked with ground fog. This would shield them from visual detection, but make navigation tricky.

"Twenty," announced an airborne controller, code-named Magic, in a radar plane far above. They were 20 miles from O'Grady.

"Ten," Magic called. Tarbutton ordered the Cobras to press ahead, positively identify O'Grady and check the landing zone.

Marine Major Scott Mykleby, lead Cobra pilot, flew his gunship towards O'Grady's coordinates.

"I can see you," O'Grady radioed. Then, a moment later, came the excited shout. "You're overhead!"

"Pop smoke," Mykleby directed.

O'Grady's little orange smoke flare was almost lost in the fog. Then Mykleby threw out a yellow smoke grenade, to mark O'Grady's position more clearly.

O'Grady warned Mykleby of the heavy firing he had heard the night before, then pulled on the bright orange cap from his survival kit.

"Buster," Mykleby radioed Tarbutton—code for proceed ahead at maximum speed.

The two Super Stallions slashed across the fog bank and climbed the steep ridge to the clearing—just large enough for them both to land. Marines piled out to form a security perimeter as Mykleby radioed: "Run to the helicopter." O'Grady pounded through the thicket, his boots slipping on the wet rocks.

From Dash Two, Berndt saw movement in the fog to the left. O'Grady's orange hat was bright in the mist. Sergeant Scott Pfister, crew chief on Dash Two, jumped from the hatch to help the exhausted pilot inside.

A Marine wrapped O'Grady in a thermal blanket. His hands were cold, wrinkled claws, his bearded face waxy. "Thank you, thank you," he kept saying.

Tarbutton ordered the formation to move up and out at maximum speed, flying only 50 feet above the rolling hillsides, so fast that obstacles rushed by in a blur. They were coming up to the final mountain range when the cockpit warning instruments gave a sharp bleep.

Tarbutton caught a glimpse of movement to his left and heard Mykleby's warning cry: "SAMs in the air!"

Mykleby saw a chalk-white smoke trail corkscrew towards the helicopters from the left, then glowing orange balls sailed towards them from the right and incandescent red tracers spat up from an automatic anti-aircraft gun on the ground. The pilots threw their aircraft into violent zigzags. Sergeant Scott Pfister returned fire with a short, rattling burst from his machine-gun.

As O'Grady hunched beneath a blanket, warmth slowly seeping into chilled limbs, an assault-rifle bullet pierced Dash Two's tail ramp and ricocheted around the troop bay. Two feet away from O'Grady, Sergeant-Major Angel Castro felt a blow on his side. He pulled out the empty canteen from his hip pouch. The green plastic was deeply gouged by the impact of the bullet.

BACK FROM THE DEAD: O'Grady hugs sister Stacy.

The Cobra pilots wanted to engage the anti-aircraft gun—but if Tarbutton broke the gunships from formation, he would have no protection crossing the coastal towns ahead. They had to hold their course and take fire.

An amber warning light flashed, signalling that one of Tarbutton's main rotor blades had been hit. Then Mykleby radioed that he also had a warning light.

Moments later, they flashed across the coastline, and the *Kearsarge* task force came into view on the horizon. "Mother in sight," Tarbutton informed the team. O'Grady blinked at the dazzling surface of the Adriatic, his face twisted with emotion. Colonel Berndt looked back from his seat in the cockpit, and O'Grady flashed a warm grin . . .

It was just after 1.30am in Alexandria when Bill O'Grady received another call from Colonel Wald. "Scott is on board the *Kearsarge*," Wald said. "He's dehydrated, but otherwise fine." Scott's father rushed to tell Stacy and Paul.

On June 10, Captain Scott O'Grady addressed reporters at Aviano Air Base in Italy. "If it wasn't for God's love for me," he said, "and my love for God, I wouldn't have got through it." But he also reserved special thanks for the "people at the pointy end of the spear"æthe Marines who had risked their lives to save him. "If you want to find heroes," he said, "that's where you should look."

Struck by
lightning

by Ruaridh Pringle

The forecast had been superb, but now, 11,000 feet up, the young climbers were trapped in a terrifying storm.

Perched on the narrow Alpine ledge with my climbing companion Hugo Glover, I realized we were in trouble. In the pouring rain, Hugo was dangling from his rope and harness, waiting to follow the three Japanese mountaineers up ahead of us.

"Are you all right, Hugo?" I had to ask twice. A puzzled look crossed his face. "I think I'm abseiling," he replied.

It was a bizarre answer. "Here, tie in," I said, making a figure of eight in the rope that he would need for the next part of the climb. After he had fumbled with it, something made me check what he had done. He had not tied on properly. "Hugo, you've just duplicated the first knot."

"Always thorough, me," he slurred. I grabbed his shoulders. "Hugo—tell me exactly how you feel." His eyes wandered. "Dunno."

As an outdoor journalist and photographer, and a keen mountaineer, I recognized the classic symptoms of hypothermia. Hugo couldn't feel his hands, feet or legs.

His speech was slow and muddled and he thought he was abseiling—going down the mountain on ropes. His cheeks and legs felt like a corpse's. I reckoned he wasn't far from total unconsciousness.

We were caught in a storm at 11,000 feet in the French Alps, halfway up the almost sheer face of the legendary Bonatti Pillar. The thought crept into my mind: *Will Hugo get off the mountain alive?*

We had met ten days earlier at Les Choselets camp site near Chamonix, a popular rendezvous for British climbers. At 26, I had far more experience than 19-year-old Hugo, but he had done some more difficult climbs. He'd just left University College School in north London, after his A levels, for his first season of Alpine climbing.

Five foot seven inches tall and stockily built, he was indomitably cheerful and a fine climber. We made a good team, and for a week feasted on short but technically difficult forays on the granite spires of the Chamonix range.

But always in the background was the Bonatti Pillar, a magnificent 2,000-foot column, one of the most famous rock-climbs in Europe. After abseiling down to its base, the only way off the Pillar was to climb almost to its peak, then traverse to a treacherous incline known as the Flammes de Pierre, down which one could abseil home on the south face. The ascent had to be fast, which meant travelling light, without much emergency clothing or equipment—the essence of Alpine climbing.

The Pillar forms part of the summit of the Petit Dru in the Drus mountain range which is notorious for electrical storms. We agreed not to go near it without a superb weather forecast.

That came on Saturday, July 20, last year. We left our details with the warden of the Charpoua mountain refuge, and the following evening bivouacked 1,600 feet

CRAMMED ON A LEDGE: **Hugo tries desperately to keep warm.**

above on a three-foot ledge, from where we would make the 800-foot descent to the Pillar's base next morning. The view was breathtaking: row after row of jagged peaks, tinged every shade of pink and red by the setting sun. Hugo was almost in tears: "I can't believe I'm actually up here."

At 4am, we slithered out of sleeping bags, abseiled down and started the climb. But, blocked by a large overhang at 600 feet, we could find no way up the Pillar. We spent an uncomfortable night a third of the way up on a square-topped flake of rock.

We restarted at first light. Soon, we noted another pair of climbers moving with impressive speed to our left. "That has to be the route," I called to Hugo. A diagonal abseil brought us to a ledge. Other features on the route began to make more sense. By midday, we were about halfway up, to be joined by three Japanese climbers: Go, Hiro and Ozaki.

But big cauliflower clouds were boiling up. Mont Blanc wore an ominous cap of cloud; the foothills had become dim shapes. *The forecast must have got it wildly wrong.*

I hoped to be off the Pillar before any storm hit us. As I glanced down, however, a dark shape was swallowing the valley in huge gulps. Thunder boomed in the

STORM RAGE

Petit Dru

Top of the climb

Second bivouac in niche during storm

Bonatti

Bivouac on Flammes de Pierre ridge

First bivouac on the Pillar

Pillar

Abseil to the Pillar's base

Start of the climb

On the sheer face of the Bonatti Pillar, at 11,000 feet high in the French Alps, the young climbers were caught in a ferocious electrical storm. Would they ever get off the mountain alive?

distance. Suddenly the storm was on us. Roped on to the mountainside, Hugo and I were stuck on the same narrow crack. I struggled to pull the bivouac bag over our heads but we were soon soaked.

After an hour and a half, the storm eased. We agreed with the Japanese to continue as a team, using the same ropes. As they climbed on ahead, there were long delays while they fixed and sent down the ropes. *Still about a third of the Pillar to climb.*

It was past 6pm when I noticed Hugo's grey, waxy look and heard his confused murmur: "I think I'm abseiling."

I rubbed his stomach and legs, trying to restore his core temperature. "Hugo, you've got to keep moving." No response. "Hugo, listen. You must warm yourself up. Move your legs." A feeble rocking started. "No, hard, dammit. If you don't warm up, and keep yourself warmed up until we get off this mountain, you will die. Understand?"

The rocking became more vigorous. "Move your arms. Get angry. Punch." I rubbed his torso and thighs until I was breathless. "How do you feel? Any warmer?"

"The numb level's going back up my legs," he replied. I rubbed his legs until I felt faint, then turned back to his body. "How about your core temperature?" I asked. "Can you tell any difference?" A pause. "Cold . . . but better." I began to breathe again. Hugo still felt like ice, but the rain was tailing off. *If I can just keep him going until he dries off.*

At last it was our turn to climb. "I can't do it," Hugo mumbled. "Legs won't work."

"Hugo, get angry," I ordered. "You hate this climb. Give it hell."

With a mighty effort of will, he propelled himself upwards. This was a strenuous and exposed part of the climb, and the last major obstacle before the slightly easier final section. Hugo was now moving well. But I was all too aware how he felt—cold, soaked to the skin and with a 20-pound pack on his back, after two days of scant food and minimal sleep.

A distant boom was followed by others, each one louder than the last. The second storm exploded on us in a chaos of wind, water and noise. No more than 150 feet from the point of descent, we were trapped.

As we clawed our way up on to a shallow ledge, our Japanese friends hustled us into a walled niche under a small overhang. Hugo and I stripped ourselves of metal gear that might attract lightning, while the Japanese erected a nylon bivouac shelter.

We crammed our lower bodies into our sleeping bag and bivouac bag. Sitting at the open end of the tiny cave, I made sure to jam Hugo between myself and Ozaki, to preserve his meagre body heat.

But as the bivouac shelter thrashed wildly in the storm and spray began seeping in, I knew we would soon both be saturated. Hugo could lapse again into hypothermia. With my arm round his shoulders, I tried to rub some warmth into him. "How are you?" I asked.

"I'm not warm, but I'm OK."

The distant crackle of thunder prompted a more pressing concern: if lightning struck, it could jump off the lip of the cave roof to the floor, like a spark plug. Climbers had been electrocuted in caves in exactly that way in the Yosemite peaks in the US.

Suddenly, our world turned white. There was an ear-splitting crack. The air filled with screams, some of them my own. A lightning strike! Then blackness, and distant thunder.

Again, there was an explosion of light and head-numbing noise. I felt a massive electrical charge pass up my legs from the soles of my feet. My right leg felt as though it were being ground in a vice. Pain was slowly fading to numbness when once more we were hammered by dazzling glare and noise.

Impotently, I counted the lightning strikes as the only means of distracting my mind from the cold, pain and terror. After the next strike, the bivouac filled with the stench of burnt plastic and singed hair. *Five.* The electrical charge that whipped through my body was so strong that I passed out with the pain. Slowly, I came to in blackness.

Should we be seeking shelter elsewhere? There wasn't any elsewhere. Out in the open, none of us, least of all Hugo, would survive the exposure. We could receive a direct hit from the lightning. We could be clawed off the mountain by the wind. Here, we were still alive.

Body bent by the cave into an agonizing, near-foetal position, I waited in the darkness. *How much longer can our luck hold out?*

A blinding flash freeze-framed the face of one of our Japanese companions, bloodshot eyes bulging in terror. I writhed in pain; my knees felt as if they were being torn off. *Ten.* There was a smell in our bivouac that I had heard of, yet never experienced: the smell of fear.

Tensely, we all waited. Sometimes there was a ten-minute gap between lightning strikes; sometimes, it was an hour. *Please take this storm away.*

A murky daylight came but the storm raged on. In 12 hours, we'd had 17 lightning strikes.

At 10.30am, there had been no lightning for half an hour. "Let's go for it," I urged. All five of us were ready to climb in a minute flat.

LONG DESCENT: **Ruaridh abseils down the Flammes de Pierre.**

My gloves, soon saturated, made it even more difficult for me to get a grip on the icy rock, and I put them in a pocket. But with bare hands, my circulation stopped. Whenever I tried to warm them, the returning circulation would inflict excruciating pain.

Now it was Hugo's turn to spur me on. "You've got to fight it, Ruaridh. Get angry." My hands puffed up with frost nip, one stage short of frost-bite, I struggled to work the ropes.

At last we were on the shoulder of the mountain from where we could traverse across to the Flammes de Pierre and start our abseil descent. There was a blinding flash as lightning hammered down on us again. Electricity seared up my arms from the rope. Everything went blank. When I recovered, I was still on my feet on the ridge. We were struck twice more on the way down. *Twenty.*

The abseil descent ate up another four hours. By late afternoon Hugo was again shivering violently. At the bottom of the Flammes de Pierre was the bulk of our kit. We'd have liked dry clothes to change into, but all we had there were saturated gloves.

"WE MADE IT." Ruaridh after his ordeal.

We had to keep up the momentum of the descent. While the Japanese hurried on ahead to do the final slopes without ropes, we decided it would be safer for us to continue abseiling. With our judgment skewed by exhaustion, we would be at our most vulnerable. *Another three hours in icy, dripping clothes.* "Not long now," I encouraged Hugo.

Finally off the steepest part of the mountain, we came to a glacier to find that the snowbridge that we had crossed on the way up had collapsed. It meant a half-mile detour over unstable ice and slush.

At last the rock leading to the Charpoua hut was within reach. Hugo turned to me and we shook hands. *We had made it.* "There's not a great deal else that can happen to us now," said Hugo. Ten minutes later, we were being pelted with hail the size of marbles in a storm that followed us over the final 500 yards.

The warden's eyes widened as we shuffled in, astonished that we had made it down on our own, not long after our Japanese friends. Seven other parties were still on the Pillar and the Petit Dru. All were rescued next day. It had been the worst storm on the Chamonix range in 25 years.

Back home in Balerno, a village in the hills outside Edinburgh, my mother greeted me with a smile. "Did you have a nice time, dear?"

Worried about the loss of feeling in my fingers, and aching numbness in my right leg, I went to my doctor. He assured me everything would eventually return to normal. "But to be honest," he added, "I haven't had that many patients struck by lightning—not 20 times."

Neither Hugo nor I have any regrets about our ordeal. Despite some appalling luck, we remained calm, and did most things right. We both learned much about friendship, teamwork and ourselves. But, especially when climbing, I am more than ever aware that every second of life is precious and should be savoured to the full.

Benny's heart

by Lawrence Elliott

After her son's senseless murder, Linda Zweigle knew she could help one dying man. In the end, though, dozens were saved.

Linda Zweigle had two sons and loved both with her whole heart. But Eric was 21 and already his own man, while Benny still came to her beaming a great grin and grabbing her in a big bearhug. The 16-year-old was only an average student at Fresno High in central California, but to Linda, a single mother who worked at a Macy's cosmetics counter, he could do no wrong.

Benny, six-foot-two and still growing, was a standout baseball player who hoped to play pro ball. But lately he'd been caught up in daydreams of having his own car to drive and work on. He loved to tinker with machinery.

Benny's talents were never more apparent than the morning he heard Linda groan, "Oh, no!" Their refrigerator had given up the ghost, and a new one was definitely not in the budget. She left for work disconsolate. Benny, pretending he was going to school, doubled back home. It took him all day to take the refrigerator apart, piece by piece, to doctor the malfunction and then put it back together. But by the time Linda came home, it was purring.

"You fixed it," she gasped. Benny smiled shyly. Then she understood. "You cut school." He nodded.

"Are you mad at me?" he asked. This time it was Linda who grabbed him in a bearhug. Her Benny had golden hands and a good heart. In time he would find himself and settle down.

It was not to be. On Friday, September 17, 1993, Benny left after dark to meet his friends at the neighborhood hangout, the brightly lit lot across from the Zweigles' house.

At a little before 9.30pm a Cadillac rolled by the lot and taunts were exchanged. Twenty minutes later the Cadillac returned, this time with the front-seat passenger leveling a gun and firing four shots from the open window. Benny was hit behind the right ear and fell like a stone, facedown.

GOLDEN HANDS AND A GOOD HEART: **Benny and Linda.**

His brother, Eric, ran into the street at the sound of the shots. He saw boys scattering. Someone shouted, "They shot Benny!"

Eric fell to his knees by the crumpled body, saw the gathering pool of blood by his brother's head, heard his brother's insubstantial breathing.

"Somebody call 911!" he begged as he ran to get his mother, and then raced back to take Benny's hand. "You're gonna be OK, bro," he said over and over. But Linda took one look and knew otherwise.

When she next saw her boy, he was in an intensive care unit, attached to a welter of tubes and monitors. He seemed to be asleep. But a doctor showed Linda the brain scan and explained that the bullet had spun around inside Benny's head; his brain looked like shattered glass. It was dead, the doctor said, and without artificial life support, his heart and lungs would fail too. What did she want to do? Nothing, she said. She wanted her son back.

Hours passed. Night turned into gray dawn as Linda tried to come to terms with her loss. Her Benny would never become a man, would never realize the potential of his God-given gifts. She had never felt such an agonizing hurt of body and soul. She thought, *How can a mother recover from such a loss?*

Someone asked her to meet with counselors from the California Transplant Donor Network. They tried to console her, explaining that through her, Benny could give life and sight to others by donating his healthy organs. Scarcely understanding, she turned away, wondering what good cutting into her Benny would do.

Yet, unaccountably, she said yes. Was it to keep Benny's spirit alive? Or to give a young boy like Benny the chance to realize his potential? She didn't know, but gave permission for Benny's corneas, pancreas, liver, kidneys, lungs, bone marrow and heart to be removed, recognizing that they would go to people she was never to know.

At 4.45pm the coroner pronounced Benjamin Anthony Zweigle dead. Linda went home thinking that a heart must somehow be connected to a soul. In the long nights to come, she often wondered who had gotten her Benny's soul.

The following morning, near the town of Modesto 90 miles away, 60-year-old Lyle Baade woke thankful for one more day on earth. He'd suffered three major heart attacks and had twice had open-heart surgery. He lived with almost constant chest pain and could no longer help out on the family walnut farm. His only hope was a heart transplant.

He went on the list for a compatible heart at Stanford University Medical Center. Some on the list were lucky, but Lyle came to know others who had died waiting. He himself had been called twice, only to be bitterly disappointed.

One time, already prepped for surgery, he was told that the donor heart was bruised and unusable. Then, just a week ago, when he and his wife, Beverly, had taken a drive to the ocean, the pager linking him to Stanford, which he wore even to bed, had somehow failed to beep. By the time he heard the urgent messages on his telephone answering machine—"We have a heart for you! Please get back to us!"—it was too late.

But that Sunday, September 19, as he and Beverly left for church, the pager beeped with word that there was a heart for him. At the hospital, there was barely time for Beverly's hurried kiss before Lyle was whisked away to surgery, where his enlarged, overworked heart was removed and the healthy, fist-size donor heart was sutured to his aorta and pulmonary artery. It needed no jump-start; it began beating at once.

As soon as Lyle was fully awake, he realized that he was a different man. He asked for a stethoscope and listened to the firm thump-thump-thump of the new heart, so unlike the faltering, squishy sound his poor sick one had made. Once home he walked so briskly that Beverly had to run to keep up. He raked leaves. He went back to his hobbies of camping and building furniture.

Lyle knew almost from the start whose heart had saved his life. Given his medical file to take to his doctor in Modesto, he saw that the donor was a 16-year-old from Fresno who had died of a gunshot wound. A check of the newspapers, which turned up Benny Zweigle's obituary, told the rest of the story.

Because donor information is supposed to be kept confidential, Lyle did not contact Linda Zweigle directly. But he did send her an unsigned message through the donor network expressing his everlasting gratitude.

There was little for Linda Zweigle to be thankful for after Benny's murder. She did everything she had to do—went to work, cleaned house, prepared meals—but it was as though she were someone else. The real Linda Zweigle was constantly waiting to hear the door bang open and the sound of her Benny shouting, "Hey, Mom, I'm home!"

Then came the anonymous letter. It was from the man who had gotten Benny's heart; he wanted to thank her. Linda was shaken by the news. A 60-year-old man. Why had they given Benny's heart to someone whose life was nearly over? Her hope that the heart had gone to a boy or girl with a whole life to live—the life that had been stolen from Benny—was shattered.

Even the arrest and conviction of the teenage boys responsible for Benny's death brought little peace to her. Tried as juveniles, they would be freed to start new lives when they turned 25, while Benny slept on in his grave.

Meanwhile, Lyle and Beverly Baade had moved to the retirement community of Ventana Lakes near Phoenix, where they were leading happy, active lives. On the afternoon of April 19, 2000, they were in a meeting of the residents that kept droning on. Lyle had to get to a 2.45 appointment for his annual check-up, so he and Beverly quietly rose from their seats.

But as they walked to the exit, a huge bearded man stopped them. It was Richard Glassel, a local crank who'd had run-ins with his neighbors. "Go back and sit down," he growled, shoving Lyle hard.

Stunned, Lyle looked down to see that the man was holding a pistol. He drew Beverly behind him, and watched as Glassel moved away from them.

"He's got a gun!" Lyle yelled.

"I'm going to kill you all!" Glassel called out as he began firing.

Lyle pulled Beverly behind a partition as he saw friends

VENTANA LAKES: the Baade's new home.

topple from their chairs and heard the cries of the wounded. People dropped to the floor, desperately scrabbling for shelter.

Suddenly the gunfire stopped. Glassel laid down the pistol and raised an assault rifle. *He really is going to kill us all,* Lyle thought. Then it was as though he were hearing a voice from outside himself, and it was saying, *You can take this guy. You can get there before he turns that rifle on you. Do it!*

Lyle came flying out of a crouch as if he were still the teenage linebacker of his high school football team, and launched into a flying tackle that brought the 300-pound Glassel down in a heap. But the gunman fought back in a rage, clawing at Lyle with one hand and scrambling for the rifle with the other.

Glassel got his finger on the rifle trigger and pulled. In the echo of its roar, a victim cried out. But then Lyle slammed the rifle to the floor and pinned it. The burly gunman writhed and heaved, but Lyle managed to hold Glassel to the ground until others wrestled the rifle away, pinned down his wrists and tied his ankles.

When the police arrived, they found that Glassel had enough ammunition to kill everyone in the community center three times over. As it was, two residents were dead and three wounded. Those who survived were saved only because of Lyle.

LIFESAVER: "You can take this guy," thought Lyle Baade as he faced the gunman.

His hand had been clawed bloody by the frenzied gunman, but Benny's heart beat steadily.

Lyle's daughter, Tammi Bowman, moved by the outpouring of gratitude from people he had saved or their loved ones, decided it was time Benny Zweigle's mother knew who had gotten her son's heart. She leaked the story to Kimi Yoshino, a Fresno *Bee* reporter.

At first Linda didn't want to hear it. "Anything you tell me is just going to make me cry," she told Yoshino. But then it sank in: the old grandfather who was walking around with her Benny's heart had saved 41 people from violent death.

For Linda, that changed everything. It was as though she had been freed of a great weight. She read the newspaper story again and again, always with tears in her eyes. But now they were tears of pride and joy. Benny's organs had saved many lives. But it was his heart that had rescued even more, and spared their families the grief she'd borne these seven years.

And at that moment, Benny's death, which had haunted her as senseless and useless, seemed to have meaning. She would never stop missing him, but her loss became somehow bearable. She believes it was Benny's voice Lyle heard that day, and in her heart, she now knows what happened to Benny's soul.

Two of our engines are missing!

by John Dyson

Spewing a cloud of flaming fuel, the cargo jet hurtled toward the runway, too heavy and too fast.

With a thunder of jet engines, the Boeing 707 lumbered down the runway of Luxembourg Airport. *She's heavy again*, Captain Ingemar Berglund thought. He knew from the loadsheet that their cargo—40 tons of oil-drilling equipment—was the maximum allowed. At last, the air-speed indicator reached 155 knots and Berglund pulled back on the controls. With just yards to spare, the jet lifted off into a cold March morning.

An hour later the plane was struggling upwards through choppy weather in thick clouds over the Alps. Berglund and his four crew clenched their rumbling stomachs. Any second now the plane would break out into smooth air and sunshine at 32,000 feet.

At last I'll get some coffee, Berglund thought.

They would land in the steam heat of Nigeria to unload their cargo, hop to Ghana to load fresh fruit, then fly back to Europe. Pilots called it the pineapple run. Berglund anticipated a peaceful, six-hour cruise over the Mediterranean Sea and Sahara Desert.

But deadly hairline cracks were creeping through a vital component of the jet.

In 28 years of service the plane—registered in Nigeria as 5N-MAS—had made almost 18,000 flights. With every new take-off and landing, the metal fitting attaching its No. 3 engine to the wing came closer to disintegration.

A sharp-eyed engineer who removed the Pratt and Whitney engine and went over the mounting with a microscope might have detected the tell-tale signs of metal fatigue. But safety inspectors were not required to go so far.

Slimly built with hawkish features and a salt-and-pepper beard, Berglund at 57 was a veteran of this no-frills cargo trade. The former fighter pilot in the Swedish Air Force enjoyed roving the globe as a freelance pilot, even though it meant leaving his vivacious Greek wife Maria home in Utrecht.

When this contract came up two weeks before, the quality of his crew had been Berglund's biggest worry. Too often he'd flown with cowboy pilots with counterfeit licenses. But the men with him that day were true professionals.

British co-pilot Martin Emery, almost too tall for his cramped right-hand seat, had flown gliders as a schoolboy and had a pilot's license before he could drive a car. The 44-year-old bachelor had flown everything from stunt planes at air shows to airline DC-10s.

Sitting behind them, monitoring the engine control panel, was flight engineer Terry Boone, 55, also British. He had spent a good deal of his career in Boeing 707s.

The other crewmen were belted into jumpseats. Ike Nawabadike, 36, from Nigeria, serviced the engines on the ground. Ingvar Einarsson, 27, from Iceland, was financing his own pilot training on 707s by looking after the cargo.

MIDAIR CRISIS

Emery looked out of his side window to check the engines. He saw only a gaping hole rimmed by torn metal and bare wires. "Number four engine has left the wing!" he said. Seconds later he looked again: "Number three has gone too!" he shouted.

"OK, Ingvar," Berglund said as they saw the sun through the clouds, "let's put some coffee on."

"Sure." Einarsson unclipped his seatbelt and stood up. But as he reached the galley, a violent down draught slammed the plane. It dropped like a car going over a cliff.

Einarsson's feet left the floor, and the others were thrown upwards into their seatbelts. The pilots felt a terrific jolt, as if the plane had hit something. In a blink, the 150-ton jet flicked on its side.

Quick as a cat, Berglund snatched the controls as warning horns and bells exploded in the cockpit, red lights flashed and instruments went haywire, signalling the failure of just about every system.

The captain's glance snapped to the standby instruments in front of him. The altimeter needle whirled like the hands of a runaway clock, confirming his worst fears. The plane was plunging sideways—down towards the snowy mountains wrapped in clouds far below.

His fighter-pilot instincts taking over, Berglund threw the controls hard left and booted the rudder the same way.

Then he swiftly cut back the remaining engines so the plane didn't roll on its back. His mind raced with questions. *Was it a mid-air hit—have we clipped a plane and lost a wing?* At this sink-rate, they had only minutes before impact. Amid the noise, Boone and Emery raced through the fire drills.

Emery looked out of his side window to check the engines. He saw only a gaping hole rimmed by torn metal and bare wires. "Number four engine has left the wing!" he reported.

Not too terrible, Berglund thought. The relative weakness of engine mounts was in fact a designed-in safety feature to allow an engine to break away in the event of a crash landing.

Twisting further round in his seat, Emery looked again. Instead of the inner engine, there was another gaping hole. "Number three has gone too!" he shouted.

"No way, Martin!" Boone scoffed. The crew were stunned.

Berglund wrestled the plane out of the death dive, while Boone struggled to restore electric power and other systems. The plane could turn left, but to turn right might be fatal. Berglund had to rely on brute force to keep the plane level. It was like manoeuvring an 18-wheel truck without power-steering.

Scared and desperate, the men aboard 5N-MAS became aware of a weird whistle cutting through the clamour in the cockpit—the wind screaming through the mangled metal on the wing. None doubted it was their death knell.

Berglund's arm and leg muscles quivered with the strain of fighting the controls, but his brain was calm. *It's the end of us*, he thought, *but we'll go down fighting*.

INGEMAR BERGLUND

"It's the end of us **but we'll go down fighting," thought Captain Ingemar Berglund as he fought the controls.**

The heavy jolt in the air had caused the faulty mounting lug on engine No. 3 to disintegrate. The engine had spun sideways, smashing into No. 4 and knocking it off the wing. Both engines landed in dense forest below.

Emery radioed air traffic control. "Mayday! Mayday! Request landing immediate!" He had to shout over the din of the alarms.

"We need emergency landing, both engines missing, right wing," Emery reported.

"Roger, turn left heading south."

As Berglund gingerly wrestled the aircraft through a left turn, Emery took a disposable camera from his flight case and snapped a picture of the damage. "If they find the film in the wreckage at least they'll know what happened," he told Berglund.

Impressed by Emery's cool, the captain nodded. He realized that Emery, too, didn't expect to survive. Like a shared secret, this knowledge strengthened the calmness from which he drew strength. *I can do this, I'm really not afraid*, Berglund told himself with surprise. He began to weigh their options. Where should they make for?

Geneva lay behind them but was socked-in by bad weather and surrounded by mountains. *No thanks*. Lyon, not far away, was one of the few airports Berglund had never seen and weather was bad there, too. *Not good*.

"OK, it has to be Marseille," Berglund decided. But it filled him with foreboding.

Berglund had flown into the Marseille airport many times and now visualized the setting. He'd have to come in from the north—too fast and too heavy and with a tail wind. The plane was likely to veer off the runway, hitting other planes or even the passenger terminal. Yet Berglund knew the runway jutted into a shallow lagoon. *If things look bad, I'll skim down on the water—if we get that far*.

Einarsson had crawled to the back of the plane and put his eye to the small window. He reported fuel spraying from a ruptured pipe, but no flames.

The captain gave the go-ahead for dumping fuel to lighten the plane.

Boone flicked the switches to open the dump-valves under each wing. Torrents of jet-fuel streamed out of the plane, merging with the fuel leaking from the ruptured tank connections, and vaporizing into a highly explosive cloud trailing the plane.

Ten minutes after losing its engines, the 707 was down to 17,000 feet and descending fast while making a big curve over the farms and vineyards of Avignon.

"Two engines missing. Request straight-in landing!" Emery reported to the Marseille region air traffic control.

"Roger."

"Request weather," Emery radioed, the shorthand for a complete weather report.

"Roger."

But the requests went unheeded. With mounting anger, Emery repeated, "Two engines missing" and then called "Mayday" six times.

"Roger," the Marseille controller replied. But Berglund and Emery could tell from his indifferent tone that he did not understand. Their explanations were falling on deaf ears and they suspected the reason.

In aviation jargon to "lose" an engine means it has stopped operating, a dangerous but controllable situation. An aircraft can still fly even after "losing" two engines. Though English was the official language of aviation world-wide, these controllers didn't comprehend the one-in-a-million situation of engines that actually drop off.

Suddenly the grey murk veiling the windshield whipped away. A scrap of coast near Marseille was in sight, with a layer of flat cloud blanketing the countryside 12,000 feet directly below.

Nawabadike slotted the red emergency handle into a hole in the floor, and cranked down the landing gear. The wheels created extra drag,

MARTIN EMERY

"REQUEST STRAIGHT-IN LANDING!" co-pilot Martin Emery told Marseille air traffic control.

making the plane even harder to control as Berglund banked to line up with the runway now 20 miles ahead. *We're going to make it!*

But a quick glance at the altimeter needle chilled his hopes. They were down to 7000 feet. At the rate they were dropping, the plane would crash before it reached the airfield.

Just then, through a gap in the cloud, Emery spotted an empty runway. It was

ON SOLID GROUND: the 707's charred right wing reveals the full extent of the damage.

the French Air Force base at Istres. He clicked his radio button. "We have an airfield ahead. Can we land there?"

The voice of controller Jean-Philippe Simonnet came on the radio. "It's OK for landing."

"Yeah!" Berglund exclaimed and started a wide turn to reach the runway.

The increased turbulence caused by the turn made the bare electric wires flail more wildly in the rich fuel-air mixture spraying out of the damaged wing. Two wires touched. A spark flashed and the volatile vapor ignited, turning the 707 into a flying blowtorch, trailing a tongue of roaring super-hot flame.

In the cockpit, Berglund was struggling with the controls. He needed to turn left but even with the controls hard over, the plane wanted to go to the right. *Something bad is happening*, he thought.

"Go left, go left!" Emery shouted.

"She won't come round!" Berglund panted, unable to keep it straight. The controls were now so heavy that with every correction he groaned aloud with effort.

The last bit of control available was the thrust of the two engines on the left wing. Berglund figured that by changing the revs, he could steer the plane like a twin-engine powerboat using only engines to maneuver.

The plane at last obeyed, but with less power, it sank even faster.

Never mind the runway, Berglund decided. *I'll crash-land her anywhere on the airfield if we get that far*.

The 707 dropped out of the cloud two miles out, 1100 feet above the ground but it was not lined up with the runway.

"Trust me, Captain!" Emery yelled, reaching for the throttles.

"OK, but keep some power on!"

Emery throttled back No. 1 engine by two-thirds and No. 2 by one-third. The plane swung to the left.

Berglund shoved the throttles forward again. The runway filled the windscreen dead ahead.

Unknown to the crew, jet fuel was leaking out of the cracks in a fuel tank in the burning wing. As the tank exploded, a fireball erupted from the wing.

In the control tower at Istres, Simonnet watched the 707 approach—now with a streaming tail of fire. *It's not going to make it.* He telephoned the base firemen to prepare for the crash.

Berglund saw the runway rushing up to meet him at 245mph—100mph faster than normal. *Too fast! Too fast!* He pulled the nose up and the 707's main landing gear touched down right on the white-painted numbers, rocketing along the runway as fast as a high-speed train. Berglund cut the power, then jabbed at the rudder pedals with his feet to brake the burning jet. There was no response. "Terry, I've lost the brakes!"

"Hit the air!" Boone yelled.

Berglund triggered the emergency pneumatic brakes. *If the tires burst, it will slow us down*, Berglund thought. But only the left side blew out.

Half the runway was already gone. Boone shoved the throttle of No. 2 engine into full reverse.

Shuddering and roaring, the jet slowed, then swung off the runway. Just 30 feet from a notice at the edge of the airfield—"Do Not Pass Here"—the 707 lurched to a halt. As fire tenders doused the flames with foam, a jeep sped over and skidded to a stop. Out of it jumped an officer who unzipped his bulging leather jacket to produce a bottle and glasses.

"Congratulations, Captain," he greeted Berglund.

After the landing of 5N-MAS, a full investigation took place and 707s throughout the world were inspected and many similar cracks in the engine fittings were found. Replacement parts were installed, and the planes were once again certified fit to fly.

Swamped in the

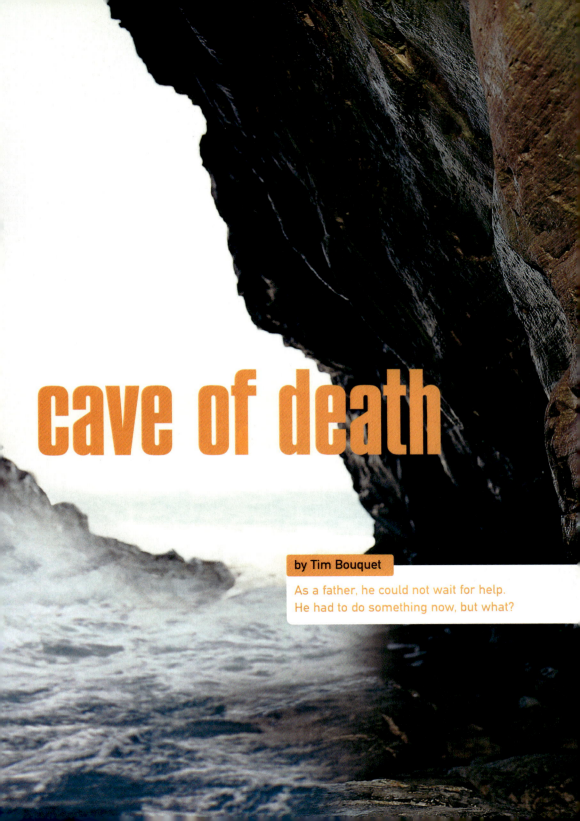

cave of death

by Tim Bouquet

As a father, he could not wait for help.
He had to do something now, but what?

"'m off to the beach," announced 11-year-old James Leeds, coming into the dining-room of the family's Cornish hotel, Willapark Manor. Nick Leeds looked up from serving wine to the 38 guests tucking into Sunday lunch and smiled at the small sparkle-eyed, black-haired boy.

"Have a good time," he replied. He had no qualms. James was mature for his age and always told his parents where he was going.

Nick glanced beyond the dining-room windows at the Atlantic rollers slicking up the popular surfing beach of Bossiney Cove, 200 yards away. He never tired of this evocative smugglers' coast of gentle coves cradled in high black slate cliffs. A mile north was Tintagel Castle, legendary birthplace of King Arthur, whose golden round table was said to lie deep under the mound of Bossiney Castle, just across the fields from the hotel.

A quietly spoken yet sociable man, Nick had bought the neglected turn-of-the-century cliff-top villa in 1982 and had worked hard to transform it into a 14-bedroom hotel, with the help of his attractive, fair-haired wife Liz.

Today, September 6, 1998, she was busy in the kitchen while Nick and their 23-year-old daughter Kate worked in the restaurant. Nick, a tennis nut, was looking forward to a quiet afternoon watching Tim Henman on television.

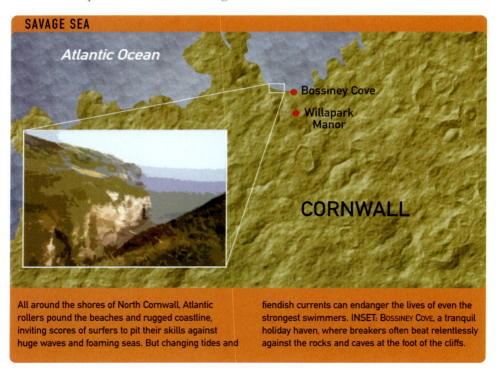

SAVAGE SEA

Atlantic Ocean

Bossiney Cove

Willapark Manor

CORNWALL

All around the shores of North Cornwall, Atlantic rollers pound the beaches and rugged coastline, inviting scores of surfers to pit their skills against huge waves and foaming seas. But changing tides and fiendish currents can endanger the lives of even the strongest swimmers. INSET: BOSSINEY COVE, a tranquil holiday haven, where breakers often beat relentlessly against the rocks and caves at the foot of the cliffs.

It was 4.45pm when Nick heard his wife screaming. He rushed into the hall. In front of Liz stood James's friend Christopher Hill in wet trunks, sobbing: "James has been swept out. I think he's hurt."

At the beach, the waves had started coming in much bigger and faster than usual. The two boys had climbed on to a 20-foot-high rock, but one wave which dwarfed all the others had engulfed them.

James's legs had been swiped from under him and the retreating wave had sucked him into the Atlantic.

James! James! echoed round Nick's head as he raced out of the hotel, still in the crisp white shirt, bow tie and waistcoat he wore for waiting at table.

He loved all their seven children equally, but he had a special bond with his youngest son. They shared a love of the sea and often played guitar together.

FATHER AND SON: **Nick and James Leeds.**

Nick cursed his leather soles as he careered clumsily in Christopher's tracks across 100 yards of damp grass to the cliff edge. The sea was pounding into the cove 180 feet below. A swarming sickness tugged at his stomach.

He sprinted down the twisting cliff path, in places no more than a slippery gully. In five minutes he was on the rock from which James had been swept.

It was next to a cave, 40 feet high and 25 feet wide, which disappeared 80 feet into the cliff like a damp black railway tunnel.

Nick stripped to his underpants, desperately scanning the huge waves and the gaps between for a glimpse of his son's dark head bobbing above frothing blue. Nothing.

As a father he could not wait for help. He had to do something.

"Throw me that float," he yelled to Christopher, gesturing at a buoyancy aid attached by a rope to a steel post.
Although Nick was only of average build, his passion for playing tennis had kept him fitter than most 52-year-olds. Even in these terrifying conditions, he might stand a chance. Clutching on to the buoyancy aid, Nick jumped.

Like his son he was a good swimmer, but he found himself being hurled around. Suddenly he could not move his legs. The buoyancy-aid rope was tangled round his ankles. Kicking and struggling, he managed to free himself.

Wave after wave dumped down on his head. His strength began to fail, but he could not give up on his son. James might have been washed into the cave.

If only he could get in there too, he could at least comfort the boy. *I just can't bear the thought of him alone and frightened.*

Three times the sea swept Nick towards the cave. Three times he lunged at the rocks, but it was worse than gripping wet soap. Swept out again, choking and gasping, he surfaced long enough to yell: "Please God! Help me!"

After calling the emergency services at Port Isaac, Liz scrambled down to the beach. She saw James's clothes and changing bag thrashing around in the angry water. On the rock she spotted her husband's watch and a single shoe.

She was a strong and optimistic woman, but at that moment her spirit deserted her.

Then she felt two arms go round her. It was Kate. The two women hugged each other and cried.

Suddenly a wave hurled Nick into the depths of the cave. On the right, a great shoulder of smooth rock extended its entire length. He threw out his arms, grabbing anything that would stop him being sucked back out.

At last! A handhold. He was more than halfway inside, where the rock narrowed to a twisted floor-to-ceiling slash, dividing the front of the cave from another chamber behind it.

Up to his shoulders in water, Nick gulped air. *What next?* he wondered.

Then he heard a voice high above: "Dad? I love you, Dad."

Nick peered into the darkness. "Round this way!" James yelled down from the roof of the cave.

He had climbed into a narrow crevice 20 feet above his father, where he was clinging on by his fingertips.

Clambering up a 60-degree face of ice-smooth slate was not easy, but eventually Nick managed to manoeuvre himself into the small space behind James.

He reached out and put his arm across the boy's back to reassure and protect him.

It was the most wonderful moment of Nick's life. "I love you too," he said. "I really thought I'd lost you."

At 5.16pm, more than half an hour after James Leeds had been washed into the sea, local coastguard Ken Richards joined Liz on the rock.

"They must be in the cave," Liz told him, praying for it to be true.

"We'll do everything to get them out," Richards reassured her.

Two helicopters and two lifeboats were already on their way. On top of the cliff, three coastguard teams were setting up ropes and lights, and getting ready to be lowered down the cliff.

The Atlantic had the same kind of heavy groundswell that had claimed the lives of two surfers just along the coast three years before. Even worse, 300 yards out was a series of sandbars. Every time 12- to 15-foot waves hit one of these, they gained an extra 15 feet in height. The biggest were coming in at intervals of six minutes. And those waves were going to get a whole load bigger before high water at 6.20pm.

"James, it's a helicopter!" Nick's spirits soared. "They've come to get us."

Squeezed into the narrow gap behind his son, Nick kept his darkest fear from James: *If the cave fills completely, we'll drown before anybody can save us.*

The water was only eight feet below—and rising fast.

Nick realized that the throb of engines was coming from directly above their heads.

He looked up and saw a sliver of daylight coming down a shaft the size of a tiny chimney. If he could just push James into it, at least his son might be safe, however high the tide rose.

But the shaft was blocked by a yellow buoy. Nick stretched up and pushed at it. It would not move. He punched at it, hoping to work it loose, but the sea had jammed it there with such force that it was stuck fast.

Then his ears popped. The air pressure in the cave had changed. He heard a rumbling to his right. Turning his head, he saw a big wave rushing down the cave. It was going to swamp them. "Breathe in," he shouted to James, flexing his muscles so his body filled the crevice to shield his son.

The water thudded into him, a solid, unforgiving mass. The noise was deafening.

Suddenly he was tumbling in the backwash. Winded and weightless in a helter-skelter of white water, Nick's helpless body cannoned into rock.

Clambering back up to his son, he saw the Port Isaac inshore lifeboat just outside the mouth of the cave.

"We're here, we're here!" Nick shouted, waving frantically. Then he saw huge waves powering in behind it. One swept two of the crew overboard, dashing any hope of rescue for father and son. The backwash flushed the battered lifeboat out of the cave as the remaining crewman tried frantically to restart the engine.

Nick was desperate. It was getting dark and the other two lifeboatmen were stranded somewhere in the cave, out of sight.

From outside, a beam of light played crazy patterns on the rock. *Another rescue boat?* But Nick knew that the waves were now too high for anybody to get into the cave. "If we can hang on until the tide turns," he told James, "we'll get out." *But when would that be?*

Still on the cliff path, Liz Leeds saw one of the coastguard team dangling on his ropes just beneath the cave's upper lip. When she saw him gesturing at the coastguard, pointing his thumb down and shaking his head, she shuddered.

"Ma'am! Ma'am!" Ken Richards shouted at her. "You must go up top for your own safety."

Unaware that the thumb-down gesture meant simply that getting into the cave was impossible, she turned and walked away—certain she would never see her husband and son again.

Nick smelt fumes. The surging tide had smashed the wrecked lifeboat back into the cave, and leaking fuel was vaporizing in the incessant spray, making it hard to breathe.

Huge waves knocked him off his perch and tossed him into a frantic whirlpool of rocks and driftwood, which crashed into his head. A layer of skin was grated from his back, buttocks and shoulders, but he was so cold he felt no pain. Each time he managed to scrabble back up to James.

"We're not going to get out of here are we, Dad?"

"Yes, we are," Nick gasped. "Just hang in there and don't let go."

Again Nick was thrown down. When he tried to climb out, his left arm no longer worked. His shoulder joint had been crushed like a ping-pong ball and his strength was spent.

"James!" he shouted up. "You'll have to make it on your own."

Terrified, James yelled for all his worth into the blackness: "My dad's dying! My dad's dying!"

Suddenly, above the noise of the surf, he heard a shout: "Don't give up! Help's coming." It was lifeboatman Mike Edkins who, along with fellow crew member Kevin Dingle, was squeezed in a tiny hole nearer the mouth of the cave.

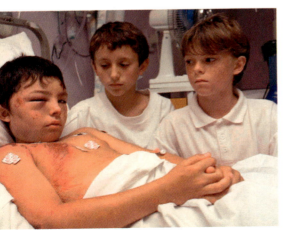

ORDEAL OVER: **James recovers in hospital.**

Nick had barely clawed his way, one-handed, back up to his son when another huge wave flushed them both right into the rear chamber of the cave.

James fractured his skull in the fall. But although his head was badly bruised and swelling, he was still in better shape than his father, who was shaking and exhausted, his useless left arm dangling limply at his side.

All at once James realized that their survival depended on him.

He heard the voice shouting again. "Keep him warm. Don't let him go to sleep."

For the next hour James stayed as close as he possibly could to his gallant father.

To stave off hypothermia and keep Nick awake, James kept on talking, saying anything that came into his head. If Nick lost consciousness he would die.

"We're going to make it, Dad," he urged through chattering teeth, searching all the time with salt-stung eyes for any sign that the tide was losing its terrible rage.

Again he saw light bobbing into the cave from outside. James could not let his father slip away now. His innate good sense overcoming his small boy's fear, he cajoled, bullied, coaxed: "Wake up, Dad. C'mon. Don't go to sleep!"

HAPPY FAMILY: **James with Nick and Liz.**

It was 8.50pm. Although the tide had turned more than two hours before, the surf in the cave had been too lethal for a search attempt.

Now, out of the gloomy depths of the cave, emerged the trapped lifeboatmen Mike Edkins and Kevin Dingle, helped by two coastguards.

Moments later two figures, one much smaller than the other, crawled out into the eerie glare of the searchlights.

After nearly five hours in the water, Nick and James Leeds clung tightly to each other for warmth and for strength. Both knew there could be no greater thing that a father could do for his son or a son for his father than to save the other's life.

Nick and James were transported to the North Devon Hospital, Barnstaple, by an RAF helicopter which had earlier plucked the third Port Isaac lifeboatman safely from the sea.

In March 1999 both father and son received British Gold Hero awards from the Association of Retired and Persons Over Fifty.

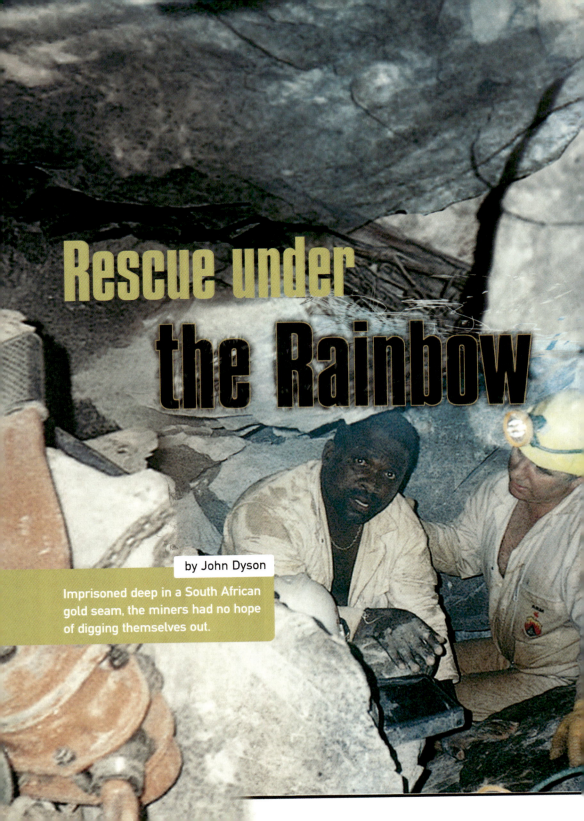

Rescue under the Rainbow

by John Dyson

Imprisoned deep in a South African gold seam, the miners had no hope of digging themselves out.

n the boardroom of African Rainbow Minerals, the gold mine's managers were discussing production targets when the windows rattled. The sudden jolt felt as if the world had run over a pothole.

Instinctively, the managers glanced at their watches. It was 1.17pm on Monday, January 10, 2000, an ominous time because the 1800 men on the day shift were still underground.

The shock wave shivered the desk of engineer Dirk Venter in charge of the mine's two volunteer rescue teams. In the office next door computers monitored seismic activity. "It's two point nine on the Richter scale," the mine's seismologist said. Venter took off.

The gold mines of South Africa—the deepest in the world and among the most dangerous—are frequently hit by localised earthquakes known as "bumps". The Rainbow mine at Orkney, 100 miles southwest of Johannesburg, "bumped" five or six times a month.

Arriving at the head of the main shaft, Venter was told that 15 men were trapped by a giant rockfall. He led his team of 11 into a huge cage-like lift. In two minutes they dropped more than a mile.

At this depth, the rocks were warm to the touch; the air, even after fans blew it through sprays of chilled water, was jungle-hot. In hard hats and with heavy lamp batteries on their belts, the team jogged towards the rockfall, snatching up ropes, telescopic ladders, hammers, crowbars, explosives and stretchers on the way.

They reached a crowd of miners shovelling away an avalanche of debris that was spilling out of a steeply sloping tunnel. This led up to another tunnel, called a "centre gully", where the 15 miners were trapped. "It looks bad," Venter reported to the emergency-control room.

1.23pm Monday

Flat on his back, team leader Julias Lefielo was bruised and stunned—and surprised to be alive. In one terrifying instant, the world had seemed to implode, the roof falling, the walls bursting inwards, the floor kicking up. Fallen rock slabs filled nearly every space.

"Help me! I'm over here!" Amid blinding, choking dust, Lefielo heard his work-mates' cries. Searching through the rubble, he found Mothesi Maema lying face down, struggling under the rocks that pinned his back and legs. Lefielo pulled him out, then sized up the situation.

Two men were dead; three more were alive but hopelessly pinned by slabs. A sixth, whose leg was broken, refused to move. The survivors huddled in shock.

Lefielo knew that inaction would kill them as surely as falling rocks. "We've got to find a way out," he said. Crawling along the partially collapsed gully, they reached a vertical shaft where the ore was channelled into railway wagons 100 feet below.

Using an orange plastic hosepipe, the men made a harness for Pheko Mosola, the smallest of the group. They lowered him down the shaft, but after 30 feet, his boots touched rocks.

"It's blocked, and I can't hear anything," he called. The crew hauled him up.

"Turn off your lamps—we'll use one at a time," Lefielo said. Their batteries were getting almost as low as their water bottles.

6pm Monday

The dramatic rescue effort was already headline news throughout South Africa, and a crowd of reporters had rushed to the site. But Larry Biggs, a tough veteran with 20 years' experience of mine rescues, paid no attention to the hubbub as he led the second rescue team to the lift.

When he reached the scene, Biggs took one look at the big rocks blocking the tunnel. "We have to blast," he said. It was risky, but there was no other way.

His team placed explosives on rocks jammed in their pathway then, taking cover around the corner, they detonated the charge electrically. Usually they waited 30 minutes for fumes and dust to clear. Now it was barely as many seconds before they returned to kick rubble down the slope and lay the next charge.

Biggs knew how it felt to be trapped—it had happened to him as a young miner. "You wait for death and ask for forgiveness over and over," he told his men. Though he'd been freed from his own ordeal after four hours, the memory of his terror spurred him on.

They worked through the night, cooling themselves in 35 degrees C (95 F) heat by draining one energy drink after another. Some men wore special coats with slabs of ice in the pockets. All of them hoped there wouldn't be another "bump".

1am Tuesday

Twelve hours after the mine collapse, more than 80 tons of rubble had been carted away, but more rocks kept breaking loose.

"*Pas op!*" someone shouted. "Look out!" Biggs heard the warning and sprang for the side-wall as a rock as big as a desk thundered past him. In such a mess of fallen rock the odds of survival were remote. *Nobody can be left alive,* Biggs thought. But his team laboured on until relieved by Venter. Then they staggered up to the surface for a few hours' rest.

7pm Tuesday

For hours, Lefielo's men had worked their way forward, forming a chain and passing stones hand to hand. Now, short of water, they were too tired and hot to move. Their skin was breaking out in itchy, red blisters, and their throats, tongues and lips were caked with dust. The cries of their helplessly pinned workmates grew fainter.

Every few minutes there was a thud, and the rock trembled from blasts on the other side. "We can't see them, but they're coming to get us," Lefielo gasped.

"We're already dead," a crew member retorted in the dark.

"We're not dead!" Lefielo replied, but he too felt the dread. Four years earlier, his wife had died in his arms after a short illness. She had been so calm and serene, he remembered. Now a calmness and lassitude began to seep into his own body. He summoned all his will to fight it.

"Follow me," he told his men. Then, as Lefielo probed between the rocks, he spotted a water pipe. It was cracked and had no water, but it gave him an idea. He took out his spanner to loosen the bolts on the clamp and broke open a small section of the pipe.

At that moment Dirk Venter propped an explosive beneath an overhead rock, took cover around the corner and detonated it. Waiting for the last lumps to tumble down the slope, he heard a faint voice.

"Listen!" he hissed.

He heard it again, then glanced down at the broken end of a water pipe attached to the rock-wall beside him. The voice was coming out of the pipe.

"*Nika amanzi*," Lefielo was calling in the dialect spoken by black and white miners. "Give us water!"

Recognizing the voice, Venter called into the pipe, "Hello. Julias, is that you? How are the guys?"

"We can't handle this any more," Lefielo replied. "Water!"

One of Venter's men hacksawed a notch in the top of the pipe, and water was hosed in. On the other side, the trapped miners drank eagerly from water they collected in their hard hats, then sat under the pipe, splashing water on their bodies.

Next, the rescuers fed a powdered energy food into the pipe, washing it along with more water. As lamp batteries began to fail, phosphorous sticks that make light when cracked were also washed down the pipe, along with energy bars wrapped in plastic.

The news that there were survivors flashed up to the surface.

1.30pm Wednesday

Lefielo's crew's spirits had soared, but as the hours passed they began to ebb again. The air carried the stench of death from their dead colleagues. They could hear the rescuers' hammers ringing on rocks, but listened as if in a trance.

"We'll get out quicker if we dig towards them," Lefielo said. "Who's going to start?" Nobody moved.

On his belly, Lefielo squirmed into a niche between slabs and, with iron spikes, clawed at the stone, opening a tunnel down the side of the gully. Another man crawled over to help.

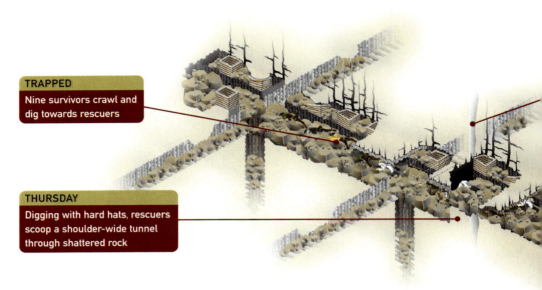

5.37pm Wednesday

About 200 feet of the tunnel had
collapsed. But there were gaps—mainly
around the "packs", thick pillar-like props that held up the
tunnel ceiling every five feet. The problem for the rescue teams, working back-to-
back shifts, was finding a route through the labyrinth.

The work was excruciatingly tedious, but was suddenly punctuated by terror.
Another earth tremor several hundred yards away caught them unawares. But, as
soon as the rubble stopped falling, they continued to dig into the tunnel.

5am Thursday

Venter's men hit a solid wall of rock. A fault had dropped about five feet. Worse,
right in their way was a pack so pressurized from the weight of rock that its timbers
were as hard as concrete.

"There's no choice," Venter said. "We have to remove the pack, then tunnel
downwards." Bit by bit, the prop was hacked loose and dragged out by hand winch,
chain and aching muscles.

1.30pm Thursday

Next, Biggs's team tunnelled down five feet, then turned horizontal again. Now
Biggs brought his three smallest men, Werner Prinsloo, Lukas Beukes and Christo
van der Linde, up to the front.

The space was so tight that, even with handles cut off, their shovels were too big.
On his knees, Prinsloo picked up stones one by one, using his hat as a bucket.
Every few minutes, he swapped places with Beukes or van der Linde. As they

246

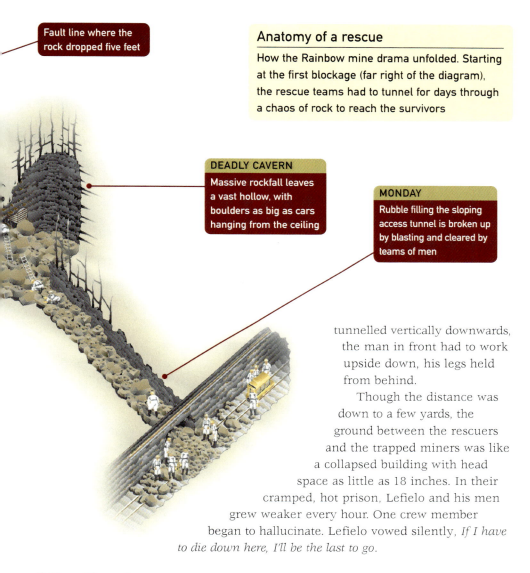

Fault line where the rock dropped five feet

Anatomy of a rescue

How the Rainbow mine drama unfolded. Starting at the first blockage (far right of the diagram), the rescue teams had to tunnel for days through a chaos of rock to reach the survivors

DEADLY CAVERN
Massive rockfall leaves a vast hollow, with boulders as big as cars hanging from the ceiling

MONDAY
Rubble filling the sloping access tunnel is broken up by blasting and cleared by teams of men

tunnelled vertically downwards, the man in front had to work upside down, his legs held from behind.

Though the distance was down to a few yards, the ground between the rescuers and the trapped miners was like a collapsed building with head space as little as 18 inches. In their cramped, hot prison, Lefielo and his men grew weaker every hour. One crew member began to hallucinate. Lefielo vowed silently, *If I have to die down here, I'll be the last to go.*

5.38pm Thursday

Werner Prinsloo was head first down the tunnel when he suddenly saw two eyes a foot and a half away through a small gap in the rocks. "We can see the men," Biggs reported to the control room. A loud cheer greeted the news.

Deep beneath the surface, the rescuers inched forward. The faint current of air flowing out of the collapsed tunnel was nauseating. Space was so constricted that a filled hat could not be passed back.

"Pull me out!" Prinsloo shouted. Biggs, sitting at the top of the vertical section, hauled on Beukes's legs. In turn, Beukes pulled van der Linde, who dragged Prinsloo until he could twist round and pass back the hat to be emptied. Then Prinsloo crawled forward again on knees and elbows, holding his arms and the hat out front—until stopped by a massive slab of rock. "I don't know what to do," he called back.

"Try going under it," Biggs suggested.

Prinsloo worked his way beneath the rock and continued. Later, taking over from Prinsloo, Beukes saw an exhausted face looking at him from six feet away. "Are you OK?" Beukes grinned, flicking a rope along the tunnel. "Come on then." Khabo Taelo grabbed the rope and, wriggling on knees, chest and elbows, slithered towards Beukes.

9.49pm Thursday

The ground shuddered; it was another earthquake. Biggs held his breath, Beukes closed his eyes and Prinsloo rolled over on his back, putting up his hands. Then, as quickly as it came, the tremor subsided. Biggs called into the dust-filled tunnel: "Are you OK?"

There was a long pause. *They're buried*, he thought. Then he heard Prinsloo's voice. "Yes, pull us out!"

Exhausted and confused, Lefielo's

TIGHT FIT: only slight men, such as Werner Prinsloo (at the hole) could get to the miners.

men now emerged, one by one. "My boss will never fit," said one anxiously. Sure enough, when his turn came, Lefielo's head and shoulders filled the tunnel from wall to wall. Prinsloo tried to pull him through but could not anchor himself.

"He won't fit!" Prinsloo yelled.

For half an hour Lefielo struggled to squeeze through. Finally, in desperation, he exhaled every breath of air to make himself as small as possible. Then, with a mighty effort, he reached out, grabbed a hanging chain and hauled himself forward. A moment later, he was out. Biggs clapped him on the back. "We're all proud of you," he said.

10.52pm Thursday

Eighty-two hours after the rockfall, the first survivor reached the surface. Never before had miners in South Africa been trapped for so long and survived.

Presenting Julias Lefielo with a bravery award, President Thabo Mbeki told him: "Your calm courage and leadership are an inspiration."

Please
save my
little girl

by Jim Hutchison

"Speak to me!" her father pleaded. But there was no sound from inside the upturned boat.

"They're going too fast," said Valerie Cottrell, watching as pleasure boats passed dangerously close in the darkness. Sitting next to her on the bridge of the cabin cruiser *Fred*, her husband, Anthony, frowned in concentration as he gripped the wheel. They were among hundreds of boats heading for marinas along the Swan River in Perth, Western Australia.

IN PERIL: **four-year-old Jaimee Lee.**

The Cottrells and their four-year-old daughter, Jaimee Lee, had boarded the 26-foot *Fred* at noon. The boat's skipper, Robert Harvey, had invited the family and four other friends to watch the fireworks above Perth's skyline, celebrating Australia Day, January 26.

Jaimee Lee had clapped with delight at the fireworks. "Look, Mummy, look!" she'd squealed, over and over. The rapture in their daughter's dark eyes made the couple especially glad they'd taken a rare day off. In addition to looking after Jaimee Lee, 31-year-old Valerie helped manage a hotel they owned. A steelworker by trade, Anthony, 28, held down a second job, working cranes on building sites.

When the fireworks ended, vessels ranging in size from ferries to small runabouts all tried to leave at once, funnelling into a dangerous crush in the river's navigation channel. Harvey decided to wait before returning to *Fred*'s mooring.

An hour or so later, just before 10pm, Anthony offered to take the helm. But when he eased the boat into the channel, the aquatic traffic jam still had not cleared.

Seeing that Jaimee Lee was tired, Valerie carried her to a bunk in the forward cabin. The little girl fell asleep at once. Valerie smiled and kissed her goodnight. She and Anthony were fiercely proud of their bright, happy daughter, their only child.

As she walked down the narrow corridor, Valerie had trouble keeping her balance—the boat was rocking violently. She reached the bridge just as Anthony turned into the deepest part of the channel, near the yacht club at Pelican Point.

Suddenly a large cruiser loomed out of the darkness behind them. Roaring past on their port side, it sent a high wake surging towards them. Then the wake from another boat smacked in from starboard. Their cruiser rolled the other way.

Valerie braced herself. Then her eyes widened with alarm as the cruiser kept toppling to port. She had a sickening realization that they were going to capsize. Her immediate thought: *Jaimee Lee's downstairs!*

In moments the boat was upside down. Part of the superstructure smashed into Valerie's shoulder and head, driving her deep underwater. Furiously she lunged for the surface.

By the light of passing boats she could see Anthony and the other adults struggling in the water. Where was Jaimee Lee?

Rocking crazily in the turbulent water, the upturned boat was almost fully submerged, except for less than three feet of bow above the waterline. The stern trailed downward at a 45-degree angle. Mind-numbing fear gripped Valerie. "Jaimee Lee is still inside!" she screamed. "Please save my little girl!"

Anthony dived under the hull, straining to reach the companionway leading to the cabin door. He quickly ran out of oxygen and had to surface. The others took turns diving, but soon they were clinging to the hull, exhausted.

Other boats quickly pulled up to assist, their crews shining flashlights and tossing out life vests. "Call for help," Valerie yelled. "My little girl's trapped in there!"

Anthony swam to the bow and hammered on it with his fists. "Jaimee Lee! Can you hear me?" There was no answer.

Valerie began to shake uncontrollably. Clinging to the hull, she choked back wrenching sobs. *Dear God*, she prayed, *don't let my daughter die.*

BOAT JAM: as the fireworks end all the boats try to leave at once.

"Mayday, boat capsized off Pelican Point. One person trapped inside." Acting Sergeant Paul Kimber, 38, patrolling the river on a police speedboat, responded to the distress call: "This is *Victor Mike Three*. We're on our way." Kimber then alerted the police patrol boat *Cygnet*, with Senior Constable Mark Mackin, 35, aboard. He was having a hectic night. He'd just apprehended a drunken skipper who was trying to ram other boats. But as Mackin leapt aboard the culprit's craft, he'd injured his right knee. Now *Cygnet* headed towards the yacht club.

A piercing scream came from inside the overturned cabin cruiser: "Daddy!" Anthony jerked round and pressed his ear to the bow. "Jaimee Lee, can you hear me?" he shouted.

"Daddy, get me out," the child wailed. "I'm scared."

Relief flooded Valerie. Now there was hope, but also increased urgency. She knew what happened when a boat overturned. Jaimee Lee must be trapped in an air pocket in the forward cabin. But all the time, water would be leaking in. It would rise until the child's face protruded just above it, pressed up against the cabin floor. Soon—in minutes perhaps—all the air would be replaced by water and the boat would sink, taking Jaimee Lee with it.

A police helicopter hovered above the river, illuminating the scene with a powerful searchlight. When *Cygnet* arrived, Mark Mackin met a chaotic scene: boats milling about, people shouting.

Ignoring the throbbing pain in his knee, Mackin leapt into the water. He was greeted there by Kimber, who had arrived minutes earlier.

"There's a little girl in the cabin up front!" Kimber gasped. In over a dozen energy-sapping dives under the bow of the cruiser, Kimber had managed to open the hatch to the forward cabin and reach up inside. Jaimee Lee had grabbed his wrist before lack of oxygen forced him to surface. "I don't have much left in me," admitted Kimber.

"I'll take over now, mate," Mackin replied.

More than 20 minutes had elapsed since the cruiser capsized, and its hull was being tossed about violently by passing boats. *If this thing goes under, it will sink in seconds*, Mackin thought grimly. There would be no chance of saving the child. None of the police boats carried scuba gear.

Grabbing a torch, Mackin swam down towards the cruiser's bow rail. The light beam penetrated less than an arm's length in the murky water.

MARK MACKIN

"I'LL TAKE OVER," said Mark Mackin, fighting his way into the boat.

Debris loomed out of the dark. He ducked under the rail, then fought his way up through a tangle of swirling rope, groping for the hatch. Reaching it, he ran his hands round the opening: it was wedge-shaped, about two feet wide by two and a half feet deep. Then, out of air, he had to resurface.

On his second dive Mackin struggled to clear the hatch of the rope that snaked out. The spaghetti-like mass coiled menacingly around him. Kicking free of the coils, lungs bursting, he again rocketed to the surface. He'd almost fatally misjudged the length of the return trip. *Another mistake down there*, he thought, *and I'm dead.*

Jaimee Lee had been trapped for nearly 30 minutes. For Valerie and Anthony, it seemed an eternity. "Jaimee Lee, speak to me!" her father yelled.

There was only silence.

Growing desperate, Mackin and Kimber dived again and again. While Kimber shoved aside debris, Mackin tried to reach into the cabin and grab the child. But each time, he encountered a wall of clothing, rope and cushions. When he thought he'd cleared it, more took its place.

Finally, he decided there was no way to pull Jaimee Lee out safely. He needed to get inside the cabin and carry the child out. But if he couldn't find enough air for the return trip, he would drown. One breath would never be enough.

By now he was exhausted. The underwater struggles were taking their toll. But

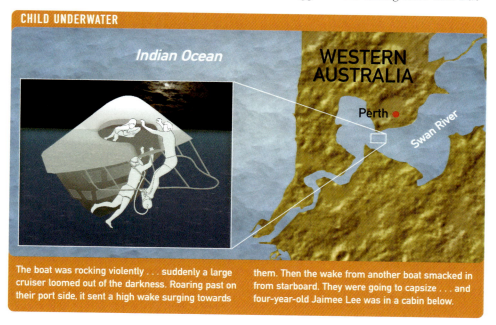

CHILD UNDERWATER

Indian Ocean

WESTERN AUSTRALIA

Perth ●

Swan River

The boat was rocking violently . . . suddenly a large cruiser loomed out of the darkness. Roaring past on their port side, it sent a high wake surging towards them. Then the wake from another boat smacked in from starboard. They were going to capsize . . . and four-year-old Jaimee Lee was in a cabin below.

Top trio: **Mark Mackin (left), Jaimee Lee and Paul Kimber happy and afloat.**

time was running out. The boat could sink at any moment. As the only qualified diver, Mackin knew he was the girl's only hope.

"We need some kind of air!" he yelled.

A fireman on *Cygnet* ran to the rail. "I've got a BA Unit," he called.

The breathing apparatus consisted of a mask that covered nose and mouth. This was linked by a hose to a cylinder of compressed air strapped to the user's back. But the equipment was for use in smoke-filled rooms, not for diving. Still, Mackin had no choice. He swam towards *Cygnet*. Leaning over the rail, the fireman strapped the BA mask over Mackin's face and opened the tap on the air valve. Mackin dipped his head underwater to test the mask. Water seeped in, and there was no air regulator, but it would have to do.

Immediately he realized there was another problem. Unlike lightweight aluminium scuba tanks, the fireman's air cylinder was made of alloy steel. Without the benefit of a scuba diver's buoyancy aid, Mackin would sink. Yet if the cylinder was held on the surface, the hose would not be long enough to allow him to reach the cabin.

Mackin and Kimber came up with a plan. "We'll go down together," Kimber said. "I'll hang the tank off my feet and hold on to the boat. That should give you better reach."

Mackin agreed, and Kimber hooked his feet into the cylinder's shoulder webbing. Mackin fastened the mask to his face with its elastic strap, gave a thumbs up and dived.

At the hatch entrance, Mackin took a tentative breath. Water leaked into the mask and trickled into his mouth, but he could breathe if he did not gulp air. Taking a slow breath, he squeezed through the hatch and pulled himself up through the water inside the upturned cabin. His head and shoulders surfaced in an air space so shallow that his head touched the inverted floor.

At first he saw only a floating mass of clothes, ropes and nets. Then his torch beam transfixed a tiny face plastered with dark hair. With just her head and shoulders above water, Jaimee Lee was clinging to a partly submerged cushion. She stared at Mackin, wide-eyed with fear. Thinking his mask probably made him look like a monster, and fearing the hose could get trapped by debris on the way out, he discarded the breathing apparatus.

Jaimee Lee lunged at Mackin, throwing her arms round his neck.

"Hello, my name's Mark," Mackin said. "I'm going to take you to mum and dad, but first we're going to play a game, OK?" The child nodded. Mackin was grateful that she didn't seem panicked. He could only get her out if she trusted him.

"We're going to count to three and see how long we can hold our breath," he said. She nodded again. Mackin counted to three and Jaimee Lee obliged by taking a deep breath.

"That's great," he said, his cheerful tone belying his anxiety. "Now let's do it for real. On the count of three, take a big breath, close your eyes and we'll swim out. I'll hold on to you tightly."

As Jaimee Lee took a breath, Mackin filled his own lungs and squeezed through the hatchway. Rope coiled about his legs. He kicked free, and suddenly they were out.

Swimming with one arm supporting the little girl cost Mackin precious oxygen. His chest pounded as he cleared the bow rail. Thrusting the girl before him, he began to kick wildly for the surface. Then Kimber's brawny arm appeared and snatched up Jaimee Lee.

When the rescuers burst to the surface, Jaimee Lee gasped for air and spluttered. Wiping her eyes, she looked around and cried, "Daddy!"

A cheer erupted and Kimber handed the child to her father.

"Lose something?" he said, grinning. Anthony wept as he passed Jaimee Lee into her mother's arms.

The Cottrells were transferred to *Cygnet*, which raced to the shore and a waiting ambulance. Jaimee Lee had been unharmed by her ordeal and soon went home with her parents.

Next afternoon Valerie took Jaimee Lee to water police headquarters. "There is no way we can adequately thank you for what you did," Valerie told the two policemen. Mark Mackin and Paul Kimber were each rewarded with a hug from Jaimee Lee.

Three minutes to live

by Tim Bouquet

A drunken stranger lunged at him in the bar, screaming abuse. Then Stephen felt a massive blow to his chest.

The cavernous bar of The Swan on Stratford Broadway in east London was packed with office workers when 22-year-old Stephen Niland arrived. It was six o'clock on Friday, April 16, 1999 and Stephen, a painter and decorator, was planning to have a quick beer with two friends before going to the cinema with his girlfriend Anna.

It was the first time Stephen had been to the four-storey Victorian pub since it had been revamped, and he noted the freshly stippled walls, new stained-glass light fittings and the ruched drapes. "Looks like a nice place," he said to his friends as they joined the crush at the bar.

Suddenly a man in front of him wearing blue jeans and a fleece turned round and lurched into Stephen.

"Shorry," slurred the man.

"S'OK, mate," Stephen smiled good-naturedly.

For about an hour and a half Stephen and his friends sat by one of the big windows, joking and catching up. Stephen had his back to the bar. Suddenly one of his friends looked alarmed. "Watch out!"

Stephen turned round.

The man who had bumped into him was now staggering towards Stephen screaming abuse. Two fellow drinkers tried to wrench him back. When Stephen saw the man was brandishing a bottle, he stood up. The chatter in the bar ebbed fast.

"Hey, let's get a cab," one of his friends suggested.

Too late. As Stephen curved his arm up to protect his head from the bottle, he felt a massive blow to his chest.

Suddenly he was reeling, sinking to the varnished floorboards. He felt as though he was passing out. He was vaguely aware of a fracas somewhere above him. A big six-footer, he started crawling towards the bar before collapsing unconscious.

Stephen Niland had no idea that he'd been stabbed in the heart with a flick knife.

Relaxing over coffee in their rooftop crew-cabin on the seventh floor of the Royal London Hospital in Whitechapel, Heather Clark and Alastair Mulcahy reflected on an adrenalin-filled 12-hour shift as duty doctors on London's Helicopter Emergency Medical Service (HEMS).

Their calls that day had included putting down in Oxford Circus, in the middle of Europe's busiest shopping street, to whisk to hospital a woman who had suffered severe head injuries in a car smash. They had also flown to the aid of an eight-year-old boy whose leg had been crushed by a lorry.

Pretty, 34-year-old Clark, an accident and emergency registrar and the newest doctor on board, was halfway through her month's training for a six-month stint on HEMS. Her trainer Mulcahy, 33, an anaesthetist and senior doctor on the team, would soon be returning to the wards before becoming a consultant.

It was 7.50pm, an hour after they had been due to go off duty, and Mulcahy was looking forward to having dinner at home with his wife. Clark, one of the country's top amateur salsa and jive dancers, was planning a quiet evening off from her hectic rehearsal schedule. Then the phone rang.

As Mulcahy went to take the call, he turned to Clark: "If this is a job, it's going to be a big one!" Nobody would ring that late if it wasn't.

"Thank God you're still there!" It was Central Ambulance Control in Waterloo which channels all the capital's 999 calls. "We've a stabbing in Stratford, in a pub. Can you get there?"

"We're on our way."

The Swan was about seven miles to the east but by now the distinctive red and white helicopter had gone back to its hangar for the night. They would have to take the HEMS rapid-response Audi instead.

Zipping themselves back into their vivid orange fireproof suits, they grabbed their nine-pound case of resuscitation equipment, instruments and drugs, and dashed to the hospital's ambulance park, Clark's shoulder-length blonde hair flying behind her.

Within seconds, the car was shooting out into the traffic on Whitechapel Road, sirens wailing, emergency lights flashing.

It was five minutes before eight.

Clark and Mulcahy shouldered their way through two sets of swing- doors into The Swan. It was now six minutes past eight, 21 minutes after someone in the pub had dialled 999.

As the doctors adjusted their eyes to the dim light, they saw that there were still people leaning on the long bar. In front of the flickering fruit machine, two ambulance men had cut the shirt off a bulky young man lying flat on his back and inserted a drip into a vein in his arm. Stephen Niland was barely conscious.

As soon as Mulcahy and Clark knelt next to him they noticed the knife slit, about half an inch wide, near his left nipple. It was right over his heart, but there was no blood.

"He looks really sick," Clark muttered to Mulcahy as she placed her fingers on the man's neck. She felt a pulse but it was very weak. He was hardly breathing, and his skin was white and running a cold sweat. Mulcahy checked Niland's eyes. The pupils were huge and staring, but unseeing. There was no time to lose.

STEPHEN NILAND

"Looks like a nice place," he said, joining the crush to the bar.

First, they had to get him breathing properly to stand any chance of transferring him to hospital. Mulcahy introduced drugs, including light general anaesthetic via the drip. Then he inserted a tube into Niland's windpipe and connected it to a self-inflating bag, which was put over his mouth and attached to an oxygen cylinder to ventilate him.

Now they had to find out whether the knife had punctured a lung causing a tension pneumothorax—where the lung collapses and squashes the heart so much it stops working. Clark would have to make small incisions in the chest wall.

"WE'RE ON THE WAY": the Swan pub.

She pulled a scalpel from her knee pouch and made a quick downward dissection under Niland's left armpit, then did the same under the right. Placing the scalpel on the floor, she grabbed the forceps to open up the muscle. Finally, she pushed her finger through the chest wall to make the final openings. Each hole had taken about 20 seconds.

She could feel that both lungs were inflated. So far so good. Again she felt the man's neck.

"No pulse!" She double-checked.

Niland was now clinically dead.

The knife must have penetrated his heart, flooding blood into the pericardium, the sac containing it, and creating such pressure it could no longer pump.

Clark and Mulcahy had one slender chance to bring Stephen back. External cardiac massage would be no good to him now. They had just three minutes before his brain, starved of oxygen, would cease to function.

Mulcahy looked at Clark. "He needs a thoracotomy!" he said.

They would open up his chest, remove the blood clots and hope to massage the heart back to life. Neither had ever performed this surgery.

"You've seen this before, so you open him," suggested Mulcahy. He ran to the car to get the surgical bag. Just two days previously, Heather Clark had watched another HEMS doctor perform the same risky procedure on a shooting victim. The man had died. In fact, only five people in the world are known to have ever survived a thoracotomy, without brain damage, outside a hospital.

259

Not even the daily drama of ten years' accident and emergency experience had prepared Clark for this.

"I'll start," she said calmly.

Oblivious to the onlookers, she made a surface incision across Niland's chest, joining up the two small holes and guiding her scalpel up to the breastbone. From her bag she selected a pair of scissors. She inserted them into one of the holes she had already made. Placing her left index finger under the bottom blade to ensure she did not go in too deep, she leant over the body and began to cut.

As she hit bone she could not help staring into Stephen's oval face. She was pleading for this to work.

Mulcahy was back. "It's going a bit slow," said the slightly built Clark through gritted teeth. "I'm having trouble cutting through the sternum. Start cutting from the other side and meet me in the middle."

Less than a minute later she was through the breastbone. Mulcahy fitted a vice-like implement known as a rib retractor to keep Niland's chest apart. As he opened it up—it was like prising open a clamshell—he was suddenly aware of voices in the bar. Momentarily he looked up. Two men were discussing a football match.

There was now an eight-inch opening. Right in front of them were Niland's heart and lungs.

Clark saw that the pericardium was bulging with a clot containing almost a pint of blood. Two minutes must have passed. She had to release the pressure.

With a pair of scissors she started to cut a hole in the sac, but it was tough, a bit like the skin of a haggis, and in places it was stuck to the wall of the heart. But finally she was able to put in her hand and scoop out the clot.

Then, as though coming out of some macabre dream, she suddenly looked up at the stunned faces of the bar's other customers and then back down to her patient and the blood all over the floor.

Now, for the first time in her life, she found herself holding a man's heart in her right hand.

About the size of a large purple-red grapefruit, it was slimy, rubbery and still warm. She would flick it with the fingers of her left hand to try and kick-start it, before massaging it with a milking motion.

She had just started to squeeze when she felt a flickering against her bloody palm. Her blue eyes widened.

It felt like a beat. It was definitely a heartbeat! She could see it now. Remarkably, Niland's heart had restarted.

The two doctors looked at each other in elated disbelief. Clark felt a surge of exhilaration. *So few survive!*

But only half the job was done. She had to mend the puncture.

"There it is," she showed Mulcahy, pointing to the small fountain of blood which had started to pump through the hole with every beat.

"Do you think you could put a stitch in it?" Mulcahy asked.

"Not in this dim light," replied Clark. She looked at him and, half-smiling, added: "You'd better pop your finger in."

Gently, Alastair Mulcahy pushed his right index finger as far as it would go into Stephen Niland's heart. He was in deep, almost up to his knuckle. At first the heart beat weakly and erratically. He felt something twitching against his fingertip. It was one of the valves.

The bleeding had stopped and the heartbeat was getting stronger. But as Stephen was being lifted into the ambulance, Mulcahy suddenly felt the beat slow.

"Careful!" He sucked air through his teeth. "Don't rush—we'll lose him!" he said.

On their way to the Royal London, Mulcahy felt the warm heart grip his finger very tightly. The beat was strong now, the rhythm regular. It meant that Niland's blood pressure was good and that oxygen was getting to the brain. Mulcahy looked into his eyes. The pupils were back to normal. He called for a sedative.

"Fifty-fifty he'll survive," he reassured Clark as she radioed the hospital and called confidently for a full cardio-thoracic surgical team.

It was now 8.37pm.

Just six days later, Niland was ready to go home. "I can never, ever thank you enough," he told Heather and Alastair. "I used to hear the helicopter flying over my house but I never fully appreciated what you did." He stared at the 70 stitches in his chest and knew just how lucky he was.

Two months later Stephen Niland, his family and friends held a charity event and raised £5,500 for HEMS, which relies on donations.

SO FEW SURVIVE: **Stephen with Heather and Alastair.**

Horror at Lynx Creek

by Jerry MacDonald

The rampaging bear turned the young couple's dream vacation into a grizzly nightmare.

"**M**atthias, come see!" Claudia Garschhammer shouted as she jumped from the canoe onto shore.

Matthias Ruppert and Claudia, both 26, had been paddling through frigid rain for three hours that day, June 9, 1994. Now Claudia had spotted a cabin where they could rest up and get warm. But as they approached, they saw notes on the door left by earlier paddlers: "Warning. Big black bear. May 13, 1994. Stole my backpack!" Another message, about a week old: "Bear tried to steal our packs as we were unloading canoe. We scared it off my making lots of noise."

PICTURE-BOOK BEAUTY: **Bowron Lake.**

Resolving to be extra careful, the two decided to press on to another campsite.

Battling waves and driving rain, Matthias and Claudia kept paddling. Blond and blue-eyed with an athlete's build, Matthias shivered as the icy waters of Isaac Lake spilled over the gunwale and soaked his hiking boots. *Some holiday*, he thought. But he had to admit that Bowron Lake Provincial Park was beautiful. Cold, clear mountain lakes and rugged portages formed a 70-mile chain in British Columbia's Cariboo Mountains, attracting canoeists from around the world. This June day was the third of their planned ten-day trip.

After paddling several more torturous hours, Claudia and Matthias spotted Campsite 21 at Lynx Creek. As the couple turned their canoe toward shore, the wind ceased, the clouds broke and a rainbow arched across the glasslike stillness of the lake. A large bull moose swam by them. It was the Canadian wilderness of picture books, and the canoeists felt a deep contentment.

Matthias and Claudia came from small German towns near the Austrian border. They had met a few months earlier at a hospital in Munich where they both worked. Matthias was a sixth-year medical student with a special interest in emergency/trauma medicine; Claudia, a slender brunette with a warm smile, was a physiotherapist. As their friendship grew, they discovered a mutual excitement for the outdoors—for getting away from the pressures of city life. After Matthias learned he had been accepted for training at Seattle's Harborview Medical Center, he asked Claudia to join him on a Canadian wilderness outing before his tour of duty began.

As they roamed about Campsite 21, Matthias and Claudia saw a small cabin. Two other campers were already there and offered to share space with them. But the German couple preferred to pitch a tent under the open sky. This would be more like the wilderness adventure they'd envisioned.

That evening Claudia celebrated the change in weather by making herb noodles and fresh bread. After dinner, they stowed their food and most of their gear in a "bear cache," a platform strung high between two poles and accessible only by ladder. In the cabin they stored their packsacks containing a first-aid kit and some clothes. They went to sleep that night exhausted but exhilarated.

About six the next morning, when the men in the cabin broke camp, Claudia and Matthias were still asleep. They were awakened as the morning's stillness was broken by a snuffling sound. A large form brushed against their tent. Near the zippered entrance they saw a dark figure moving outside.

Claudia and Matthias sat bolt upright in their sleeping bags. "A bear!" Matthias said under his breath. To frighten the animal off, they began whistling and yelling. When they stopped, they could hear only their own panicked breathing. Had the intruder left?

Suddenly the bear's claws came ripping through the tent. "Get under your mattress—quick!" Matthias yelled. He pushed Claudia down and threw her foam pad over her. He scrambled to get under his own pad, but it was too late. The tent collapsed as the bear pounced. Matthias was pinned by the 275-pound creature.

Play dead, he thought. This had been the advice of hiking guide-books he'd read. But an instant later the bear raked its claws across Matthias's back and legs, sending a searing flash of pain through him. Next it began to bite and tear chunks of flesh from Matthias's left buttock and hip. Trapped under the wreckage of the tent, Claudia could only listen helplessly to Matthias's screams. When she spied a small hole in the tent above her head, she thrust her fingers through and ripped the fabric. Pushing her head out, she found herself face to face with the bear, blood dripping from its jaws. Matthias called out, "Claudia, help! It's killing me."

As the savagery of the attack increased, Matthias felt his mind becoming strangely detached. The medical student found himself analyzing his injuries as if they were someone else's. *The bear must have hit the sciatic nerve*, he thought when a bite sent pain through his body and numbed his left leg.

Claudia realized that if Matthias was to live, she had to do something. *I must stay calm*, she repeated to herself. Moving slowly, keeping out of the bear's sight, she crawled from the tent, stood up and sprinted the 30 feet to the cabin.

I'm going to die, Matthias thought. Then he realized with horror that the bear could continue attacking him without killing him if no arteries were cut. *Let the agony end,* he pleaded silently. *If only I could lose consciousness.* An image flashed before him of his mother in Germany. Matthias was an only child, and he feared his mother would never get over his death.

Her heart pounding, Claudia scanned the inside of the cabin. There, next to one of the packsacks, lay a 12-inch wood-handled hatchet. She grabbed it and ran out the door as Matthias gave another agonized scream. Thrashing about, he had managed to get his head out from under the tent. Instantly the bear lunged and sank its inch-long canines into the side of Matthias's skull. With its jaws clamped, the bear yanked him upward, trying to free him from the tent. Its teeth scraped along Matthias's scalp, peeling the skin away.

Claudia moved behind the bear and crept closer. Less than an arm's length away, tensing her body, she swung the hatchet at the back of the bear's neck. Stunned, the animal dropped its victim and headed into the forest.

Matthias, on the ground, was covered in blood and barely conscious. "You must walk!" Claudia urged. "Quick, before the bear returns!"

"I can't get up," he replied weakly.

Still clutching the hatchet, Claudia put Matthias's arm around her neck and dragged him to the cabin. Once inside, he collapsed on the floor, bleeding from puncture wounds all over his body. A gaping hole marked his left buttock. Half his scalp was peeled back. "What should I do, Matthias?" Claudia pleaded.

Concentrate! he told himself. *React calmly and you have a chance.* "Get the first-aid kit and thermal blanket in the packsack," Matthias said. He knew he had a better chance of surviving if he stayed warm. "Don't bother with my head wounds. The others are more serious." Then he told Claudia to bandage his bleeding leg and buttock.

Following Matthias's instructions, Claudia positioned him on the cabin floor so that if he lost consciousness and vomited, he wouldn't choke to death. As Claudia wrapped him in the blanket, he told her what she already knew. She'd have to go for help alone.

But first, Matthias realized, he needed water from the lake to prevent dehydration. Claudia opened the door to get some—then slammed it.

"It's back!" she said, her face going white. The bear was standing over the tent, nosing at the blood-soaked nylon.

WILDERNESS ADVENTURE: **It was not what Matthias and Claudia had planned.**

"Don't go out," Matthias ordered. "It's too dangerous."

Claudia knew Matthias needed help right away. She grabbed the hatchet and a piece of firewood and stepped onto the porch. She screamed at the animal, waving the weapon and heaving the wood. The bear retreated to the forest. Now Claudia sprinted to the lake to fill a metal canteen. When she returned, she built a fire in the potbellied stove. "If the bear comes, you must fight for your life!" she said and pressed the hatchet into Matthias's hand.

Opening the door a crack, Claudia peered out: the bear was back. Once more she screamed and threw wood; again the animal retreated. Claudia latched the door behind her and secured it with rope. Then she raced to the lake, jumped into the canoe and set off for the ranger cabin over seven miles away. The craft zigzagged in the water; it was her first time paddling alone. Blisters on her hands broke open. She blocked out the pain and pressed on. Hoping to attract campers, she stayed close to shore, screaming for help. Nobody answered.

Matthias drifted in and out of consciousness. Suddenly he heard a scratching sound. He turned to the window six feet away and gasped. Standing on its haunches and scraping at the metal screen was the bear. Attracted by the smell of Matthias's blood, the animal had come back. With one swipe, it could rip the screen and crawl inside.

OK, Matthias thought, *I'll show you I can still fight!* He got to his feet. Gripping the hatchet, he took one step toward the window and collapsed on the floor.

Shifting his weight to his good leg, he pulled himself back up. Gathering strength, he let out a roar of rage and pain and threw himself across the room at the window. He managed to swing the hatchet at the sill in front of the bear's face.

Had he hit it? He couldn't tell. But the last thing he saw before losing consciousness was the animal lumbering toward the woods. When Matthias came to, he realized the bear could return at any moment, so he struggled to secure the shutters on the windows. Then, crawling across the floor, he shoved the wooden table toward the door and lay beside the stove, utterly spent, in a pool of his own blood.

As his body grew colder, Matthias thought about his future, about graduating from medical school, about a recipe for his favorite bread—anything to stay conscious. He tried not to think of the bear, but he couldn't help himself. *An animal of such strength could surely break down the front door of the cabin if it wanted to.*

It was 10.15am. Claudia had been gone over two and a half hours. Matthias willed himself not to panic. There was no telling how long it would be before she could return with help. If she had to go all the way back to the park entrance, he reasoned, it might take days. Already he was frighteningly short of breath. How long could he hang on?

Around 10.30, near the northern end of Isaac Lake, Claudia spotted a ranger boat. She waved frantically, and a few moments later Reg Plett and Damaris Kunzler pulled alongside. Claudia wept as she told them about Matthias.

At first Plett and Kunzler couldn't quite believe their ears—there hadn't been a bear mauling reported in the more than 30 years the park had been open. With their boat at full throttle, Plett radioed for a helicopter to be on standby.

At 10.55, four hours after the attack, the ranger boat arrived at Campsite 21. Keeping a sharp lookout for the bear, the three rushed to the cabin. "Matthias!" Claudia shouted. "We're here!" No answer.

"Matthias! Answer me!" Claudia pleaded, putting her shoulder to the door and pushing hard. Finally it gave way. From the darkness a weak voice muttered, "Who's there?"

Claudia rushed to Matthias and, lightly touching his face, whispered everything would be OK.

About eight hours after the attack, Matthias Ruppert was wheeled into surgery at G. R. Baker Memorial Hospital in Quesnel, 75 miles away. For two hours surgeons worked to sew up the damage the bear had inflicted. It took 200 stitches to close the wounds in Matthias's face, neck, arms, leg and buttock. No vital organs had been damaged, but he had come within an hour of bleeding to death. He was just regaining consciousness when Claudia came to his bedside. "Thank you for saving my life," she said softly. "Thank you for saving *mine*," Matthias replied.

Two days after the attack, ranger Reg Plett destroyed an eight-year-old black bear snared near the cabin at Lynx Creek. With no sign of other bear activity in the area then and for days afterward, park officials are confident they caught the right bear.

Matthias Ruppert was transferred to Harborview Medical Center in Seattle, where he spent seven weeks undergoing surgery and recuperating. By September 1994, he was well enough to begin his training. He still limps and has panic attacks recalling that June day. But the event left another legacy as well. "I feel more for my patients, their fright and their pain," he says. "I hope I carry that through the rest of my life."

Rescue in Sichuan

Chengdu

by Ian Cunningham

Only the British aid workers could save the Chinese truck driver, trapped in his cab 700 feet down a mountainside.

ROAD TO THE ROOF of the world: trucks labour up 12,000 feet to the Tibetan plateau.

Over the past hour, the bus had been jolting along a steep single-track road, 12,000 feet up on the Tibetan plateau. From his rear seat, Dr Kevin Ilsley looked out at the thickly forested mountain slopes that fell away alarmingly only feet from the bus's wheels, and at the leaden, threatening sky. After six weeks away from home doing humanitarian-aid work in the Tibetan village of Dengke, the 42-year-old GP was looking forward to getting back to his wife and three children in Bromyard, near Worcester.

As chief medic of the Care and Share Foundation's Project Dengke, Ilsley had been responsible for the expedition's medical programme. Other members of the 30-strong team from nine nations—many of them from Loughborough University—had helped install running water at Dengke's tiny hospital, as well as renovating it and the local school. Now, on September 25, 1992, they were on the fourth day of their five-day journey to Chengdu, capital of China's Sichuan province, before flying home via Hong Kong.

Suddenly the bus shuddered to a halt on the muddy, unmade road that snaked along the side of Erlang mountain. After a few minutes, Ilsley decided to find out what was going on. Rounding a corner, he saw they had come to a stop behind a truck carrying enormous tree trunks while a Chinese man squatted in the road repairing one of its tyres. Near by, a knot of people, most of them from the other Project Dengke vehicles, were peering over the edge of the mountain.

From them, he discovered that a second timber truck, in edging past the first, had misjudged the width of the road and plunged down the mountainside, swallowed from view in the dense grey-green forest. Arne Brantsaeter, a 33-year-old Norwegian doctor on the team who spoke fluent Chinese, asked a man from the broken-down lorry how many people had been in the stricken vehicle. "Three," the man told him.

271

DEATH FALL?: a truck had crashed down the mountainside. As a doctor and a Christian, Kevin Isley felt he had to help.

Kevin Ilsley eyed the near-perpendicular mountainside. As a doctor and a Christian, he felt he had to help. Trying to sound braver than he felt, he told the expedition's leader, scientist and senior lecturer Dr Mel Richardson: "If there's any chance of survivors, I'm going down. Does anyone want to come with me?"

This is horrific, thought Mel Richardson. *Even if anyone could survive a drop like that, should I let team members risk their lives?* They had drugs and expertise, but no safety equipment, and there was no way of knowing what terrain they would face once they got beyond the belt of forest a few hundred feet below.

Urging the others away from the road's crumbling edge, he said: "Let's yell down to see if there's any sign of life." An eerie, ghost-like scream echoed up through the mist. "All right," he told Ilsley. "Take a team down."

Arne Brantsaeter and Jon Martin, a 27-year-old Lincolnshire doctor, had already volunteered. When Ilsley asked for an engineer to join them, Danish-born Peter Kofoed, in his mid-twenties and built like a Viking, came forward. Quickly Ilsley emptied morphine, dressings and surgical equipment into a rucksack, then said to the others: "Right. Let's go."

Slowly the four began edging their way down the precipitous slope, slipping and sliding, grabbing branches to steady themselves. Within minutes they were covered in mud and soaking wet. Twice Jon Martin had to shake leeches from his fingers. Ilsley tripped over a fallen tree trunk and fell heavily. *I can just see the headlines,* he thought. *"Foolhardy doctor breaks leg in futile rescue attempt."*

For about half an hour the four slowly worked their way down, dropping like monkeys from tree to tree where the ground was steepest. They saw traces of the truck's headlong plunge—broken trees, pieces of sheared-off metalwork and plastic sheeting, an occasional log.

They had descended about 700 feet when, to their surprise, they saw two Chinese men clambering up towards them. Bloody and bruised, they had been thrown clear of the truck when it hit a tree. "They say the third man's still alive, but he's trapped in the cab," Arne told Ilsley. Moments later, Peter Kofoed called from ahead: "Over here—I've found it." Leaving the two survivors to continue their painful progress up the mountain, the rescuers forced their way on through the forest.

The lorry had come to rest only 200 feet from a near-vertical 50-foot drop to the valley floor. It lay, mercifully the right way up, in a narrow gully, pointing up the mountain at an angle of about 45 degrees. Its remaining logs, flung loose, had cannoned into the front of the cab, crushing the passenger side to a width of barely eight inches.

Two Chinese from the broken-down lorry on the road above had reached it already and were trying to force back the cab's mangled passenger door, using pieces of metal that had fallen off the truck. The reek of spilt petrol was almost unbearable.

Climbing up the opposite side of the narrow gully to draw level with the driver's door, which had been completely sheared off, Ilsley and Brantsaeter peered inside. Stretched along the bench seat lay a muscular, moustached man of about 40. Blood trickled from cuts on his head, and both his shins were cruelly pinned in the tangle of crushed metal that was all that remained of the far door. In the dim light, Ilsley could just make out the man's feet, in bloodstained white socks.

Arne spoke quietly in Chinese to the man, who was groaning as he drifted in and out of consciousness: "Don't worry, we're doctors, we'll get you out." Fortunately, they could just reach the man's right arm. Arne gave him a shot of morphine.

The driver's moans subsided, but the two Chinese men's efforts to free his legs seemed to have no effect. "This is hopeless," said Ilsley. "We need more help if we're to have any chance of getting him out." Peter, the youngest and strongest, set off on the laborious climb back to the road to collect more men and equipment.

The other three turned their attention back to the injured man. If they did succeed in freeing him, how on earth would they get back up the mountain carrying his dead weight? Brantsaeter's mind went back to the survival training he had done during his military service. "Anoraks," he said. "We can make a stretcher with our anoraks. We just need to cut down some saplings and thread them through the arms."

Suddenly, Kevin Ilsley felt for the Swiss Army knife his children had bought him as a present to take to China. "Look, Dad, it's even got a saw," ten-year-old Andrew had told him proudly. He pulled it out, opened the saw blade and began cutting down some of the saplings that flourished at the gully's edge. *Things are looking up*, he thought as the blade sliced cleanly through the thin stems. *We've got to get him out now.*

It was almost an hour later and the grey sky was already darkening when Ilsley heard crashing in the foliage overhanging the gully. Suddenly a large object flew past, narrowly missing his head. Looking up in alarm, he saw his colleague Grant Freeman, an engineer in his early thirties. The object was a large wheel-jack, which had slipped out of Grant's hand. Close behind Grant came Sam Brooks, also an engineer, and Gareth Clegg, a medical student.

Picking his way through the scattered logs to the far side of the cab, Grant Freeman was horrified to see the pair of bloody feet protruding from the tangled metal. He also noticed that one giant log, at least four feet wide, had come to rest in the worst possible position: with one end resting precariously against the cab roof, directly above the driver's feet.

"We can attempt to jack the metal back and free him," Freeman said, "though anyone who tries is likely to bring that tree trunk crashing on to his head." The alternative was even more drastic: to amputate his feet.

Never mind the risk, Freeman told himself. *I must have a go.* With the heavy jack in his hand, he climbed cautiously on to the narrow foothold formed by the gap between the cab and the upright rear stanchion. Less than six inches above his head, the thick tree trunk was held tenuously in place by the front edge of the cab roof. *If that log slips,* he thought, *it'll smash my head like an eggshell.*

Gripping the corner of the cab with his left hand, he leaned across and down, trying to insert the jack into a narrow opening between the stanchion and the shattered cab door. At last he got a purchase. Using short, cautious strokes so as not to dislodge the log, he began to crank.

Jon Martin gave the driver another shot of morphine, but when Arne Brantsaeter asked how he was, the reply was ominous: he couldn't feel his legs. The three doctors began to fear his spinal cord was broken. If so, trying to get him up the mountain could paralyse, even kill, him. Would their efforts prove futile after all?

For Grant Freeman, operating the heavy jack from such an awkward position was taking its toll. His breathing was laboured in the thin mountain air, and sweat plastered his T-shirt to his back. As the metal stubbornly refused to part company with the stanchion, he thought miserably, *This is impossible—there's just too much metal to shift.*

Suddenly the log began to bounce alarmingly. In near-panic, he realized that one of the Chinese rescuers was clambering over the trunks that had fallen in front of the cab, threatening to dislodge the log resting on the wreck and bring it crashing on to them both. He called our desperately to Peter: "Get him off there!" Chased away by Peter, the man jumped clear.

For about half an hour Freeman laboured relentlessly, ignoring his blistered palms and the pains in his spine. Millimetre by millimetre, the metal finally started to give. *It was working.* At last, with more and more space opening up around the man's feet, he gasped: "Try and pull him clear from the other side!"

As Ilsley and the others pulled the driver by his shoulders and arms, Freeman saw the bloody feet disappear. The man was free. Freeman collapsed on the bank, elated and exhausted.

Gently Kevin Ilsley and his medics manoeuvred the driver out of the cab. One of his shins was cut to the bone where the metal door frame had bitten into it, and both his socks were filled with blood, but Ilsley noticed that he was now moving his feet: *Maybe his spine's OK after all.*

As the rescue team lifted the man on to the makeshift stretcher, Ilsley's initial

MAKESHIFT STRETCHER: **Sam Brooks (right) and Grant Freeman with Dr Arne Brantsaeter.**

euphoria at freeing him began to evaporate. The prospect of manoeuvring their burden up hundreds of feet of almost vertical mountainside was daunting. But in the fading light, there was no time to lose. With Ilsley in front, holding a lead rope he had attached to the front of the stretcher, the team set off up the gully.

As they climbed, the soft mud churned treacherously beneath their feet. Glancing back, Grant Freeman could see clearly where the gully abruptly fell away to the river below. *If anyone slipped now,* he thought with a shudder, *he could go all the way down.* The effort of heaving the stretcher high enough to keep it horizontal brought fresh torment to his aching muscles. *Keep going,* he exhorted himself. *Keep at it.*

Every few minutes, Ilsley had to stop to brace the stretcher with his rope so that the team could manhandle it a few feet further. Time and again the driver slipped down the stretcher until the rope securing him threatened to cut into his throat.

Near the top, the climb became almost perpendicular. Ilsley and his team could move only a couple of feet at a time, alternately scrambling and crawling their way upwards.

At last, craning his neck to try to spot the road, Ilsley saw a cluster of anxious faces just 100 feet above. To his surprise, the driver, who had prompted the disaster by changing his truck's wheel in the middle of the road, was shouting impatiently at the two Chinese rescuers helping with the stretcher. "He says he'll go without them if they don't come straight away," Arne Brantsaeter translated.

Staggered by this callousness Ilsley burst out: "But we're saving this man's life!" The team were dismayed as the two Chinese abandoned the stretcher and scrambled up to the road. After a few minutes the lorry drove away, never to be seen again.

HERO OF THE DAY: Worcester GP Kevin Ilsley, tends the injured truck driver.

But by now others were making their way down to haul the stretcher the last 20 feet up the mountain. Relieved of their burden, both Kevin Ilsley and Grant Freeman found themselves unable to move any further up the slope. Friends let down a rope for them each to climb in turn. At last Ilsley, limbs trembling with exhaustion, found himself back on level ground—four long hours after he had set off down the mountain.

In Chengdu shortly before Ilsley flew home, a Chinese girl asked him about the rescue. "Why did you go down the mountain? You did not know these people."

"We had no choice," Ilsley tried to explain. "We're doctors."

"But you didn't know them," the girl persisted. For the first time, Ilsley realized that had they not arrived, the driver would have been left to die.

Looking back, he says: "It's hard not to reflect that Providence played a part. We were way beyond where Europeans are normally allowed to go. We were doctors and engineers, and we had the basic equipment we needed. I do believe God was with us on the mountain that day."

MEL RICHARDSON

"YOUR FRIENDS SAVED OUR LIVES." The project leader had been concerned for his team.

In February 1993, project leader Dr Mel Richardson received a letter, translated into English, via the provincial governor's office in Chengdu. It was from the driver Liu Dehua, now fully recovered, and his mates Lu Chuansheng and Gao Qirong: "We are extremely grateful that you and your friends saved our lives . . . You should understand that we wouldn't be in this world now if you and your colleagues didn't realize that we had that terrible accident and came to save us so bravely. All our families also greatly appreciate your kindness to bring us back to this lovely world . . . Next time we all would like to invite you to our homes when you come to Sichuan."

Under their signatures, they had added: "The three luckiest people in this world you saved."

Hit by 25,000 volts

by Colin Brennan

The train driver had reported a pile of burning rags on the track, but police discovered it was the body of a young man.

Lee Taylor was on his way home after a day studying on his business course at university in Crewe when his friends spotted him: "Come on, Lee, tomorrow's your birthday. Let's celebrate."

A popular 22-year-old with olive skin and dark hair, Lee knew there was no escape. But after a few drinks at the college bar, he slipped away for an early night. Tomorrow's football was on his mind. An outstanding player, Lee was toying with turning professional. The outlook was good. He'd been booked to play next day for a Welsh club.

Out in the foggy November night, Lee passed four men in their early twenties loitering outside a busy pub. Moments later he noticed that they were following him.

There'd been reports of attacks on students by a local gang. Scared, Lee began to run. At once they were after him. "Get him," one shouted.

Super-fit, used to running five miles in the Black Mountains near his Welsh home in Talgarth, Powys, Lee scaled a roadside gate leading on to wasteland.

Glancing back, he thought he had shaken the gang off. He eased his six-foot frame over a fence on to what appeared to be a small bridge.

There was an immense flash. Searing pain shot through Lee as a massive electric jolt spat him into the air like a spark from a fire. He had touched a live cable above a railway gantry, zapping a lethal 25,000 volts through his body.

Screaming, his body on fire, Lee fell 20 feet before landing heavily, his limbs locked rigid. He regained consciousness to feel his shoulder vibrating. Dimly, he could hear a noise in the distance. *I'm lying against a railway track*, he realized. Lights were coming towards him. Desperately he tried to roll over, then blacked out.

Half a mile away, the alarm had been raised in the British Transport Police station: not long after midnight the driver of a train bound for Rugby had seen what he'd taken to be a pile of burning rags on the track, a few miles north of Crewe.

On receiving this report, Sergeant Vernon Grinney and two colleagues set off to walk the line. In the gloom they came upon a shape like a black rubbish bag. It was smouldering. Bending down Grinney gasped as he saw that it was a man, burned black as charcoal except for the whites of his eyes. Mercifully a light rain had fallen, extinguishing the flames that had eaten deep into his body.

Grinney saw that he was young. Tears came to his eyes as he thought of his own teenage children. Pulling off his anorak, he draped it gently over Lee.

As the two other men went to guide the ambulance crew down the steep embankment, Vernon Grinney was left alone with what he was convinced was a dying man. Instinctively, he offered his hand for comfort. To his surprise Lee grasped it firmly. Trying to keep Lee alert, he whispered reassuringly to him until the paramedics arrived. When he carefully let go of the young man's hand, pieces of shredded skin remained in his palm.

Lee was rushed to nearby Leighton Hospital. Dr Teri Gilpin, senior house officer on duty, could scarcely recognize him as human. His face was grotesquely swollen and burned black. His hair had turned a bluish colour and was standing up on end. From the waist up his flesh was burned to the muscle and in places right down to the bone. Even Lee's eyes had changed colour, from green to a fish-like grey.

Dr Gilpin, an attractive, blonde 24-year-old who had qualified only a year earlier, forced her nerves aside. Lee could die at any moment from fluid loss or the effects of the huge electric jolt on his heart rhythms. Swiftly she hooked him up to intravenous drips, gave him oxygen and blood, and called for X-rays to check for spinal injuries.

"Lee, you've had an accident," she said loudly to him. "You are in hospital and we're helping you." Watching his face for any acknowledgment as the anaesthetist put him to sleep, she noticed that his breathing was becoming laboured. The ugly burns stretching round his chest were acting like a tourniquet, tightening the skin and constricting his lungs. He was suffocating.

An image from a medical textbook flashed up in Gilpin's mind. It was of an emergency procedure, though she'd not seen it performed. "I know what I have to do," she said. Watched by a shocked Grinney, still by Lee's side, she made three deep incisions in Lee's chest, cutting through the burned flesh, down to his waist.

But Lee was still fighting for breath. Gilpin tried again, this time sawing deeper until, finally, blood trickled out and she knew she had reached living tissue. As it split open, the pressure on his lungs was released. Almost immediately Lee's chest expanded and his breathing eased. Watching him being wheeled away to intensive care, his hands encased in plastic bags, his body wrapped in protective cling film, Teri Gilpin wondered if he would survive until morning.

The next day, November 11, 1994, Lee was rushed to Whiston Hospital in Liverpool. Consultant surgeon Ian James, in charge of the burns unit, operated immediately, cutting dead skin from Lee's body, before deadly toxins could build up, poisoning his system.

Lee's parents Carol and Robert arrived. As they walked the featureless corridors it seemed as though the staff avoided them. "They think he's going to die," Carol said. "But they don't know Lee. He's a fighter."

LEE TAYLOR

"LEE, YOU'VE HAD AN ACCIDENT," she said loudly. Lee Taylor before a massive electric jolt spat him into the air like a spark from a fire.

She began talking to the nurses, trying to impress on them how special her son was. She spoke of Lee's kindness, how he'd worked with children in summer camps in the US. He was going to be a footballer, Carol said; as a student he'd coached at a university in North Carolina and had a great future.

At last they were taken to see him. Lee lay swathed in bandages. Apart from the gentle hiss of the life-support machines, the room was deathly quiet.

Ian James, a tall, lean Scot, quietly explained that Lee would be kept in a drug-induced coma to protect him from the appalling pain. "Sixty percent of Lee's body has been burned—he was a tomato skin away from losing his stomach, liver and throat—and he has lost almost a quarter of his muscle tissue. He has broken his hip, leg and several ribs. His right lung is punctured." He did not tell them that he put Lee's chances of pulling through at less than one in 100.

James continued: "We need to operate again soon to cut out more dead skin and muscle. But the wounds won't heal by themselves. Lee will need massive skin grafts. We have harvested his own skin from his legs. But it's not enough. We have to ask— can one of you donate skin from your thighs?" Carol immediately offered hers.

Lee was receiving regular blood transfusions. He had so little skin that at first the blood oozed through his dressings on to the floor. Over the next few weeks he received extensive grafts of his own and his mother's skin, on his chest, abdomen and back.

On the way to theatre, Robert walked beside his unconscious son. "Forget the operation, Lee," he whispered. "This is football. You've got to get out and win."

For five weeks Lee lay in a coma in intensive care, unaware of the hundreds of goodwill messages from friends and relatives. Finally able to breathe without a ventilator, he was moved to the burns unit.

Lee dreaded the early mornings, when the nurses came to change his dressings. Because he was becoming resistant and addicted to the morphine given to him as a painkiller, the dose had to be restricted. At first, Lee passed out as the nurses inched off and replaced the bandages. Later, he steeled himself not to moan.

You have to let them get on with it, he told himself, trying to think up new ways of blocking out the pain. He imagined himself up in the snow-capped Alps, high on a diving board above a lake, his fit, tanned body glistening in the sun, the way it used to look. He pictured himself springing into the air, straightening into a thin streak, feeling the wind whistling past his flesh. As he hit the icy green water a rush of cool relief suffused his whole body. He went deeper and deeper and for a few precious seconds, the pain was eased.

Over the next 19 weeks, Lee underwent 30 operations and received more than 170 pints of blood. His kidneys failed twice, his lungs collapsed and had to be drained. Some of the skin grafts didn't take and had to be redone.

Yet in two months he was sitting up. By four months he was raising his arms above his head—he'd been told it could take three years. "His courage is remarkable," Ian James told Carol.

At the end of March 1995, Lee was moved to Bronllys Hospital, a few miles from his home. At one point his weight had dropped to five stone, less than half his previous weight. He now looked as frail as an injured bird. He still couldn't get out of bed without help. He could walk, slowly and laboriously, only a few steps.

The superficial burns on his face were healing; there would be no scars to mar his good looks. But the wasted muscles on one side of his neck meant that his head was pulled permanently to one side.

At the hospital, physiotherapist Kumari Dias explained that Lee's only hope of recovering full movement was through exercises to stretch his scars and muscles. Manipulation would bring fluid and mobility back to his joints and weight training would rebuild his strength.

WALKING WOUNDED: **Lee says farewell to hospital staff in Liverpool.**

"You won't like me," warned Kumari, a small, determined woman. "I'll have to push you and it will be painful." She couldn't understand why Lee chuckled. Later it became clear—it was *he* who pushed her.

Lee worked doggedly. He desperately wanted to be able to hold his head up straight. When he looked at his body in the mirror he often felt a black rage sweep over him. Then he'd angrily submit to another hour of exhausting physical manipulation, stretching his shoulder muscles, working to get them in balance.

After one particularly punishing session, when Kumari had used her own physical strength to stretch and pull him, she urged: "Let's stop there." But Lee insisted on going on. Back in his room, he slumped over his bed, white with pain. "You're a hard man," said Kumari—and the name stuck.

Some weeks later, Kumari saw the "hard man" through the windows of the hospital. Bent and hobbling like an 80-year-old, he was practising walking, going round and round the building. Still pitifully thin, he looked like an animated scarecrow. Kumari had to turn away.

In July 1995, just eight months after his accident, Lee and his father went out on the football pitch near their home in Talgarth to knock a ball around. Robert was proud of his son. He didn't mind showing his scarred legs and he was regaining weight. "This is good for you," he said. Lee wasn't so sure.

The hip he had broken was giving him trouble. "It's no use, Dad," he said in frustration. "I'm too stiff and slow. I can't dribble the ball the way I used to."

PAINFULLY BRAVE: Lee courageously fought his way back to life.

Yet some months later he was back jogging in the hills and when, in January 1998, Lee was asked to take part in a charity hospital match against Builth Wells Football Club, he was overjoyed to be given the chance to play again.

Lee returned to university to complete his business degree. Following his graduation in summer 1997, he faced one final operation, on his neck. Balloons placed under the undamaged skin on the left side of his throat were inflated slowly over a few weeks, stretching the skin, then it was surgically pulled across the remaining scars. Now he can wear a shirt and tie without discomfort.

Lee was asked to appear on a Granada Television show in Manchester with surgeon Ian James and Dr Teri Gilpin, whose respective skill and quick thinking had saved his life. He'd been told that in the week following his accident Teri Gilpin had phoned the hospital twice a day to check on his progress. Lee was looking forward to thanking her personally.

Teri was apprehensive as she waited in the hospitality room. *What would Lee look like?* He'd been so badly injured that she had never thought of him as a person. She could picture only his singed eyebrows and grotesquely charred skin.

A tall, attractive figure walked into the room and started to thank her. It was such a shock that she burst into tears. *My God, this is the man I saved*, she thought, as he hugged her. *He is real and alive—and he has his whole life ahead.*

Capsized!

by Derek Lundy

The lone yachtswoman's boat had capsized far from land. She knew that no one could save her.

sabelle Autissier was aboard her 60-foot yacht, *PRB*, in what some sailors call the hole, the part of the Southern Ocean so remote that not even search-and-rescue aircraft can reach it. At 1900 miles west of Cape Horn—deep within the zone of Antarctic drift ice—she was as far from land as any human, short of an astronaut, can be. And from the west, a powerful low-pressure system was stalking the 42-year-old Frenchwoman's boat.

On this February day in 1999, Autissier—as famous in her homeland as a rock star—was the leader by a narrow margin in the Around Alone 1998–99, a 27,000-mile solo race around the world. During the previous five months, she had sailed close to 17,000 miles, enduring loneliness, fear and grinding fatigue.

Now, before the storm hit, she needed to sleep to be in good shape when it roared over her. But when the autopilot failed to react fast enough to a quick shift in the wind, the boom swept across the deck like a scythe and smashed up against the lee rigging. In two seconds *PRB* was thrown on its side, mast in the water.

Autissier began to struggle out of the cabin so she could administer the prescribed remedy: ease the rudder and mainsail. This was her fourth solo around-the-world race, and she'd seen a lot worse. The boat, she was sure, would pick itself up again.

To Autissier's astonishment, *PRB*—propelled by a wave that struck at the precise moment of the knockdown—continued its determined roll. She barely had time to duck inside and slam shut the watertight door before *PRB* turned upside down, its 15-foot keel in the air, its mast and sails plunging 85 feet into the sea.

More than a ton of water flooded the forward compartment as the forehatch jammed halfway open. But the bulkhead held and Autissier was able to seal off the rest of the boat. The view through *PRB*'s big cabin windows gave her the sensation of being inside an aquarium. Looking down, she watched the sails tear and the mast fracture. Oil leaking from the now-inverted engine covered everything, fouling the cabin.

Autissier activated her EPIRB (emergency position-indicating radio beacon). She knew that no commercial ships were within 1000 miles, and that only a fellow racer could save her.

The Around Alone race begins in America and runs in four legs with stops in South Africa, New Zealand and Uruguay before finishing back in Charleston, South Carolina. In this race, competitors pilot deep-sea racers along the planet's fringe—the remote, ice-threatened and wearying seas of Antarctica. The Southern Ocean embodies what Melville called "the full awfulness of the sea."

Autissier had experienced that awfulness before. In a ferocious storm during a 1996–97 around-the-world race, Canadian Gerry Roufs had vanished within 100 miles of where Autissier was now capsized. Autissier, sailing *PRB*, had led the search. She'd been pounded by the same 65-knot winds as Roufs and was already exhausted, with seven-storey-high seas roaring down on her.

PRB was knocked over by waves six times, Autissier flung against the cabin top of the boat. "I am in survival conditions," she reported. "I am at my physical limits." She couldn't distinguish the waves from the clouds.

For hours she slogged into the wind but made little headway. Roufs's EPIRB hadn't been activated. Without those coordinates, Autissier's task was hopeless. The search-and-rescue directors released her from any further obligation, and Autissier resumed the race. Looking for Roufs had been the most difficult experience of her life.

"I was resourceless," she said. "It was so frustrating, terrible, because life was on the table, and I couldn't do anything."

When race officials picked up Autissier's signal, two fellow racers were close by. Frenchman Marc Thiercelin was less than 100 miles downwind of Autissier. Giovanni Soldini, an Italian, was about 200 miles north—and upwind.

It was crucial to get to Autissier quickly. Within the next 30 hours or so, the Southern Ocean low that was bearing down would be directly over her, bringing 40-knot winds and 25-foot seas. Even using the EPIRB coordinates, a rescuer might take days to find her. And there was no assurance that *PRB*'s bulkhead—the only thing keeping it afloat—would continue to hold.

Race operations notified Soldini and Thiercelin of the accident. Thiercelin's land crew reported his boom had broken and it

HIGH TENSION: Isabelle Autissier was being chased by a storm.

would be difficult, if not impossible, for him to beat back to Autissier's position. Soldini, who had spent three years and millions of dollars preparing for the race, didn't hesitate. "I'm going now," he e-mailed. "I won't let up until I find Isa."

On February 15 at 1730 hours Greenwich Mean Time, Soldini turned his boat, *Fila*, to the south.

Working by flashlight in the almost pitch-black cabin, Autissier pushed her canting keel as far out as it would go. But the righting capability of such a keel is predicated on big waves, and in the relatively mild conditions then prevailing, the sea lacked the force to initiate the upright roll.

Before her electronics shut down, Autissier managed to get off a quick call by satellite phone to her shore team in France. All they heard before the connection failed was "I'm upside down."

PLOTTING A COURSE: **Isabelle Autissier at her high-tech navigation station.**

Autissier began to stack everything she could near *PRB*'s stern to balance the weight of the water in the flooded forward compartment. An escape hatch in the boat's transom was her only way out. Hunkered down on the cabin ceiling, she kept an anxious eye on the pieces of mast and boom gyrating below. She worried that they might smash through the hull or a window.

Short, wiry Giovanni Soldini, 32, knew exactly what his friend Isabelle was going through. In 1998, during a transatlantic speed-record attempt in *Fila*, he and four friends crewing for him capsized during a storm. The boat was quickly thrown upright again, but one crewman, Andrea Romanelli, was never seen again.

For the first 12 hours, Soldini held a direct course toward Autissier's EPIRB coordinates. But at 0630 hours on February 16, he reported that *Fila* was now forced to tack into near-gale-force winds—and he was still 50 miles away. When the wind changed, he closed the gap to 40 miles in two hours, pounding through 25-foot seas. As he moved around his boat, he had to hang on to avoid being trampolined into the ceiling or flung across the cabin as *Fila* flopped from crest to crest.

By 1300 hours he was eight miles away. Then the wind dropped to 25 knots, creating a short-lived window of good weather. Soldini arrived in the search area after nightfall. The EPIRB position was only approximate—it could be off by a mile or more, a distance that might as well be 100 miles given the heavy seas and poor visibility.

By first light Soldini saw no sign of *PRB*. He began methodically to sail the lines of a search grid. After half an hour he climbed to the first mast spreader to get a better look over the 25-foot waves. Still nothing.

The storm was just hours away and *PRB* might not survive it. He scrambled down and was preparing to jibe onto a new course when suddenly, miraculously, the boat was there.

Soldini sailed close to *PRB*. He shouted repeatedly but got no response. He made another pass, but there was still no sign of Autissier. His joy turned sour. He grabbed a hammer and threw it hard at the overturned hull.

Down in her cabin, Autissier heard something slam into the boat. She stuck her head out of the escape hatch. First she saw *Fila*, then Soldini waving, laughing, and shouting.

Autissier got into her life raft and for the last time floated away from *PRB*. Soldini manoeuvred close, and Autissier climbed aboard. Soldini e-mailed to race

KEELED OVER: "PRB" and her life raft, alone on the bottom of the world.

SEARCHING AN OCEAN

Pacific Ocean

Auckland

Soldini Receives Distress Call

NEW ZEALAND

Autissier Capsizes

Punta del Este
URUGUAY

ANTARCTICA

| _PRB_ | route ▶ |
| _FILA_ | route ▶ |

Isabelle Autissier knew that no commercial ships were within 1000 miles . . . only a fellow racer could save her.

headquarters, "I have Isa inboard with me. Isa and I are going back to the race."

As the boat, now set on autopilot, sailed itself through the storm that soon overtook them, Soldini and Autissier wedged themselves in below, drinking tea and red wine. They talked for hours about sailing. They also talked about sailors who hadn't been so lucky. For Soldini, finding Autissier was a chance to right the balance.

"He lost a life, and he saved a life," Autissier said later.

Before dawn on March 3, a half-dozen press boats pitched and rolled off Punta del Este, Uruguay. Soon *Fila*'s form appeared, illuminated beneath its lights and by a spotlight from a press helicopter. As he drew closer, Soldini set off flares in celebration. The sight of the luminous, fragile-looking boat coming in from the sea evoked what matters in these races: the courage, skill and endurance of the sailors and their willingness to support each other. The next day, when Soldini and Autissier were asked why they kept going back to the Southern Ocean, the passion of their answers was astonishing.

He just loved to play the game, Soldini said, because it allowed him to search for his own limits. To find that edge and run down it was what made him feel truly happy.

For Autissier, this was her last solo race through the Southern Ocean. Four times was enough. But what truly mattered was how she'd sailed the Great South. "I've tried to do it in the proper way," she said. "To do it with all my heart, my skill, to do everything I could do—and to do it until the end."

On May 8, 1999, Giovanni Soldini sailed into Charleston harbor to win the Around Alone race in 116 days, 20 hours—breaking the record by four days, 21 hours.

65 hours in a frozen tomb

by Louise Mills

Swamped by a landslide, the young ski instructor was in danger of freezing to death.

"**G**oodnight, Sal." Stuart Diver kissed his wife, switched off his bedside lamp and lay back with a feeling of pleasure. It was Wednesday, July 30, 1997, and the end of a long, tiring day for the couple, both 27. It was peak season in Thredbo, a bustling Alpine town of some 4000 in Australia's Snowy Mountains. Stuart had worked eight hours as a ski instructor, and his wife Sally had put in a long shift at a local hotel, where she organised conferences.

Stuart had met Sally—bright and energetic—at the Royal Melbourne Institute of Technology eight years earlier, and with their shared passion for the outdoors, they were soon

DREAM START: Sally and Stuart on their wedding day.

inseparable. One rare time when they were apart, Stuart drove six hours from Thredbo to Sydney to propose to her. "What about getting engaged today, Sal?" he asked. She laughed her bubbly laugh and replied, "Oh, yes!" Following their marriage in 1995, their dream was to start their own outdoor adventure business. They now lived in the Bimbadeen staff lodge, a four-storey concrete-block structure set on a slope opposite Thredbo's main ski slope.

A steady snow was now covering the roof of their lodge and, as Stuart slept, the first warning sign came: a sudden thundering roar. His eyes flicked open. His bedside clock read 11.37pm. Within moments, the bed trembled, and the roar grew louder. Stuart and Sally screamed as the windows, walls and ceiling crashed around them.

Seconds later when the tumult subsided, Stuart tried to sit up, but bashed his head against something hard. It felt like concrete. With mounting horror, he realised the building must have collapsed, and that he and Sally were trapped in a space no bigger than a coffin. Neither could move.

"Help me, Stuart!" Sally cried. Stuart ran his hand along her body and discovered a big concrete beam across her waist, pinning her to the bed. Their wrought-iron bed-head had fallen forward, trapping her head. Miraculously both had missed him.

Now they heard a rumbling, rushing sound. *Water!* If a water main had ruptured above them, it could flood their tomb and drown them. A split-second later, an icy, reeking mixture of water and heating fuel rushed through gaps above Stuart's head, filling the small space.

"Stuart!" Sally screamed, as water poured over her face. Desperately, Stuart heaved at the bedhead to no avail. He placed his hand on Sally's mouth, trying to keep her from drowning. But their cavity continued to fill. Beneath his hand, Stuart felt Sally's submerged face contort in horror. Stuart pushed himself onto his elbows. The water had just started lapping his lips when suddenly it drained away. Stuart reached down to his wife. She was dead. He wished he would die too—if only to be with Sally. *Just do it*, he pleaded, *and make it quick*.

Paul Featherstone, 47, a Sydney-based senior paramedic, arrived in Thredbo at 5am. As he got out of the bus that had transported him from the local airport, the stocky, silver-haired father of four gaped in astonishment. Two chalets—Bimbadeen and Carinya lodge—had disappeared in a massive landslide, pancaked under a tangled mass of mud, timber, concrete slabs, wall-partitioning, bricks, roof sections, upturned cars, trees and boulders. It looked as though someone had emptied a giant vacuum cleaner.

Police and firefighters had arrived on the scene soon after the landslide, Featherstone learned. But a senior police officer had declared the site too unstable to try rescuing anyone. Now, six hours later, it was still off limits.

As a member of the New South Wales ambulance service's special casualty access team—an elite group that specialized in treating patients in rugged terrain—Featherstone was used to emergencies. But he had never seen anything like this. *It's hard to imagine anyone surviving*, he thought.

Stuart Diver lay stunned in the icy mud all around him. "You've taken my wife!" he shouted out, choking with grief. Within minutes, however, his despair gave way to a fierce determination. Stuart sensed Sally's spirit with him. If he gave up without a fight, he felt he'd be letting her down. He vowed to survive as long as he could.

Now another torrent of water swamped him. This time he jammed his left hand against the wall and the other on the muddy bed. Then he pushed upwards, straining to keep his nose and mouth above the freezing water.

Stuart had completed two wilderness-survival courses that taught the urgency of preserving core-body temperature in subzero conditions. Already his hands and feet were numb. When the water subsided, he put his hands under his armpits to conserve heat. He wiggled his toes vigorously. He must do everything he could, he decided, to store heat.

By the time a wintry sun rose over Thredbo, more than 200 firefighters, police, ambulance and other rescuers had arrived. In a makeshift headquarters, police area commander Charlie Sanderson explained that at least 11 men and seven women were under the rubble. "Screams were heard soon after the tragedy," he said, "but there's been no sound since then. We have the gravest fears for them all."

A team of geophysicists finally declared the site stable at 10am and Sanderson briefed workers on rescue procedure. Three siren blasts, he warned, would mean the rubble was slipping. "Then get the hell out!"

At 10.30am, 11 hours after the accident, Paul Featherstone joined emergency-service workers and volunteers on the landslip. Hand-to-hand in a human chain, they passed pieces of shattered concrete, furniture, bedding, bricks and timber to waiting trucks. Firefighters crawled over the landslip and peered into gaps, yelling: "Rescue team above—can you hear me?" But the only sounds were from birds overhead and the gurgle of water beneath the tangle.

Stuart had been inundated five times by sudden bursts of water. Thirst and hunger gnawed at him. He pondered drinking the next gush. But with fuel and possibly sewage in it, he knew it could be toxic. Even worse than his thirst was the cold. It clawed at his body. He tried to keep his feet moving, but soon lost all energy. Then he felt a cotton cover at the end of the bed. Stretching down, he ripped a piece of the material free. It just covered his stomach and thighs, helping conserve body heat. Next he found a fleece jacket he had left on the bed and struggled into it.

Now, as Stuart sank into a deep, sluggish state, he heard a faint noise. Somewhere, a man was shouting. *People are looking for me!* he realised. He felt a surge of excitement.

"Hello!" he shouted over and over. No response. His spirits sank. He'd been trapped for 29 hours.

By dawn on Friday, August 1, one body had been recovered. The chances of finding a survivor now, Featherstone believed, were growing slimmer and slimmer. When someone is exposed to extended subzero conditions, body temperature drops, blood flow to vital organs slows, organs shut down, and the victim dies of hypothermia, usually within 24 hours.

Clearing continued throughout the morning. Suddenly an alarm blasted three times. Featherstone moved with the others to the edge of the slip. As he waited for the all-clear, music drifted from Thredbo's chapel where townspeople were praying for victims. "Amazing Grace, how sweet the sound, that saved a wretch like me . . ."

Work finally resumed and, later as the sun set, the temperature dropped to around minus eight degrees C [20F].

At 5.30 the next morning, more than two days after the disaster, firefighter Steve Hirst was moving debris when he heard a sound somewhere below him. Lying on his stomach, Hirst yelled: "Rescue party working overhead. Can you hear me?"

"I hear you!"

"What's your name?"

"Stuart Diver."

"What's your condition?" Hirst shouted.

"I'm OK."

"Is there anyone with you?"

"My wife Sally, but she's dead."

News of the survivor spread quickly, and the recovery team tore at the rubble where the voice had been heard. After an hour, workers exposed a huge slab of concrete. Through a jagged, half-metre-wide opening, they heard Stuart's voice, stronger now. "He must be just underneath," Hirst said. He and six other rescuers wriggled through the gap into a small chamber, and began clearing more rubble. Soon they discovered another concrete slab six feet lower. After more than three hours of digging, a rescuer's light illuminated a crack in the lower slab.

"I can see your light!" Stuart called. "It's above me." Silence shrouded the chamber as the men were struck by a sickening realization: Stuart was underneath yet another slab.

GUIDING LIGHT: illuminated helium balloons allow rescuers to dig through the rubble.

A fireman saw Stuart poke four fingertips through the crack. Squeezing them gently the fireman said, "Mate, I've never felt hands so cold."

Featherstone now crawled into the tunnel, pressing close to the crack. "G'day, Stuart. My name's Paul Featherstone. I'm a paramedic. How are you feeling?"

Suddenly the warning siren blasted three times and a colleague pulled Featherstone from the tunnel. Immediately, he ran to the site controller. "That guy could die unless I'm down there to settle him," Featherstone said. "I'm going back." This was a risk, he added, that he had to take. "Give me a skeleton crew of spotters," he suggested. "They can watch for movement while I'm in the hole."

The controller reluctantly agreed, and Paul Featherstone scrambled back down the tunnel.

He handed Stuart a mask, which he clamped over his nose and mouth, and connected it to an oxygen cylinder. Next Featherstone passed Stuart a warm-air hose, attached to a generator on the surface, to place inside his fleece. The paramedic then gave Stuart a pulse-oximeter, which he attached to his thumb. This would allow him to monitor Stuart's pulse.

Featherstone knew his patient's kidneys and liver could malfunction, increasing lactic acid and potassium in his blood to toxic levels, a condition known as acidosis. If Stuart moved suddenly or his heart rate rose, toxins might flood his system, triggering a heart attack. When the pulse-oximeter's beep quickened, the paramedic would need to calm him.

Suddenly Stuart began weeping. "I've got to tell you how Sal died," he said. "It's tearing me apart."

Deeply moved, the paramedic replied quietly, "Fire away."

As Stuart described how he had tried to save Sally, Featherstone struggled for the right words to say. "You did all you could possibly do," he said eventually.

Finally, he grabbed a bottle of electrolyte-and-nutrient solution and through the crack, inserted a tube from its stopper into Stuart's mouth. Featherstone restricted him to two half-mouthfuls every 20 minutes because he knew Stuart's stomach would have shrunk and any more might cause him to vomit and choke.

After clearing rubble, and when they were sure of Stuart's exact location, the rescuers started cutting a manhole in the slab above Stuart's feet, using a diamond-tipped circular saw. Dust billowed, and the tunnel filled with a deafening squeal. The pulse monitor began emitting rapid beeps. Stuart's pulse, already over 100, went up to a worrying 150.

HOW STUART DIVER WAS SAVED

1 After digging seven feet rescuers realize Stuart is under another concrete slab

2 A nourishment tube and warm air hose are passed to him through another hole

3 He is moved until his head is beneath the hole, then lifted to the surface

HELLHOLE: an ambulance paramedic contemplates the hole through which Stuart was rescued.

"Stop work!" Featherstone ordered. When the drilling stopped, he reassured Stuart. "Everything is safe. We're making the noise to get you out as quickly as possible." His words helped. Stuart's pulse immediately dropped and his respiration slowed.

Finally, after cutting through the slab immediately above Stuart and clearing other debris, the hole over his feet was large enough for a tunneller to enter. After three more hours of digging, Featherstone slid into the cavity to prepare his patient for moving. "But before we can get him out, we must set up an IV," Featherstone said. The better Stuart was hydrated, the less likely he'd suffer heart failure when moved.

A doctor now reached into the cavity, inserting an intravenous line into a vein in Stuart's ankle. Featherstone took his temperature. It was 34.7 degrees, three below normal. His patient was hypothermic, but his pulse was strong, and he didn't appear physically distressed. *So far, so good, but we're not there yet*, Featherstone thought.

The paramedic manoeuvred a harness round Stuart's waist, then gently pulled him feet-first until his head was beneath the manhole. Through the gap, Stuart glimpsed a patch of open sky. He smiled. "I thought I'd never see daylight again."

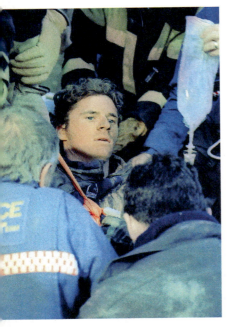

Sole survivor: **Stuart is pulled free.**

Featherstone realized the following moments would be critical. If acidosis was imminent, it could strike when Stuart was hauled from the hole.

"Before we bring him out," the paramedic told colleagues, "we need to make a phone call." With his mobile phone, he called Stuart's parents, who had driven from Melbourne the day after the landslide. Featherstone knew this might be their last chance to speak to their son.

"How're you doing, Tiger?" Steve Diver asked.

"Happy to be out of here, Dad," Stuart replied. Then the phone connection broke.

The pulse-oximeter now beeped rapidly. Featherstone placed a steadying hand on his patient. "No, mate," he said. "We have to take this slowly." Stuart's pulse returned to normal.

"OK, Stu, here we go," the paramedic said. "Let us do the grunt. You just relax."

While two firemen pulled from above, Featherstone and another paramedic held Stuart under his arms. Soon his head was partly out of the hole. On the surface, rescuers slid a rescue board through both holes in the concrete slabs, and Featherstone positioned it behind Stuart's back. "Let's do it," the paramedic said. With a concerted heave, rescuers hoisted Stuart to the surface. It was 5.17pm, Saturday, August 2—65 hours after the landslide.

Stuart looked all around him. "That sky's fantastic!" he exclaimed. "Well done, guys."

The only survivor of the landslide, Stuart was airlifted to Canberra Hospital.

There, doctors were astonished to discover that he had suffered only frostbite, dehydration, superficial cuts and hypothermia.

Stuart returned to his parents' home in Melbourne to continue his recovery. A few days later, Paul Featherstone came by to see him.

Featherstone insists he's no hero. "It's what I do," he says of his work. "You can only do your best. And often, that's enough."

Before Sally Diver's funeral service in Melbourne, Stuart looked into her coffin in the chapel. *She looks so beautiful*, he thought, *so at peace*.

Stuart kissed her gently. "See you later, Sal," he said. On one finger, along with his own wedding ring, he was now wearing Sally's wedding and engagement rings. "Part of her will always be with me," he says. "Always."

There's a girl on the tracks!

by Warren R. Young

A horrified crowd on the subway platform watched in horror as a train thundered towards the child on the line.

t was a moment frozen in time by terror. Nearly 100 people waiting on the subway platform beneath New York's 86th Street and Lexington Avenue stood transfixed. A few screamed, but they could barely be heard. For, thundering into the station at 30mph was a heavily laden, rush-hour train—a million pounds of screeching, stainless-steel and fateful momentum. And in its path, the onlookers could see a young man, his face pale with concentration, trying to jump up from the tracks four feet below.

With terrible certainty, they could see that he was not likely to make it. The train was hurtling toward him, ponderously swaying to within an inch or two of the metal-capped edge of the platform, like a gargantuan sausage slicer. The man's first jump carried him only high enough for his chest to strike the edge of the platform, and he fell back to the track.

Now the train was merely feet away. He gathered himself for one last desperate attempt. Then he felt himself rising, and it seemed just possible after all that at least his torso might get clear. But the last thought he had before the train reached the spot was: *There go my legs!*

Over the Edge

Less than two minutes earlier, 34-year-old Everett Sanderson, an unemployed musician, had been on his way home after visiting his mother. It was 5.10pm, January 16, 1975, and around him swirled the normal evening bustle, as people hurried down from the city's streets or up the stairs from the express-train level below. About every two and a half minutes, at this time of day, another local train came through, and one of them had left half a minute before.

At this moment, chance was guiding several strangers—and one particular train—each on a path which would soon converge with Everett's. Changing from express to local was 20-year-old Miguel Maisonett, a slender, clean-cut black youth sporting a neat Afro hairdo. Miguel was deep in thought about his future. He had just collected his final paycheck as a city health-department rat inspector; his job had been eliminated because of spending cutbacks. Ever since age 15, when he had dropped out of school to support himself and his younger brother (who had continued through high school and was now in college), Miguel had managed; but now jobs were scarce.

Approaching the stairs leading up to the same uptown-local platform was Transit Patrolman Rex Johnson, on his beat. Coming through the turnstiles was Mrs Joanna DeJesus, whose right eye was bandaged from a recent operation. With her were her button-cute, four-year-old daughter, Michelle, and Mrs DeJesus's sister, Margarita Esquilin.

Half a mile to the south at 77th Street, in the front cab of his train, 60-year-old motorman Daniel Miller had just released the brakes in response to a green "all-clear-ahead" signal light. Now he swung the master-controller handle to the "power" position, sending 600 volts of direct current into the 40 electric motors hooked to the train's 40 axles. The 70-second run through the tunnel to 86th Street had begun.

The DeJesus trio moved through the thickening crowd and stopped about two feet from the bright yellow stripe painted along the platform's steel-capped edge. Just then, Michelle wriggled her hand free from her mother's, hopped toward the edge to

LIFE ON THE LINE: **86th Street Station.**

look for the train—but slipped and fell onto the tracks. The screams and shouts for help began: "There's a girl on the tracks!" "Somebody get her! Save her!" All Mrs DeJesus could see was the bright-red coat and motionless form of her child, face down on the wooden ties with her feet across the nearest rail.

"Stand Clear!"

Everett and Miguel, 85 feet apart, each stepped to the platform's edge to see what had happened. Everett was about 35 feet uptown from the center of the commotion, Miguel 50 feet below. Both could see the helpless figure on the tracks. And both expected somebody in the crowd to jump down and pick up the stunned child.

Fifteen seconds passed. The crowd felt a gush of wind caused by the oncoming train, then heard the first distant grumble as it barreled through the rock-walled tunnel toward them. Down on the tracks, Michelle began to rouse. Her eyes tightly closed, she cried, "Mommy! Mommy!"

The shouts for somebody to save the little girl kept up, but nobody moved. Ten more seconds ticked by—it was almost half a minute since the fall. Then Everett, his own son in the custody of his ex-wife, asked himself, "What if it was *my* child down there?" And in a jumble of gallantry and foolhardiness, he jumped down to the tracks and started running.

Years ago, as an Ohio schoolboy, Everett had played football and basketball and once, at a track meet, had carried off all the awards. But he had never run in conditions like these, dressed in a heavy jacket, down in the trough of a subway— and with a little girl's life at stake.

On the other side of the crowd, Miguel, too, had decided to try to save the girl. Unlike Everett, however, he was thoroughly familiar with the tracks, for as a boy he and his friends, in a daredevil game, used to jump down and run across them between trains. Now, he leaped down and began sprinting.

By the time Miguel had run ten feet, he could hear the sound of the train swelling hugely in the tunnel behind him. He knew that it would reach the station in seconds. But then he saw the other man running toward him, closer to Michelle and with a better chance of reaching her. With an easy vault perfected by years of boyhood practice, Miguel swung his body up onto the platform.

By this time, Officer Johnson was up the stairs and aware of the desperate situation. He knew there was no way to cut off the power from the station, nor any fast way for him to contact the train to stop it. Headlight flashes flickered in the dark tunnel, and the noise level rose. Facing the unseen train and waving his flashlight from side to side, as regulations prescribed for an emergency, the six-foot-three-inch, 200-pound officer began running backward, shouting, "Stand clear! Get back, everybody!" The train would reach the station in about ten seconds.

Motorman Miller, at this point, had been pouring power into the 4000-horsepower electric motors to carry the train up and over a steep little slope in front of the 86th Street station. Because of this incline, Miller could neither see Officer Johnson's warning flashlight nor yet peer into the station to spot any trouble. Near the station entrance, he cut off the power. Normally, the train would be allowed to coast far into the station, then gradually be braked.

A MILLION POUNDS of fateful momentum: the 4,000 horsepower loco came down the platform like a gargantuan sausage slicer.

Silent Prayer

Miller's 25 years of bringing subway trains into stations had taught him never to be surprised to see objects in his train's path. Usually, they were unimportant. Newspapers blowing along the rails were commonplace. Once in a while, however, an "object" might be human—two or three suicides had jumped to their deaths under his wheels, waiting until the last instant when he could do nothing. And, once, a drunk on the tracks was saved by Miller's quick stop. So now, as always, his right hand was firmly wrapped around the brake lever.

Everett was so busy running that he never saw Miguel hop down and back up, nor did he notice Officer Johnson waving his light. All his thoughts were focused on the girl. She was still 20 feet away when he suddenly felt the asphalt tremble. Two brilliant headlights glared in his eyes as the front of the train, 12 feet tall and nine feet wide, abruptly filled the mouth of the tunnel.

The 240 feet now separating the train from little Michelle looked like far less to Everett, as the monster rumbled toward him still going almost 30mph, or 44 feet every second. Everett could see the motorman, his expressionless face giving no sign that he saw anybody on the track, looking even more remote because he was so far up—his feet, like those of the people on the platform, were about at Everett's eye level. Everett kept running.

Sometime during the first two seconds after the train entered the station, Motorman Miller spotted the child and the man on the tracks. He slammed the brake handle into "Emergency Stop," locking all the train's wheels. Sparks flew like fireworks as they skidded, grinding their metal against the rails with a tortured screech. Immediately, the train slowed, but it would still pass the spot where Michelle lay in only five seconds!

Everett was only a step from Michelle. In the train cab, Motorman Miller silently prayed, "Oh God, I hope I don't hit them!" On the platform, Miguel was also in the path of the train, kneeling and leaning over the edge toward Everett with outstretched arms. With three seconds to go, Everett seized Michelle in his right hand and, possessed of a strength he never knew he had, hurled her into Miguel's waiting arms. The impact knocked Miguel onto his back, with the child sprawled on his chest, safe at last.

A Single Second

For the first time, Everett recognized his own predicament. The train's speed had by this time been cut in half—to 16mph, or some 24 feet per second—but it was 40 feet away. There were two seconds to go.

Everett placed his hands on the edge of the platform, jumped for his life—and failed. By now, there was a single second left before the train would pass the spot where he was. Everett got ready for one last, desperate jump. Then, with the train

BADGE OF COURAGE: the medals presented to Everett and Miguel for their heroism.

so close that its mammoth bulk seemed virtually on top of him, he felt himself rising like an elevator. Hands belonging to Officer Johnson, Michelle's Aunt Margarita and Miguel were lifting him by the jacket and his arms. Everett hoped that his torso would clear the train, but he felt sure his legs would be amputated.

As the train passed, Motorman Miller lost sight of Everett. With a sinking feeling, he thought the first car must have caught Everett's legs and pulled him under. But he was puzzled by the absence of the familiar, sickening *thud* he always heard when a train passed over the body of a suicide. For more than three seconds, the train kept skidding. Finally, it stopped, 26 feet beyond where Everett and Michelle had been. Miller stepped out on the platform to see what had happened.

A pile of human figures on the platform were struggling to their feet. The three rescuers had tugged so mightily on Everett that some of them fell—with Everett, unharmed, landing among them. (Later, he would find a mark made by the train on the edge of his right shoe.) For the next few minutes, while Motorman Miller and Officer Johnson made sure of the happy outcome, the crowd patted Everett on the back and kept telling him he was a hero. At last, everybody went about his business—Miguel went home in a taxi, Mrs DeJesus took another cab to a hospital to make sure Michelle was not really hurt, Officer Johnson resumed his beat, and Motorman Miller announced that the train would continue its regular run. Everett Sanderson got on the train, too, and rode it to his stop.

The grateful New York Transit Authority presented Everett and Miguel with medals for civilian heroism, plus a five-year pass for free subway travel for Miguel and a life-time pass for Everett. Miguel found a job in the mailroom of the Transit Authority. Everett, for his part, decided to pursue a new career, in the nutrition field. He was presented with the prestigious bronze lifesaving medal of the Carnegie Hero Fund Commission and $1000.

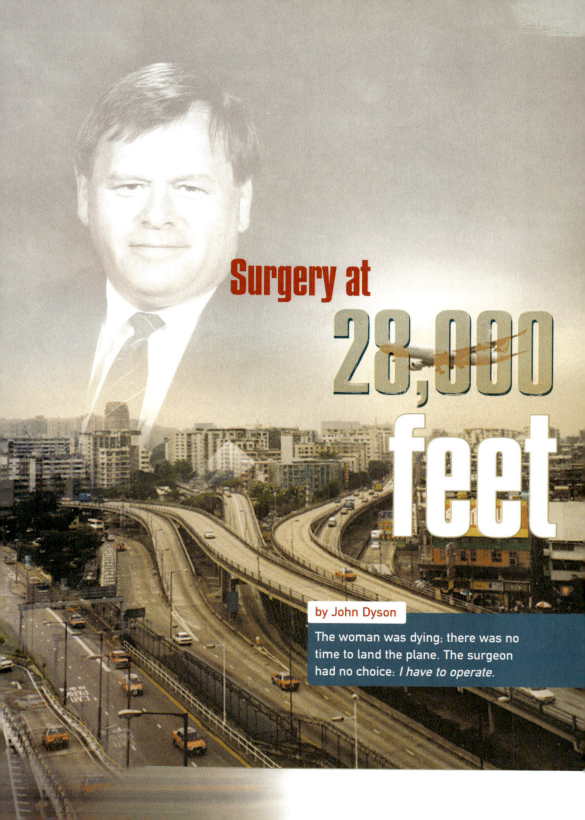

Surgery at 28,000 feet

by John Dyson

The woman was dying; there was no time to land the plane. The surgeon had no choice: *I have to operate.*

Paula Dixon hugged Thomas Galster tightly as he steered his Yamaha motorbike through the outskirts of Hong Kong towards Kai Tak airport. Only two weeks earlier dark-haired Paula, 38, had left Aberdeen. Separated and waiting for a divorce, she was lonely and in need of a holiday with her sister who lived in Hong Kong. On her first evening, she met Thomas, a tall 30-year-old factory manager from Stuttgart, Germany.

It had been a whirlwind romance. Three days before her trip was over, Thomas had pushed back his chair in a crowded restaurant, dropped to one knee, and whispered, "Will you marry me?"

"You're joking!" Dixon responded.

"I've been looking for you all my life," he said.

She hugged him ecstatically. "The answer's yes!"

Now, as they rode slowly through the balmy twilight, Dixon was already dreaming about starting a new life. She would fly back to Britain, but return as soon as she could to Hong Kong—and Thomas.

Suddenly a blue car pulled out from a side road. As Thomas braked hard, the motorbike hit the car's door. Dixon catapulted forward, slammed onto the car's boot and slid to the road.

Dazed, she struggled to her feet. Thomas ran to her. "Are you hurt?" he asked.

"Just a scratch," she said shakily. Her left forearm had a bleeding three-inch graze. "What about you?"

"I'm OK—but I'm taking you to the hospital," he replied.

Paula shook her head. "It's not that bad," she said. "I want to get to the plane. Please, darling, just take me to the airport."

At the British Airways check-in desk, Barbara Murray waited impatiently beside a trolley piled high with luggage. *Why is Paula so late?* she wondered. The two friends had come on this holiday together. Check-in for their return flight would close in 15 minutes.

Finally Paula arrived, looking pale. "We were knocked off the bike," she said, showing Murray her bruised arm.

"You ought to get it looked at," Barbara replied.

"No," Paula said. "The sooner I get home, the sooner I'll be back." She embraced Thomas, and with a final wave, the women passed through passport control.

Attention Call

The huge Boeing 747, carrying 331 passengers, would take nearly 15 hours to reach London. Paula and Barbara had the four middle seats in Row 53, at the very back, to themselves. As they boarded, Paula stopped a flight attendant and asked for some painkillers. "Could I also have something to clean my arm?"

Page 303. INSET: Professor Angus Wallace.

"I think it needs more than that," said the attendant, seeing the gash. Moments later, "Sammy" Burleton, the cabin service director, was told that a passenger might have a broken arm. "Call for a doctor," she said crisply. "I'll warn the captain that we might have a problem."

An announcement went out over the public address system: "If there is a doctor on board, would you please make yourself known to a member of the cabin crew?"

Remedial Action

Tom Wong, in economy class, snapped open his seat belt. The slim 26-year-old in blue jeans looked like a student. But Wong, 26, was a newly qualified doctor, heading back to his job at Ninewells Hospital and Medical School in Dundee.

Upstairs, in business class, another hand went up. "Can I help?" Angus Wallace asked. The burly 46-year-old Scotsman, Professor of Orthopaedics and Accident Surgery at Nottingham's Queen's Medical Centre, had been in Hong Kong examining medical students. He had planned to spend the flight reading medical papers after enjoying a quiet dinner.

Instead, the surgeon made his way to the back of the plane, where Wong was already examining Paula. The younger doctor stepped aside for the professor.

Stooping, Wallace gently pressed Paula's bruised forearm. The woman winced, but her colour was fine and she mentioned no other symptoms. Even if the arm were fractured, the doctor decided, she could continue on the flight. "We can take off and splint her arm when we're in the sky," he told Sammy.

At 10.30pm, the 747 blasted down the runway and lifted into the night. When the "fasten seat belt" sign switched off, Wallace looked through the plane's medical kit and found a splint and bandages. He and Wong returned to Row 53. Deftly, Wallace cradled the splint round Paula's elbow, and Wong wrapped the arm in bandages. "That should hold you," Wallace said.

"You're spoiling me," Paula replied, thanking them.

Well after midnight, Hong Kong time, Dixon was still awake. Her injured arm ached only a little, but the altitude had made her feet swell. She leaned forward to unlace her ankle boots. As she twisted her body to reach with her good arm, she felt as though something had stabbed her under the ribs. "God, the pain!" she groaned, clutching her side.

Angus Wallace couldn't imagine what the problem might be when a flight attendant asked him to look at the passenger he had treated a couple of hours before. "What's the matter?" he asked when he got to Paula.

"My chest," she said, panting.

Wallace pressed his fingers against her ribs. "Why didn't you tell me about this before?"

"It wasn't sore then," she said.

"I think you've fractured some ribs." Turning to Sammy, he said, "We'll give her a painkiller. Would you open the medical kit?"

But when Wallace returned with the syringe, he saw that Paula was worse. Her colour was blue, and her breathing shallow and rapid. He tried to listen to her chest with a stethoscope but could hear nothing over the roar of the jet engines. Then he pressed his fingers against her windpipe and was horrified.

Paula's trachea—the airtube under the skin at the front of the neck—had moved to the right. *It can't be.* Wallace pressed again. *No doubt about it.*

Emergency Debate

Quickly he walked the length of the darkened cabin while Wong was woken. "Tom, I want your opinion," Wallace said, when the two conferred in the galley. Wong checked Paula's chest and windpipe and confirmed that she was having difficulty breathing. Wallace suspected that the left lung was collapsing.

"I need to talk to the captain," Wallace said. In the cockpit he perched on the folding seat behind Captain Barrie Hattam and explained the problem. "A broken rib must have punctured her left lung." Paula needed an operation. "How soon can we land the plane?"

"New Delhi's our best bet," Hattam replied. "We could be on the ground in an hour and a half."

"Forget it," Wallace replied. *She could die in less than an hour,* he thought, then said, "I'll have to take action myself."

Each time Paula breathed out, a little more air leaked through the hole in her left lung into her chest cavity. The bubble of air building up there was compressing her damaged lung, deflating it. The more she struggled for breath, the bigger the bubble grew. When the left lung was fully deflated, the second lung would start to go. Gasping in agony, Paula would suffocate. She had, Wallace gauged, about 45 minutes.

In a hospital the procedure to relieve the problem was routine: a hollow needle would be inserted into the chest cavity, allowing the air to escape. Here, Wallace would have to improvise.

"I need some kind of tubing," he told the cabin crew. "What have we got?"

A drinking straw? *Too weak,* Wallace thought. The plastic barrel of a pen? *It won't hold in place.* Then a flight attendant brought the oxygen mask used in safety demonstrations. Wallace's eyes lit up, and he snipped off a length of its plastic tubing.

In the medical kit he found a urinary catheter—a thin tube designed for insertion into the bladder. One end was sealed, like the bottom of a bottle, but its last inch or so was perforated with tiny holes to allow liquid to enter the tube and flow out. *So could air,* Wallace thought.

"This will work, but it's too floppy," he said. "I need something rigid to go in the centre of the tube so I can push it into the chest."

A flight attendant found a wire coat-hanger. Wallace untwisted the hooked end and straightened out the hanger. Measuring it against the catheter tube, he bent the wire back and forth until it broke into a length—about 18 inches—a little longer than the tube.

The wire had to be sterilized, but there was no disinfectant. Someone produced a bottle of Courvoisier XO Imperial brandy—40 percent alcohol. Wallace nodded quickly. Cleaning the wire, he laid it on a tray that Sammy had covered with a white cloth. Then he cleaned the tubing from the oxygen mask and finished by splashing brandy over some scissors.

Wallace knew he needed a one-way valve to trap the released air and prevent it from going back into Paula's chest. Opening a small bottle of mineral water, he pierced two holes in its blue plastic cap. Next, he drank half the water, replaced the cap and threaded the piece of oxygen tubing through one hole, leaving the other open. "That's our valve," he said, putting it on the tray.

Rubber gloves, scalpel, swabs and sutures were in the medical kit. Sammy also produced a roll of sticky tape from her cabin bag.

The last hurdle was anaesthetic. The medical kit held lignocaine, a powerful drug for cases of cardiac arrest. Wallace knew it could also be used as a local anaesthetic—but how much could safely be given?

"Wait a minute," said Tom Wong. "I've got a BNF." He hurried to retrieve a small purple book from his hand luggage. The *British National Formulary* lists every known drug. Wong quickly thumbed to "lignocaine" and, in a moment, worked out the right dose.

"Good," Wallace said, drawing off that amount into a syringe. He checked his watch. Fifteen precious minutes had sped by.

The flight attendants had made an operating theatre by taping curtains and blankets round Row 53 and flipping on the reading lights. Paula sat up in her seat, her face covered with beads of sweat. Breathing shallowly, she felt as if she were drowning.

"You've got a collapsed lung, and I have to operate," Wallace told her. "You're not in a fit state to give consent," he added, inviting no argument. "So I'm just going to do it."

Dixon took the measure of this man. "What are you waiting for, doctor?" she gasped, managing a weak grin.

Vital Decision

Squeezing between the seats, Wallace faced his patient. If he punctured one of the arteries that lay beneath each rib, Paula could bleed to death in minutes. *I could be*

THE DRAMA UNFOLDS

A. Paula and Thomas leave for the airport.

C. Later, he cuts the tubing on an oxygen mask and then inserts it into a plastic bottle to make a valve.

B. Angus Wallace (right) inspects Paula Dixon's newly splinted arm.

C. Removing the coathanger from the catheter.

up on a manslaughter charge by morning, he thought. *But if I don't do something, she'll die anyway.* He pushed the anxiety out of his mind.

Placing sterile hand towels over her chest, Wallace tore open a surgical wipe to clean the skin. Next he injected the anaesthetic. It would numb only half the thickness of her chest wall, but that was the best he could do.

The insertion point would be in the space between the second and third ribs. Wallace threaded a curved suture needle and quickly flicked it in and out through the skin. He tied the thread in an open loop, like a purse string, ready to be drawn tight round the tube later. With the scalpel he made a small incision—barely a quarter of an inch—where the drain was to go. There was only a little bleeding.

Now came the critical moment. Gripping the surgical scissors like a screwdriver, Wallace put his right knee on the edge of the seat beside Paula. *The chances of hitting an artery are ten percent,* he calculated. But an arterial wall is tough and rounded. He hoped the scissors would be blunt enough to push it aside. Positioning the closed point of the scissors in the incision, Wallace bore down.

As the steel cut through the muscle and tissue into her chest, Paula felt as if she were being skewered on a meat hook. Her chin jerked upwards and she shuddered.

Wallace then twisted the scissor blades 90 degrees to widen the hole. The scissors were two inches into the chest cavity. As Wallace drew them out, Wong quickly passed him the wire-reinforced catheter tube. Wallace positioned it in the hole he'd made and thrust downwards.

Dixon groaned loudly and grimaced in agony. She tried to focus on reasons to survive. Her three grown children. Thomas. *I am coming back to you. I am, I am.*

Wallace pulled the coat-hanger out of the catheter, leaving the tube in the chest. "Be brave, lassie," he said.

Hurrying now, he connected the catheter tube to the oxygen tube that was threaded into the water bottle. Then he drew the purse-string suture tight, sealing the skin against the catheter to make the hole airtight.

In a moment Sammy Burleton exclaimed, "You've got bubbles! Is that what you want?" From the end of the tube in the water, bubbles were streaming forth.

"That's exactly what I want," Wallace replied. He glanced at Wong. "Is there blood in the water?"

"No blood," Wong answered, grinning. "Well done, Prof!"

Wallace adroitly put another stitch around the tube to hold it in place on Paula's chest. Where the two tubes joined, he sealed them with sticky tape. At last he looked up at his patient. Her colour was returning, and she gave him a sunny smile.

Theatrically, Sammy Burleton wiped Wallace's brow like a practised nurse. The doctor joined in the laughter. After making sure that Paula was stable, he walked forward through the darkened cabin, past dozing passengers. Their 747 was now piercing the night sky at 575mph, 28,000 feet over India.

Reaching the galley, Wallace spotted the brandy he'd used to disinfect the instruments. Weak with relief, he picked up the bottle and took a gulp.

Just before landing at Heathrow airport, Wallace checked on Paula one last time, finding her cheerful and composed. "Thank you, doctor," she said, planting a grateful kiss on his cheek. Then he shook hands with Tom Wong. Neither spoke of the professional risks they had run or medical history they had made. It was the first time a collapsed lung had been operated on in midair.

Two weeks later, completely recovered, Paula Dixon flew back to Thomas Galster in Hong Kong. Shortly after she arrived, he gave her an engagement ring.

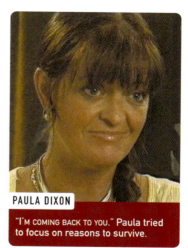

PAULA DIXON

"I'M COMING BACK TO YOU." Paula tried to focus on reasons to survive.